Presentation Graphics

contents

introduction

Advertising needs to make an immediate appeal. This requires the work of professional designers, drawing on inspiration yet maintaining a carefully thought-through balance. We see hints of the rigor that advertising production imposes on its professionals in the creative strategies developed to win client approval, and in the range of ideas and design techniques used in the production process. Advertising production is very much a behind-the-scenes activity, but with its focus on presentations this book reveals all, from the first idea sketches to the final form of the ads, with the process explained by the designers themselves. The insights to be gained by the reader in these pages give a picture of this creative world more complete than completed artwork itself can offer.

Three designers active in different parts of the world, all contributors to this book, share their thoughts on the subject of presentations.

Peter Aerts / Belgium
n.v.Van Hees Vlessing Lagrillière BBDO s.a. : Art Director

Born in 1964 in the village of Mortsel, near Antwerp. He took a 4-year degree in graphic design, then decided on a career in advertising and studied at the School of Communication Arts in London. After placements at CDP, HDM, Alan Brady & Marsh, TBWA and DMB&B, he returned to Belgium and is now an art director with BBDO Brussels.

A good ad can be drawn and presented on the back of a bus ticket. But what will your client see? The idea or the bus ticket? We can't expect an advertiser to have the same insight into our idea roughs as our colleagues. He might not make a distinction between the idea and the execution. You have to find out if he can judge an idea without any executional details. The way you're going to make presentations to him is best discussed at the beginning of the partnership. He'll learn how you work, and that a rough drawing is in no way linked to the amount of effort you're putting into his ad. That ideas come first and execution later.

Ideally, you can present the sketches you put up on your wall. A clear drawing with handwritten text will sometimes do. I am always wary of pushed and Mack'ed layouts because there is a tendency to loose yourself in executional details. Stylistic elements are very important in the finished ad, but they might get you into difficulties if you include them in idea layouts. The client might get hung up on elements that can't be changed afterwards. Try to stick to the intention. It's all about making the client see what a strong ad you can come up with. A weak idea doesn't get any better, no matter how sleek your layouts look. But it's an even greater shame to see a great idea go in the bin because the client couldn't see it.

Katsunori Aoki / Japan
Sun-Ad Co.,Ltd. : Art Director

Born in Tokyo in 1965. He joined Sun-Ad Co., Ltd.
in 1989. He has received many awards including
the JAGDA New Designer Award ('92), Tokyo TDC
Bronze Prize ('93), Japan Magazine Advertisement
Award: Gold Prize ('92, '94), Traffic Advertisement
Award: Gold Prize ('94), Tokyo TDC Members'
Silver Prize ('95) and Tokyo TDC Award ('95, '96).

Presentations embody the ideas of the moment.
This book offers a collection of materials prepared
for presentations which, when held up against the
final form the advertisement takes, may seem lack-
ing in some way. In some cases materials
are created for the purposes of comparison, to
help have a proposal accepted. Other times, the
idea's going to be a winner from the start. So what
is to be used for the presentation depends very
much on the circumstances at the time.   Of course
different approaches are needed according to
whether the proposal will be easy or difficult to
grasp. To make sure the client is fully sold on the
ideas put forward, everything has to be carefully
explained. The various sketches and comps shown
in this book together with the completed artwork
should certainly help readers to imagine how this
works. It represents for the designer, though, a
struggle through the choppy seas of the design
process before finally arriving at what for him or
her is the best possible solution. Presentations
are simply a way-station in that process, providing
an opportunity for communication with the client to
discuss progress and decide the final form of the
ad. As such, they give a fascinating glimpse of
each designer's personal style, or more simply,
different designers' ways of doing the job.

Cristina Amorin / Brazil
Giovanni Comunicações : Art Director

Her career in advertising began in 1982 and she
joined Giovanni Comunicacoes in 1996 as Art
Director. The many trophies, medals and awards
she has received include the Cannes Festival,
London Festival, Clio Awards, FIAP, New York
Festival, Brazilian Advertising Film Festival, Art
Club Yearbook (Rio, Sao Paulo) and Columnist

Prize Awards. She was elected the Brazilian
Advertising Association's Art Director of the Year in
'94 and '96, when she was among the top three art
directors in Rio for awards received. In 1996 she
received the Rogerio Steinberg Trophy.

In the advertising business, every presentation
requires more from the client than from the
 presenter.
The client's perception of the concept or basic
idea, and his capacity of imagining how it will look
after being finalized, are the secret of any successful presentation. Without this, it is completely
impossible to have an ad approved or even under-
stood. In other words, there's no good presentation
without a good client, and the credit for my best
works is necessarily shared with them.
Thanks to a Product Manager called Marcio and a
Marketing Director called Juan Manuel, both from
Smith Kline Beecham, the campaign for Phillips
Dental Cream with its strong images such as a
caterpillar on the toothbrush was possible. Thanks
to Marcos Libretti, from Globo Radio System,
myself and my partner got the 'Say No to Wild
Traffic' campaign, showing vehicles metamorphos-
ing into beasts.
Thanks to Waldyr Lima, from CCAA English
Courses, we showed a huge audience how strange
tongues can be funny while expressing the happi-
ness of managing a new language. Thanks to Paulo
Éboli, from O Globo newspaper, we inserted
recording tapes into magic slots created in the very
small spaces of classified ads. Thanks to these and
many other clients of my advertising agency,
Giovanni Comunicações, I have a good number of
memorable presentations to talk about. And thanks
to presentations like these, I feel enthusiastic
about being an Art Director.

We would like to express our deepest thanks to
all the designers who have contributed their work
and assisted in the preparation of this book.

P · I · E Books Editorial Department

introduction

　広告は一瞬にしてメッセージを伝える。そこには論理性を超えたあらゆる角度から計算されたプロのクリエイターの仕事がある。広告制作の厳しさは、クライアントをうなずかせるクリエイティブ・ストラテジーと、そして発想と表現技術を模索する制作プロセスにかいま見ることができる。本書は、通常目にする事のできない貴重なそのプロセスを、初期のアイデアスケッチから完成まで、プレゼンテーションを中心にクリエイターのコメントを交えながら紹介しています。ページごとに繰り広げられるクリエイター達の創造の世界、表現の追求は、完成作品以上に完成されたクリエイティブの世界です。

　世界のクリエイティブ現場より、本書に掲載されている活躍中の3名のクリエイターの方々にプレゼンテーションをテーマにそれぞれの考えを語っていただきました。

ピーター・アーツ／ベルギー
ヴァン・ヘス・ヴレッシン・ラグリエール
／BBDO：アートディレクター

1964年アントワープに近いモーツェル村生まれ。4年間でグラフィックデザインの学位を取得した後、広告業を目指し、ロンドンの、スクール・オブ・コミュニケーション・アーツで学ぶ。CDP、HDM、アラン・ブレーディー＆マーシュ、TBWA、DMB&Bで働いた後、新進のアートディレクターとしてベルギーに戻る。そして今日VVL/BBDOブリュッセルで多忙な毎日を送っています。

　優れた広告をバスの乗車券の裏にスケッチしてプレゼンテーションすることもできます。しかしクライアントは何を見るでしょう？　アイデアでしょうか、乗車券でしょうか？　広告主に対して、自分たちの同僚と同じようなアイデアの下絵に対する洞察力を望むことはできません。広告主はアイデアと技法の区別ができないかもしれないのです。あなたは、その人物が技法的なディテール無しでアイデアを判断できるかどうかを見きわめなければいけません。彼に対して行うプレゼンテーションの方法については、パートナーとなって間もない時期に話し合うのがベストです。そうすれば彼はあなたの仕事を知り、ラフスケッチとあなたが広告に注ぎ込む仕事の量とは何のつながりもないことを理解できます。まずアイデアが最初で、技法は後からだということを知ってもらえるのです。

　原則から言えば、壁に掲げるスケッチがあればプレゼンテーションできます。手書きの文章が入った明快なデッサン一枚で充分な場合もあります。私はいつも押しつけがましく派手なレイアウトに用心しています。技法的なディテールにこだわりすぎると自分自身のコンセプトやアイデアが失われる傾向があるからです。技法的な要素は完成した広告では非常に重要ですが、それらをアイデアのレイアウトに含めてしまうと苦しい立場になる場合があります。クライアントが細かい要素にこだわってしまい、後で変更できなくなるかもしれません。意図に忠実であるよう努力してください。自分がどれほど強力な広告を作り出せるかをクライアントに見せることが全てなのです。いくらレイアウトの見かけが良くとも、貧弱なアイデアが良くなるわけはありません。けれども、そのことをクライアントが理解できなかったばかりに、素晴らしいアイデアがゴミ箱行きになるのを目にするのは、最も残念なことです。

青木克憲／日本
㈱サン・アド：アートディレクター

１９６５年　東京生まれ。１９８９年㈱サン・アド
入社。
受賞歴
'９２年JAGDA新人賞。'９３年東京TDC一般銅賞。
'９２年、'９４年日本雑誌広告賞金賞。'９４年交通
広告賞金賞。'９５年東京TDC会員銀賞。'９５年、
'９６年東京ADC賞。

プレゼンテーションは、生ものです。ここに掲載し
たものは、その素材で、最終形と照らし合わせても
味けなく感じるでしょう。ある時は、ひとつのものを
通すための比較する素材であったり、またある時は、
どの方向に転んでも満足のいくものであったりと、
その時、その状況に合わせて素材は揃えられます。
さらに、「分かりやすいもの」、「分かりにくいもの」を
通すための話のもっていきかたは、かなり違います。
これらをきちんと納得してもらうには直接、説明し
なければなりません。この本に収められたそれぞれ
の素材を最終形により、いろいろ想像をしてもらえ
ればいいのではないかと思います。ただし、自分が
関わった仕事はいろいろな波を乗り越えてベストな
もので定着しています。プレゼンテーションは、広告
主とディスカッション、コミュニケーションをとっ
て最終形を定めていく、中間地点にすぎません。そ
うゆう意味においてクリエイターの幅のふりかた、
というか個々のやりかたが、かいまみることができて、
おもしろいと思います。

クリスティナ・アモリム／ブラジル
ジオバーニ・コミュニケイショス
：アートディレクター

１９８２年広告の仕事を始める。１９９６年よりジョ
バーニ・コミュニケイショスでアートディレクター。
受賞歴
国内、海外で、数々のトロフィーやメダルを獲得。
カンヌフェスティバル、ロンドンフェスティバル
クリオ賞、FIAP、ニューヨーク・フェスティバル、
ブラジル広告フィルム・フェスティバル、アートク
ラブ年報（リオとサンパウロ）、コラムニスト・プ
ライズ賞（リオと全国）。'９４年、'９６年ブラジル広
告協会アートディレクター・オブ・ジ・イヤー。
'９６年リオのコラムニスト・プライズ賞で最も受賞数
の多いアートディレクターとしてロジェリオ・スタ
インバーグ・トロフィーを授与。96年グランプリ・

アニュアル・コマーシャル賞、アニュアル・アウト
ドア賞。

　広告の仕事では、どんなプレゼンテーションでも、
プレゼンター側よりクライアント側に求められるも
ののほうが多いのです。

　コンセプトや基本となるアイデアを感じ取るクラ
イアントの力、そして仕上がった時にどう見えるかを
想像するクライアントの能力こそ成功するプレゼン
テーションの秘訣なのです。これがなければ、広告を
認めてもらうことはもちろん、理解してもらうこと
すら不可能なのです。言い換えるなら、良いクライ
アントがいなければ良いプレゼンテーションはでき
ません。そして私の最高の仕事に対する賞賛は当然
クライアントと分かち合わなくてはいけません。

　スミス　クライヌ　ビーチャムのプロダクトマネー
ジャー、マルシオとマーケティングディレクター、
ジャン・マニュエルのおかげで、フィリップス　デン
タルクリームのキャンペーンでは歯ブラシにのった
芋虫という強烈なイメージが使えました。システマ
グローボ　ラジオのマルコス・リブレッティのおか
げで、私と私のパートナーは自動車を獣に変化させた
『乱暴な運転をなくそう』のキャンペーンを作るこ
とができました。CCAAイングリッシュ　コーシズの
ウォルダ・リマのおかげで、聞き慣れない言葉がいか
に面白くなるかをたくさんの人たちに示しながら、
新しい言語を話す喜びを表現できました。オー　グ
ローボ　ニュースペーパーのパウロ・エボリのおか
げで、案内広告の非常にわずかなスペースにマジッ
クスロットを作り、録音テープを差し込めました。
こういった方々や、私の広告エージェンシーである
ジョバーニ・コミュニケイショスが持つその他たく
さんのクライアントのおかげで、本当に忘れられな
い数多くのプレゼンテーションを経験できました。
こうしたプレゼンテーションがあるからこそ、私は
アートディレクターという仕事に夢中になれるのです。

最後に、本書制作にあたりご協力頂いたクリエイター
の皆様に、心よりお礼申し上げます。

P･I･E BOOKS　編集部

Presentation Graphics

Copyright ©1997 by **P·I·E Books**

All rights reserved. No part of this publication may be reproduced in any form
or by any means, graphic, electronic or mechanical, including photocopying and
recording by an information storage and retrieval system, without permission in
writing from the publisher.

P·I·E Books

Villa Phoenix Suite 301, 4-14-6 Komagome, Toshima-ku, Tokyo 170 Japan
Tel:03-3940-8302 Fax:03-3576-7361
e-mail: piebooks@bekkoame.or.jp

ISBN 4-89444-045-8 C3070

Printed in Hong Kong

P·I·E Books wishes to extend thanks to the following design firms for allowing us to use their work on this book jacket.

Front right: Nakatsuka Daisuke Inc.
Front left: J. Walter Thompson

Back right: Tokyu Agency Inc. Hokkaido Branch
Back left: Abbott Mead Vickers BBDO Ltd.

Presentation Graphics

editorial notes

下記のレイアウトフォーマットに従い、制作プロセス、作者コメント、制作スタッフが表記されています。

The artwork involved in the design process, the designer's comments and the credits are shown as in this example.

コメントをいただいた制作者の方々のお名前は、186, 187ページに記載されています。

The authors of the comments are listed on pp 186, 187.

A クライアント名、広告使用目的
Name of client and purpose of ad

B 出品制作会社名
Name of design firm

C クライアントからのリクエスト、作品コンセプト、広告の目的等
Designer's comments on the client's request, the purpose of the ad and the concept behind the artwork.

D アイデアから完成まで、プレゼンテーションを含めた制作プロセスでのコメント
Designer's comments on the design process, from initial ideas to the presentation and completed work.

E 制作スタッフ／DF：デザイン制作会社　国名　制作年度
CD： クリエイティブディレクター
AD： アートディレクター
D： デザイナー
P： フォトグラファー
I： イラストレーター
CG： コンピューターグラフィックスデザイナー
CW： コピーライター
PR： プロデューサー
PL： プランナー

Creative Staff/DF: Design firm; country and year of production
CD: Creative director
AD: Art director
D: Designer
P: Photographer
I: Illustrator
CG: Computer graphics designer
CW: Copywriter
PR: Producer
PL: Planner

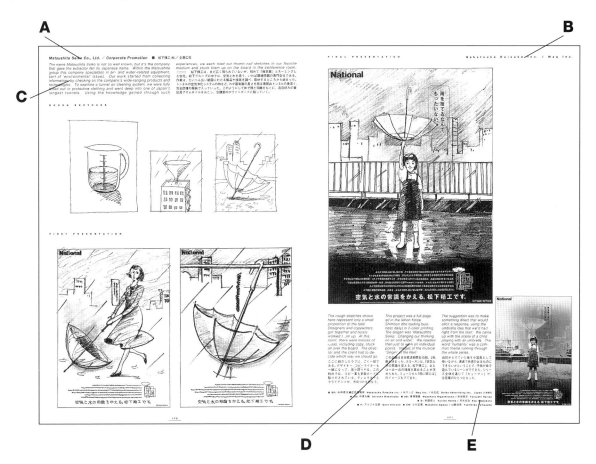

The client requested a campaign against traffic violence, using the principle that the radio is the driver's best friend and the only way to contribute to more civilized and calm behavior while driving.

クライアントの要望は、ラジオは、ドライバーの最良の友であり、運転中の上品で落ち着いた行動にとても貢献しているという事を基に、交通暴力に反対するキャンペーンを行うことでした。

ROUGH SKETCHES

FINAL PRESENTATION

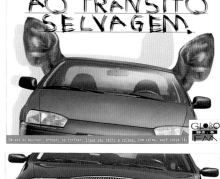

We tried associating driving behavior to primitive civilization by using a popular expression that compares everything with the jungle. That's how the idea of substituting animals for cars appeared, and consequently the slogan: 'Say no to wild traffic', with the message: Instead of honking, yelling and getting mad, turn on the radio and relax. Stay calm. You'll get there.

すべてを野生のジャングルにたとえるという大衆向きの表現を使って、ドライバーの行動を原始文明に結びつけようとしました。ここから車を動物に置き換えるというアイデアが生まれ、最終的にテーマは「乱暴な運転をなくそう」、メッセージは「クラクションを鳴らしたり、大声だして怒り狂うより、ラジオをつけてリラックス。落ち着いていれば、そのうち着きます」になりました。

The basic concept from the art department came from its own campaign theme: absurd images outlining the most absurd traffic situations in big cities, with chaotic typography symbolizing the agitated character of crazy cars.
Finally, through deliberate exaggeration we successfully showed everything we are fighting against.

制作の基本構想は独自のキャンペーンテーマに基づいていました。大都市の非常に馬鹿げた実際の交通事情を描く不合理なイメージと、狂った車の激しいキャラクターを描く無秩序なシンボルです。最終的には、誇張した表現という意図に合わせ、反対すべき事柄すべてを表すことに成功しました。

The idea was finalized with the use of pictures of different cars created with the help of computer graphics. The result was exactly what the client wanted. An image of friendly solidarity with the community for the Radio Globo System, identifying Globo FM as the most dedicated radio station for drivers.

このアイデアは、コンピューターグラフィックで制作した色々な車の絵を使って仕上げました。出来上がりはまさにクライアントが求めていたものでした。ラジオ・グローボ・システムの団体としてのイメージと同じく、優しい連帯感があり、グローボFMがドライバーに最も献身的なラジオ放送局であることを証明しています。

■ DF: Giovanni Comunicações Brazil (1996)

■ CD, CW: Adilson Xavier   ■ CD, AD: Cristina Amorim   ■ Typographer: Paulo Moraes

To position Phillips Dental cream, our client requested a campaign that polarized the product among its competitors. This way, the different attributes of Phillips Dental Cream would be explored. ▬

クライアントはフィリップス・デンタルクリームを売り出すために、この製品を競合品と差別化するキャンペーンを望んでいました。このため、フィリップス・デンタルクリームの色々な特性を探ることになりました。

ROUGH SKETCHES

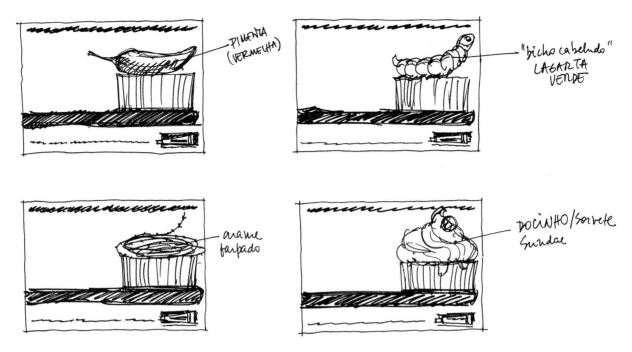

FINAL PRESENTATION

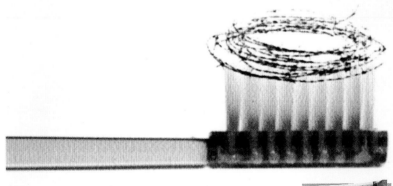

Queima e diz que é proteção. Parece até certos cremes dentais.

Presente nos melhores sorrisos.

É assim que seu creme dental coloridinho trata aftas e acidez?

Presente nos melhores sorrisos.

Teeth are very sensitive. They hate violence.

The whitest and healthiest choice.

If this reminds you of your dental cream, change to Phillips.

The whitest and healthiest choice.

It burns and claims that it protects. Even looks like some dental creams.

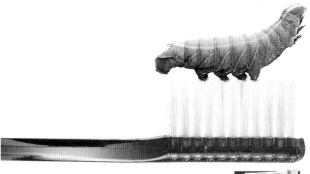

The whitest and healthiest choice.

Is this the way your nicely colored dental cream treats aftas and acidity?

The whitest and healthiest choice.

Using these differentials, we did a parallel outline of the product among its competitors by showing absurd images of dental creams that are colorful or tasty, but harmful and excessively abrasive. Phillips Dental Cream, by contrast, is white, like teeth, and contains Milk of Magnesia to fight sores and mouth acid.

色々な特性を利用して、「カラフル」で「味は良い」けれども歯に悪く研磨剤が多すぎるデンタルクリームという不合理なイメージを描き出し、フィリップス・デンタルクリームと競合品を比較するアウトラインを作りました。フィリップス・デンタルクリームの優れた点は、歯のように白く、フィリップス・ミルクオブマグネシアの処方を含んでおり、歯茎の腫れや口の中の酸と戦う力があるということです。

The visual concept of the campaign was to show competitors' products symbolized by strange elements such as burning caterpillar, wire, dessert and hot peppers. This was done so the consumer would have a clear view of how these products treat teeth and gums, compared with the positive attributes of Phillips Dental Cream.

このキャンペーンのビジュアルコンセプトは、燃えるイモムシ、針金、デザート、トウガラシなどの異様な要素を使って競合他社の製品をシンボル化する事でした。歯と歯茎のトリートメントにおける競合品の影響を、フィリップス・デンタルクリームの望ましい特性と比較して、消費者に明確に伝えるためです。

To finalize the campaign it was necessary to take pictures of each element separately. At the end, these pictures were set up to have the right visual impact with the help of computer graphics.

キャンペーンを完成させるために、それぞれの要素を別々に撮影する必要がありました。最後にコンピューターグラフィックを利用して、適切な効果と望ましいインパクトが得られるようにこれらの写真を合成しました。

■ DF: Giovanni Comunicações Brazil (1996)
■ CD: Adilson Xavier ■ AD: Cristina Amorim
■ P: Meca ■ CW: Felipe Rodrigues ■ Typographer: Paulo Moraes

Our client asked us for a campaign that would modernize the image of the magazine to match the profile of female readers. These women are part of a younger generation who intend to bring up their children differently from the conservative families they grew up in.

██████ クライアントの依頼は、女性読者に合わせて雑誌のイメージを新しくするキャンペーンをしたいというもの。こうした女性は自分たちが育った保守的な家庭とは違う方法で子供を育てたいと考えている若い世代の女性達です。

R O U G H   S K E T C H E S

F I N A L   P R E S E N T A T I O N

Drag Princess.

Pais&Filhos
Prepare-se para fortes emoções.

Lorem ipsum dolor sit amet, consectetuer adipiscing elit, sed diam nonummy nibh euismod tincidunt ut   bloch

Hell's Angel.

Pais&Filhos
Prepare-se para fortes emoções.

Lorem ipsum dolor sit amet, consectetuer adipiscing elit, sed diam nonummy nibh euismod tincidunt ut bloch

We made a list of the concerns of mothers worried how their children will grow up. Then we took some contemporary issues, such as drag queens and punks, and dressed up babies as a 'drag princess' and a 'hell's angel'. The text reads: Be aware of the changes in the behavior and personality of your children.

私たちは子供の未来を心配する母親の様々な懸念をリストにしました。次に、ドラッグクィーンやパンクといった現代の事象を使って適当な服装のタイプを作りました。テキストは次の通り。「あなたの子供の行動とパーソナリティーの変化に気を付けましょう。ペアレンツ・アンド・チルドレンを必ず読んでください。」

Together with the art department, we looked for a solution that would value the baby's image, the principal element in the ads. The Drag Princess is shown wearing earrings, heavy makeup and a colorful necklace. The Hell's Angels have bandannas round their foreheads, flashy collars, nose piercing and dark sunglasses.

制作チームと共に、広告の重要な要素である赤ちゃんのイメージを高める方法を探しました。「ドラッグプリンセス」はイヤリングと華やかなネックレスを付け、化粧を濃くしています。「ヘル・エンジェル」は額にバンダナを巻き、派手な首飾り、鼻のピアス、黒いサングラスを付けています。

The final touch of the campaign was done with the help of a computer. All elements were applied to the pictures of children and the result was a funny and attractive campaign, establishing a young and friendly image for Parents & Children Magazine.

広告の仕上げにはコンピューターを利用しました。すべての要素を赤ちゃんの写真に加えた結果、コミカルで魅力的な広告になり、若々しく親しみのあるペアレンツ・アンド・チルドレン・マガジンのイメージが出来上がりました。

■ DF: Giovanni Comunicações Brazil (1996)
■ CD: Adilson Xavier ■ AD: Cláudio "Gatão" Gonçalves
■ P: Nana Moraes ■ CW: André Lima ■ Typographer: Paulo Moraes

Hell's Angel.

Pais&Filhos
The Parents Magazine.

Be prepared for the mood and personality changes in your sweet baby. Read Pais & Filhos. bloch

Drag Princess.

Pais&Filhos
The Parents Magazine.

Be prepared for the mood and personality changes in your sweet baby. Read Pais & Filhos. bloch

It was very simple. 'Ray-Ban' brand had advertised very infrequently and there was a need to renew interest in this market leader to maintain its lead. The client requested a campaign to position Ray-Ban as 'THE sunglasses'. They left the creative interpretation of the brief open. ▬▬ 非常にシンプルでした。「レイバン」ブランドはごくたまにしか

宣伝を行わないため、マーケットリーダーであるこのブランドに対する関心を新たにして、リーダーの位置を保つ必要があったのです。クライアントはレイバンを「最高のサングラス」に位置づけるキャンペーンを望んでいました。また制作にあたっての指示は、あまりありませんでした。

ROUGH SKETCHES

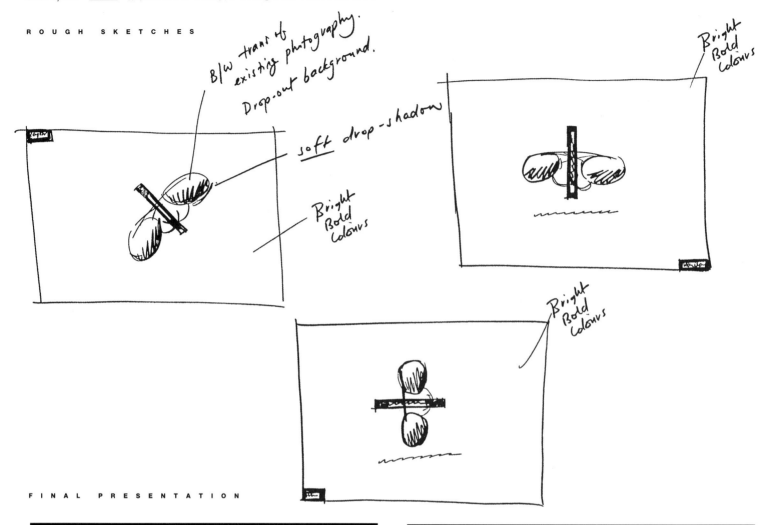

FINAL PRESENTATION

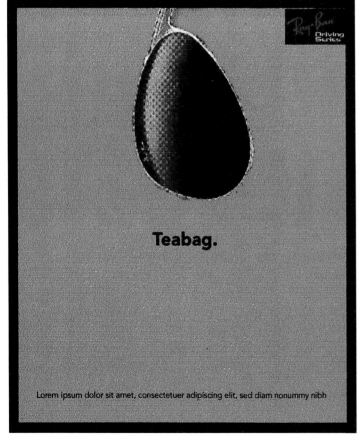

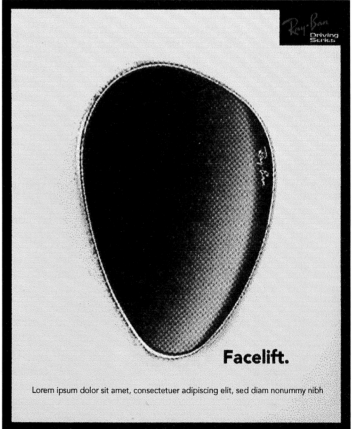

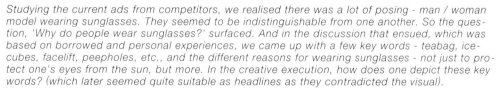

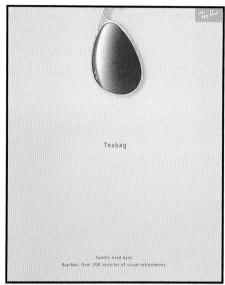

Teabag

Soothe tired eyes.
Ray-Ban. Over 200 varieties of visual refreshment.

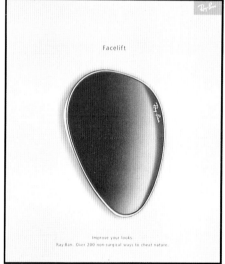

Facelift

Improve your looks.
Ray-Ban. Over 200 non-surgical ways to cheat nature.

Peepholes

For secret surveys.
Ray-Ban. Over 200 ways to disguise your intentions.

Studying the current ads from competitors, we realised there was a lot of posing - man / woman model wearing sunglasses. They seemed to be indistinguishable from one another. So the question, 'Why do people wear sunglasses?' surfaced. And in the discussion that ensued, which was based on borrowed and personal experiences, we came up with a few key words - teabag, icecubes, facelift, peepholes, etc., and the different reasons for wearing sunglasses - not just to protect one's eyes from the sun, but more. In the creative execution, how does one depict these key words? (which later seemed quite suitable as headlines as they contradicted the visual).

競合ブランドの最近の広告を調べるうちに、サングラスをかけた男女のモデルがポーズをとっているものが多いことに気付きました。お互いに区別のできない広告ばかりのように思え、ここから「なぜサングラスをかけるのか？」という問題が浮かび上がりました。そして他人や自分の経験に基づいてアイデアを確立するディスカッションの中で、「ティーバッグ」、「アイスキューブ」、「美容整形」、「のぞき穴」などいくつかのキーワードを思いつきました。さらにサングラスをかけるさまざまな「理由」──単に日光から目を守る以外のいろいろな理由──をあげてみました。クリエイティブな表現の中に、このようなキーワードをどう描写できるだろう？（後に、ビジュアルと相反するためのコピーに最適だと考えられた）。

The more we discussed the 'reasons' concept, the more certain we were that this seemed the obvious way to go - insight! Identifying with the consumer is one of the basic tenets of successful advertising and this campaign fulfilled it.

「理由」というコンセプトを話し合うにつれ、これこそ進むべき道だと思えました。──先が見えてきました！消費者の立場に立つことが、広告を成功させるための基本であり、このキャンペーンはこれを満たしていました。

When first presented, the clients required a little convincing. It was unlike usual advertising and we took a big step by not including a human element. The clients were naturally nervous. A good sign! Copy was kept succinct and relevant, creative execution was simple and uncluttered. The reader needed to invest perhaps 15 seconds to read and comprehend the whole ad. Message delivered, brand name cleanly displayed. Did the job!

最初のプレゼンテーションのとき、クライアントを多少説得する必要がありました。通常の広告と違って、人間を登場させないという思い切った手段を使ったからです。クライアントが心配になるのも当然です。これは良い兆候なのです！コピーは簡潔で深い意味を持つものに、表現方法はシンプルにすっきりさせました。おそらく15秒あれば読者は広告すべてを読んで理解できます。メッセージを伝えるために、ブランド名はきれいに表示しました。これで完成です！

■ DF: Dentsu, Young & Rubicam Malaysia (1995)
■ CD: Suzanne Schokman / Basil Antonas
■ AD: Lim Hock Chuan ■ CW: Tina Tan

A fresh print/poster campaign is required to overhaul Code 10's image. The product is a present brand leader in the hair styling gel segment. But due to its aging product life cycle, other brands are emerging in the market. Some are targetted at the same age group currently dominated by Code 10 i.e. ages 14-29. It's imperative that while a fresh brand image is needed, the advertising should position the product as far superior to its competitors by virtue of its holding properties. Code 10 Extra Hold and Super Hold formulas allow the user to style his/her hair anyway he/she deems fit. Whatever the style, this gel will hold it for some 8 hours or so. This positioning is especially important in the face of intense competition. However this 'holding power' claim is not unique to Code 10. Other brands such as Wella invariably have connotations of 'extra hold' explicitly stated on product packaging. Therefore, a strong creative piece is needed to win consumer's preference.　■■■■■　コード10のイメージを一新するための新鮮な印刷物・ポスターによるキャンペーンが必要でした。この製品は現在、整髪ジェルのブランドリーダーです。しかし長期に渡り販売されているため、他のブランドも市場に現れてきています。こういった製品の中には、コード10が今のところ優位を占めている年代と同じ、つまり14〜29歳をターゲットにしているものもあります。新しいブランドイメージが必要であると同時に、この広告によって整髪力の良さを示して、コード10を競合品よりはるかに優れたポジションに据えることが重要でした。コード10・エクストラホールドとスーパーホールドを使用すれば、男女を問わず自分にフィットするどんなヘアスタイルにでも整髪できます。このジェルならスタイルがどんなものでも、約8時間ほど保てるのです。激しい競合があるため製品の位置づけは特に大切です。しかし、この「ホールド力」に力をいれているのはコード10独自のものではありません。ウェラなどのブランドも、常に「エクストラホールド」の意味を表す事柄を製品パッケージにはっきり表示しています。そのため消費者の支持を得るには強力な広告を作る必要がありました。

R O U G H   S K E T C H E S

Code 10 The Birth of... "HARDWARE"

CW: Let's see what we can pull off for Code 10. This long period of creative stagnation ain't good.

AD: Lemme finish my lunch, will ya? (Art Director shovels organic and non-organic matter into mouth. 30 seconds later...)

AD: Burp!

CW: Can we start thinking now?

AD: You start...

CW: Let's go through the client's need for an image overhaul and examine the market forces.

AD: Burp.

CW: Maybe not.... Let's check what the competition's been doing.

AD: Burp.

CW: Oh heck, let's get right down to the problem and find a solution.

AD: I don't have that much hair left on me to be inspired.

CW: Code 10's 'Super Hold' formula is a great USP for this market. Many of us have straight, stubborn hair.

AD: (sarcastic) You should know.

CW: So this is the gel to set things right. How do we get that point across in as simple a way as possible?

AD: (a little inspired now) You know, with a hair styling gel like that, you don't need clothes to attract chicks.

CW: So name me someone who's got a great hairdo but walks round absolutely naked.

AD: A lion!

CW: Let's shoot a lion's mane and tell the world Code 10 gel is the best.

AD: Let's try harder. Find a subject that has really stubborn hair, then style it.

CW: You can forget about using me as your talent.

AD: I'm not even thinking of something human.

CW: Like a broom?

AD: Or a brush?

CW: And a mop?

AD: Exactly!

コード 10 'HARDWARE' の誕生、

CW（コピーライター）：コード10について何がひねり出せるか考えてみようよ。こんなに長い間、制作が止まってるのは良くないよ。

AD（アートディレクター）：....昼メシ、終わらせてもいいだろ？（有機物や非有機物を口の中にかき込む。30秒後...)

AD：ゲップ！

CW：始めてもいいかな？

AD：勝手にどうぞ....

CW：じゃ、クライアントのいうイメージの一新ってのを検討して、市場での競争力を調査しようか。

AD：ゲップ。

CW：いや、違うな....競合他社が何してるかチェックしようか。

AD：ゲップ。

CW：おい、なんなんだよ。さっさと問題にとりかかって解決しようよ。

AD：髪の毛の残りが少なくて、インスピレーションが浮かばない。

CW：コード10の「スーパーホールド」はすごいんだ。この市場では最高に売れてる。かたくてセットしにくい髪の人って多いからね。

AD：（皮肉ぎみに）そりゃお前にはその気持ちが分かるだろうさ。

CW：つまり、バッチリうまくいくジェルだってこと。この点をできるだけシンプルに伝えるにはどうすればいいかな？

AD：（少しインスピレーションを感じて）いいか、こういうヘアスタイリングジェルがあれば、女の子を引っかけるのに服なんていらないんだ。

CW：じゃ、すごいヘアスタイルできめてるけど、完全に丸裸で歩いてる奴っていうと。

AD：ライオン！

CW：ライオンのたてがみを撮影してコード10最高って宣伝しよう。

AD：もっとハードにしてみようか。メチャクチャ髪がかたい何かを見つけて、スタイリングする。

CW：僕を使うのは勘弁してよ。

AD：人間っぽいものなんてまったく考えてないって。

CW：ほうき、とか？

AD：もしくはブラシかな？

CW：それとモップ？

AD：その通り！

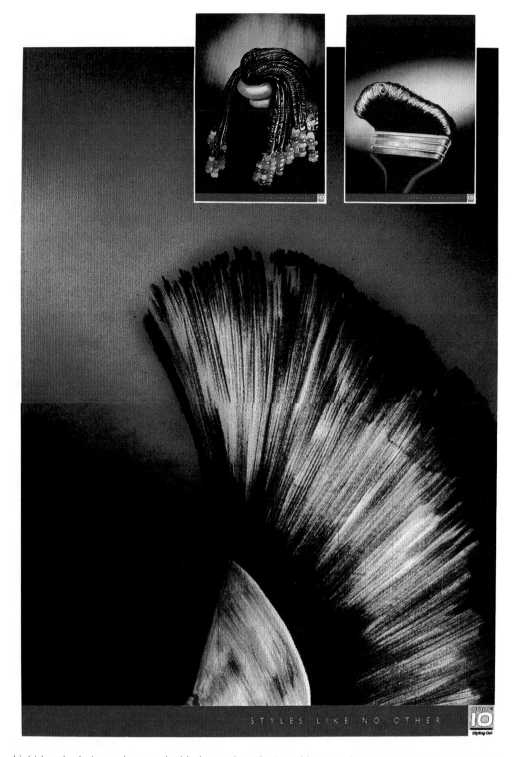

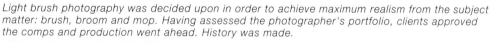

STYLES LIKE NO OTHER

Light brush photography was decided upon in order to achieve maximum realism from the subject matter: brush, broom and mop. Having assessed the photographer's portfolio, clients approved the comps and production went ahead. History was made.

ブラシ、ほうき、モップの3種類の対象物から最高のリアリズムを引き出すために、軽くブラシのかかった写真を選びました。写真家のいろいろな作品を調べ、クライアントの承認を得て、チームは制作を進めました。歴史的瞬間です。

After the colour separation stage, placement of the logos was finalized. Point size was drastically reduced to allow the subject matter maximum leverage for attention-grabbing purposes. It was also decided that the logos in each poster would be repositioned where the Art Director saw fit; i. e. not in the conventional bottom-right corner of the layout. This was, once again, to allow the subject matter to have maximum 'breathing space'. It was felt that the brush, broom and mop had to be the mainstay of each piece, not the logo nor the size of the tagline.

色分け作業の後、ロゴの配置を仕上げました。ポイントサイズは思いきり小さくして、できるだけ対象物が目を引く役割を果たすようにしました。さらに、それぞれのポスターのロゴを、レイアウト上の右下隅という従来の位置ではなく、アートディレクターが最適と判断した場所に配置し直しています。これもまた、対象物にできるだけ「必要な余裕」を持たせるための処理です。ロゴやキャッチフレーズのサイズでより、ブラシ、ほうき、モップをそれぞれのポスターの主軸にする必要があると思われたからです。

■ DF: Dentsu, Young & Rubicam Malaysia (1996)
■ CD: Dharma Somasundram / Basil Antonas ■ AD: Izwar M. Zakri ■ D: Rubie Choo
■ P: Fai of Ikhlan Fotografi Lim ■ CW: Anthony Wong

The client's brief was simple and straightforward. The current personality of the beer is as follows: it is a beer for young, modern people and aimed primarily at a Chinese audience. The consumption of beer during social occasions (pubs, bars, coffee shops·and the like) is a given. The task for the Agency was to devise appropriate occasions relevant for the consumption of Tiger Beer. ■■■■ クライアントの要望は、シンプルでストレートでした。このビールは若者とモダンな人々向けで、主に中国の人々をターゲットにしています。社会生活の中でビールが消費される状況（パブ、バー、コーヒーショップなど）がテーマでした。私達に求められたのは、タイガービールを飲むのにふさわしいシチュエーションを考え出すことでした。

THUMBNAIL SKETCHES

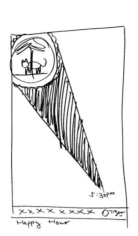
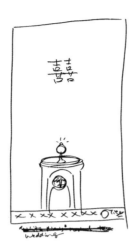

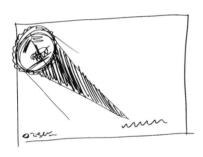

FINAL PRESENTATION

鬼佬涼茶

鬼佬涼茶

欢 乐 时 光

囍

Given the task at hand, the Agency creative and servicing teams began by brainstorming for ideas on different occasions for beer drinking. The team delved into research and personal experiences, noting that outdoors (picnics, beach outings, etc.) the home (parties, barbecues, etc.) special functions (business dinners, cocktails, weddings) and particularly happy hours at pubs rated highly as occasions for the consumption of beer. Having isolated these occasions / places, the teams settled on the three that were most highly rated i. e. happy hours, special functions and outdoors.

この仕事のために、エージェンシーの制作・営業は、まずビールを飲む様々なシチュエーションのアイデアを出すためにブレーンストーミングを行いました。調査結果や個人の経験を掘り下げてビールを飲む状況について考え、アウトドア（ピクニック、海水浴など）、家庭（パーティー、バーベキューなど）、特別な行事（仕事上のパーティー、カクテルパーティー、結婚式）、パブのサービスタイムを選び出しました。これらの状況・場所を別々に評価した結果、サービスタイム、特別な行事、アウトドアの3つが最もふさわしいという結論に達しました。

Several ideas were proposed as the outcome of the brainstorming session. The aim was to stay away from showing beauty shots of the beer since the 'occasions' were the communication point to be highlighted. This execution had the added advantage of making the ads stand out against other beer advertising that normally shows beer in all its glory. However, we couldn't ignore the identification of the beer label. Having decided to highlight the occasions, we set about finding the best way to express them, while identifying the beer within each execution.

ブレーンストーミングの結果としていくつかのアイデアが提案されました。狙いはビールの美しい写真から離れることでした。「シチュエーション」こそが強調して伝えるべきポイントだからです。この表現方法には、ビール自体を前面に押し出して見せる通常の広告より目立つという利点もあります。しかし、ビールのラベルを識別させることも忘れるわけにはいきません。シチュエーションを強調することに決め、これを表現しながら、その中でビールを識別させる最善の方法を探しました。

We decided on a direction, therefore, that would emphasise the occasion, while using the beer or its packaging to underscore the occasion. Thus for the happy hours ad, the beer cap becomes the fulcrum of the 'clock'. The shadow the beer cap casts becomes the hand of the 'clock', demonstrating happy hours - in other words, time for Tiger. For the outdoors ad, the cap was the sun denoting a hot day, perfect for outdoor occasions. The headline, 'Western herbal tea' shows insights into our Chinese audience who often refer to beer as Western herbal tea. The Chinese believe that herbal tea has a cooling effect on hot days, and ascribe the same qualities to beer. Weddings score highly for consumption of beer during special functions. In this case, the ring-pull of the beer can represents a wedding ring, with a drop of Tiger beer being the gold on it. This execution also underscores Tiger's tagline 'Good As Gold'. The clients were pleased with the ads and the rationales given for proposing the above occasions. They felt the Agency had met the brief.

この方向性から、私たちはシチュエーションを強調すると同時に、ビールやパッケージを使ってさらに際立たせることにしました。そのためサービスタイムの広告ではビール瓶の蓋が「時計」の支柱になっています。この蓋の落としている影が「時計」の針になってサービスタイムの時間を表しています。一言い換えれば、タイガーの時間です。アウトドアの広告では、状況に合わせて、蓋は暑い一日を象徴する太陽になっています。コピーの「西洋のハーブティー」は、ターゲットである中国の人たちに向けて考えられたものです。彼らはビールのことをよく西洋のハーブティーと呼ぶのです。中国人は、ハーブティーは暑い日に、涼しさを感じさせる作用があると考えており、ビールにも同じ性質があるとみなしているのです。結婚式は特別な行事の中でビールを消費することが多いとされたものです。ここでは缶ビールのリングプルが結婚指輪を表し、タイガービールのしずくが指輪の上の黄金になっています。この表現は、タイガービールのキャッチフレーズ「黄金のような素晴らしさ」を強調する意味も持っています。クライアントはこの広告に満足し、このようなシチュエーションを提示するやり方にも納得してくれました。私達が要望を満たしてくれたと感じたようです。

■ DF: Dentsu, Young & Rubicam Malaysia (1996) ■ CD: Dharma Somasundram / Basil Antonas
■ AD, CW: Khoo Wei Hung ■ P: Barney Studio ■ CW: Angeline Ang

Sega Enterprises Ltd. / Event Announcement ■ ㈱セガ・エンタープライゼス／イベント告知

This ad was to promote a special Sega Event at Toshimaen amusement park. The client requested something that would be conspicuous despite its limited exposure. We thought the poster should give an exciting pre-taste of the event, rather than list all the relevant information. The project brought together Sega, known for its computer games and Toshimaen, one of Tokyo's leading amusement parks, so the point was to convey the news that two different forms of

entertainment could be enjoyed at one location. ■■■■ としまえんの園内で行われるセガのイベント告知ポスター。限られた出稿量の中で、埋没しない表現であること。イベントの細かな内容を訴求するよりは、ポスター自体が楽しいイベントの前奏曲になっている方が大切だと考えた。デジタルゲームのセガとアミューズメントパークのとしまえん。2つのエンターテイメントが1つの場所で楽しめるというニュースを、表現の核にした。

ROUGH SKETCHES

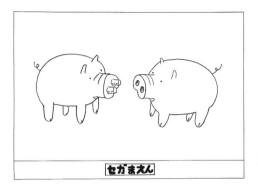

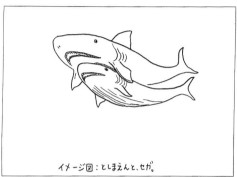

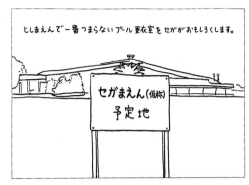

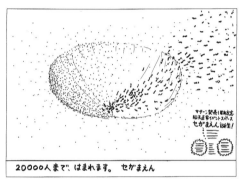

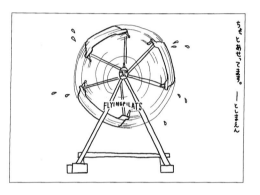

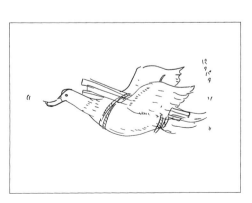

としまえん に、うまい話がやってくる!!

As the event was to be held at Toshimaen, I wondered whether we could successfully build in Toshimaen's unique advertising style. As we tried out various ideas, the duck-and-leek visual stayed with us, both from the viewpoint of the objectives of the campaign and as an interesting design. Duck-and-leek is derived from a well-known Japanese dish.

としまえんで行われるイベントなので、としまえんの広告の持つユニークな表現トーンをうまく取り入れられないかと考えた。色々なアイデアを考えていく中、カモネギのビジュアルは、企画の意図からも、絵の面白さからもぬけていると思った。

We imagined the duck flying over the streets of Tokyo rather than in the mountains, but it was after all only symbolic, and we decided on an approach that would emphasize the absurdity of a duck carrying leeks on its back.

山の上ではなく、東京の街の上を飛んでいるシチュエーションなども考えたが、あくまでシンボリックに、カモがネギをしょっているというバカバカしさを見せていく方向に割り切った。

There are times when an initial idea can be developed and expanded, getting better all the time. There are other times when the very first image turns out to be the most promising, despite all sorts of processing. The latter proved to be true in this case.

最初のイメージからどんどんふくらませて、変えていって良くなる場合と、いろんなプロセスを経ても、最初のイメージをくずさずに持っていくのがうまくいく時とあるが、今回の仕事は後者の方であった。

■ DF: ㈱博報堂 Hakuhodo Inc. Japan (1995)
■ CD: 宮崎 晋 Susumu Miyazaki ■ AD: 永井一史 Kazufumi Nagai
■ D: 石井 寛 Kan Ishii / 藤本政恭 Masayasu Fujimoto / 柳川価津夫 Katsuo Yanagawa
■ P: 小林敏伸 Toshinobu Kobayashi ■ CW: 呉 功再 O Konje / 林 裕 Yutaka Hayashi

Daini Den Den Inc. / Boutique Sachiko Co., Ltd. / Takarajima sha / Hitachi Co., Ltd. / Titleist Japan, Inc. / Mainichi Shinbun Newspaper Advertising Promotion ■ 第二電電㈱／㈱ブチック・サチコ／㈱宝島社／㈱日立製作所／日本タイトリスト㈱／毎日新聞　広告プロモーション

For Newspaper Day on 20th October, we were asked to come up with something interesting on the subject of newspaper advertising for an 8-page supplement. We considered various possibilities such as a tie-up with the editorial department to make a newspaper-type supplement, but we thought that newspaper ads where the ads themselves become news would stimulate readers to make a reappraisal of newspaper advertising. And by making newspaper ad

unlike anything that has gone before, we would encourage an awareness of the potential of newspaper advertising for the future.
　■　10月20日の新聞広告の日に、新聞広告をテーマに、別刷りの8ページで、何か面白い企画ができないかという話があった。編集とタイアップで紙面をつくる等、様々な方向性が考えられたが、広告自体がニュースになるような新聞広告を作ること、それが結果として新聞広告を再認識してもらうことにつながるのではないかと考えた。また、今までにない新聞広告を作ることによってこれからの新聞広告の可能性も感じさせたかった。

MONOCHROME COMP IDEAS

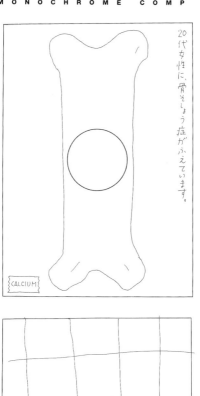

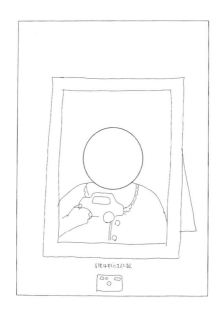

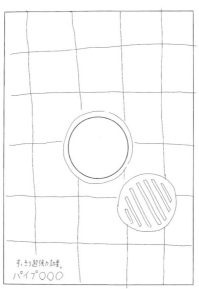

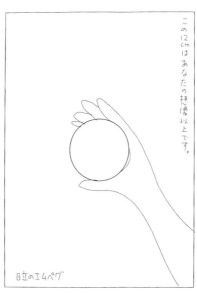

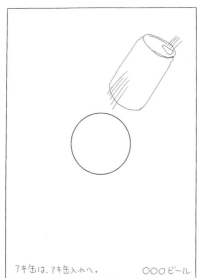

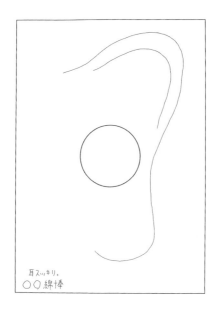

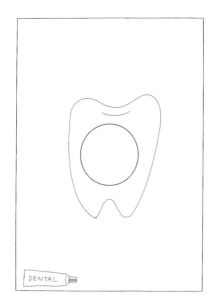

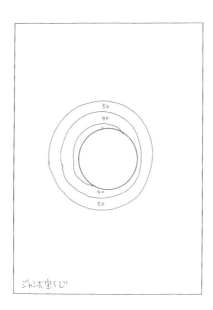

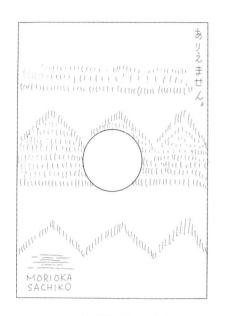

ありえません。

MORIOKA
SACHIKO

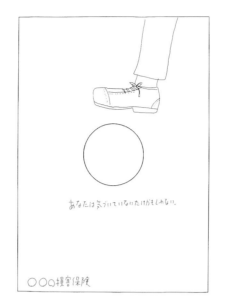

あなたは気づいていなかたかもしれない。

○○○損害保険

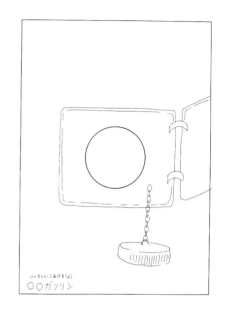

いいガソリンにしてあげよう。

○○ガソリン

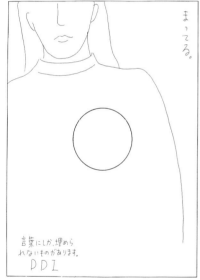

まってる。

言葉にしか、埋めら
れないものがあります.

DDI

KEIBA

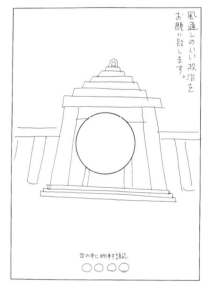

風通しのいい政治を
お願い致します。

世の中に物申す雑誌。
○ ○ ○ ○

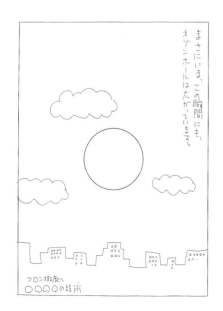

まさにいま、この瞬間にも、
オゾンホールはたがっています。

フロン撤廃へ
○○○○の技術

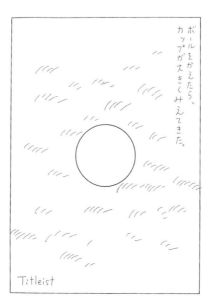

ボールをかえたら、
カップが大きくみえてきた。

Titleist

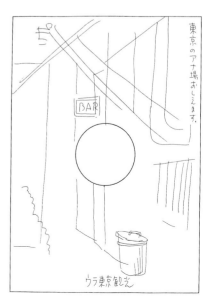

東京のアナ場おしえます。

BAR

ウラ東京観光

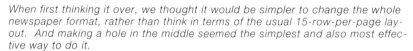

When first thinking it over, we thought it would be simpler to change the whole newspaper format, rather than think in terms of the usual 15-row-per-page layout. And making a hole in the middle seemed the simplest and also most effective way to do it.

まず目立つ新聞広告をと考えた時に、15dの枠ありきで企画を考えるよりも、その新聞自体の体裁が変わっているほうがカンタンだと思った。その中で、真ん中に穴を開けるという手法がシンプルかつ最も効果的であった。

Although we maintained a general overall coherence, we got each of the clients to exploit the hole idea in a different way to keep it interesting.

全体としてはゆるやかな統一性を持たせつつも、飽きのこないようにそれぞれのクライアントで、穴の解釈や見せ方に変化を持たせるように工夫した。

The hole was a rather heavy-handed procedure, and so in contrast, each of the ads was produced carefully in a standard way to achieve an overall balance.

穴を開けるということは、相当あざとい手法なので、逆にそれぞれの広告はスタンダードでていねいなつくりにすることによって、全体のバランスをとった。

■ DF: ㈱博報堂 Hakuhodo Inc. Japan (1996)

■ CD: 宮崎 晋 Susumu Miyazaki　■ AD: 永井一史 Kazufumi Nagai　■ D: 石井 原 Gen Ishii / 佐野研二郎 Kenjiro Sano / 丸山もも子 Momoko Maruyama ㈱リューズ RYUS' Inc.)

■ P: 坂田栄一郎 Eiichiro Sakata　■ CW: 前田知巳 Tomomi Maeda / 斉藤賢司 Kenji Saito

Budweiser Japan / Beer Product Ad ■ バドワイザー ジャパン／商品広告

The client wanted to feature the long-necked bottle centrally in the ad. An earlier TV commercial had featured the bottle as a submarine. The main issues were how we would use this symbol in the graphics and how we were to design a single page ad featuring a big Budweiser label, which is Budweiser's overall design strategy. Summer is the season of the highest demand for beer and we needed to produce something that would fizz and make everyone who saw it thirst for a Bud.

■ バドワイザーの夏のブランドキャンペーンの広告。クライアントの意向でロングネックボトルをメインに立てていくことに決定。CFが先行してボトルを潜水艦に見立てることになっていた。グラフィックとしてそのシンボルをどう描くかということと、バドワイザーのトータルの表現手法であるビッグラベル（ラベルを大きく見せる）をどう一枚絵の中に表現していくかが課題であった。ビールの最需要期である夏に、見てすぐ飲みたくなるというビール本来のシズル感も求められた。

ROUGH SKETCHES

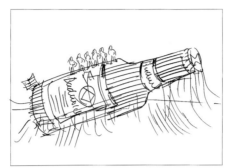

FIRST PRESENTATION

Thought of expressing the liberated feeling after drinking a Bud by using Bud girls to create a Budweiser oasis. A big visual to give a sense of scale, combined with Japanese Bud girls. In this way I wanted to create a world of ready access that anyone can identify with.

バドを飲んだあとの開放感。それをバドガールを素材に、バドワイザーのオアシスとして表現しようと思った。またスケール感あるビッグビジュアルと、日本人バドガールを合わせることによって、間口の広い共感性のある世界をつくりたいと考えた。

We wanted a poster that would avoid being pedantic or contrived and would have instinctive appeal. We looked into adding some copy, but decided that visuals alone would be more powerful and more appropriate to Budweiser.

理屈っぽさや企画性はなるべく排除して、生理的に訴えられる様なポスターにしたかった。コピーを入れることも検討したが、ビジュアルだけでコミュニケーションした方が強いし、バドワイザーらしいと判断した。

We had to put the picture together, and once we got to the comp stage we took pains with the overall composition. After repeated test photo shots, we got the positions of the Bud girls and their poses through simulation on a Macintosh.

合成で絵をつくらざるをえない状況の中、全体の構成にはカンプの段階から気をつかった。テスト撮影を繰り返して、バドガールの位置や、ポーズなどもMac上でシュミレーションして詰めていった。

FINAL PRESENTATION

■ DF: ㈱博報堂 Hakuhodo Inc. Japan (1996) ■ CD: 五十嵐一也 Kazuya Igarashi ■ AD: 永井一史 Kazufumi Nagai
■ D: 石井 原 Gen Ishii / 佐野研二郎 Kenjiro Sano / 加藤 昇 Noboru Kato / 大庭良之 Yoshiyuki Ohba ■ P: 江面俊夫 Toshio Ezura / 伊藤之一 Yukikazu Ito

The specific objective was to attract young women in their teens and twenties, the target group for SHIBUYA 109 fashion building, with a lively '109-style summer' image, and the client requested an energetic ad that would bring to the fore a sense of active, sporty summer-time. We started production with the aim of creating a 109-style design featuring the exhilaration of summer, something that would be distinctive and stand out among other advertising, and would have the sort of impact to get it noticed by young girls in the target group.

SHIBUYA 109のターゲットゾーンである10代〜20代の女の子に向けて、活気あふれる「109らしい夏」をアピールするという目的に従い、アクティブでスポーティな夏の雰囲気を前面に押し出した元気な広告を、というクライアントからの要望に基づいて制作を開始。夏の爽快感、躍動感を他の広告に埋もれない「109らしい」表現に仕上げ、差別化をはかること、またターゲットの女の子たちの話題になるような、インパクトのある広告であることなどもあわせて求められた。

R O U G H　S K E T C H E S

C O L O R　C O M P S

冒険王。SHIBUYA109

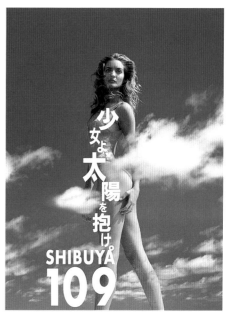

少女よ太陽を抱け SHIBUYA109

We worked up the idea of featuring lively young girls against a background theme of bold summer under a blue sky. We looked into two angles: visuals dominated by a large figure of a girl almost reaching the sky, and flirty poses of flashy girls enjoying summer to the full.

青空の下の大胆な夏をテーマに、元気な女の子を主役に据えた企画を開発。天まで届くほど巨大な女の子がそびえ立つビジュアルと、夏を思いきり満喫している派手な女の子の悩殺ポーズの2案から制作を検討。

We narrowed it down to the large figure of the young girl and did a presentation with color comps of 4 different poses. We paid special attention to the color of the blue sky and the light, and were careful not to lose the human scale when we put the shots together. We completed the designs to give the catch phrase maximum impact.

巨大な女の子案に絞り、ポーズ違いの4案を、カラーカンプでプレゼンテーション。青空や光などの色彩や、合成の際に人間のスケール感が失われないように留意し、キャッチの強さが際だつデザインに仕上がっている。

At the presentation we were asked to change the catch phrase to something closer to the target age group. On the visual side, we were able to reproduce just the right image and overall we successfully put over the idea of a 109-style bright and lively summer.

プレゼンテーションにて、キャッチをもう少しターゲットに寄ったものに変更したいという意見があり再提案する。ビジュアル面でもイメージを忠実に再現でき、109らしい元気いっぱいの夏を表現することに成功した。

■ DF: ㈱レマン Les Mains Inc. Japan (1994)
■ CD, AD, D: 大橋清一 Seichi Ohashi ■ D: 相良多恵子 Taeko Sagara
■ P: 武内俊明 Toshiaki Takeuchi ■ CW: 岡田俊則 Toshinori Okada

Shibuya in Tokyo is the fashion center of choice for teenage girls, including the so-called 'kogyaru'--the trend-setting young teens newly in the spotlight. Our brief was to come up with an ad to boost the numbers visiting the 109 building in this fashion war-zone, and for summer '96 we proposed pop designs aimed directly at the target age-group. The plan was to start the campaign earlier than usual, and we were requested to produce a wide range of design proposals, from images of high summer to the fresh feel of early summer, and also something close to teenagers' real world that did not push the seasonal theme. ■■■■■ 時代の空気を楽しむ、いわゆるコギャルを含めた10代の女の子たちがファッションの中心地として認知している街・渋谷。この流行激戦区のなかで、109が夏に向けて集客数を伸ばすための広告を、というオリエンテーションのもと、'96年はよりターゲット層を意識したポップな表現を提案。通年よりも早めの時期からの露出で広告を展開するということもあり、夏まっさかりのイメージのものから、初夏のさわやかな雰囲気、さらには彼女たちの日常に近い、あまり季節を意識させないものまでの幅広い企画が要求された。

THUMBNAIL SKETCHES

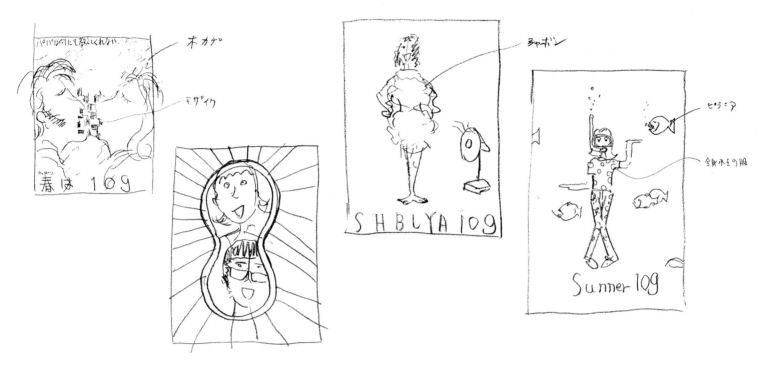

MONOCHROME COMPS

ナイスな夏が、はみだしちゃうよ。

夏の、よりどりみどりちゃん。

夏の、よりどりみどりちゃん。

ナイスな夏が、はみだしちゃうよ。

On a theme of 'thrilling summer' we came up with early-summer proposals of the soap bubbles and electric fan idea, and the snorkeling among piranha fish idea, as well as an idea closer to the target group on 'girl and boy together in summer'. We wanted to produce designs that would stand out for their wittiness.

スリリングな夏をテーマに、シャボン＋扇風機、ピラニア＋シュノーケルのひと足早い夏を先取りした案と、ターゲットに近い「彼と彼女の夏」をモチーフにした案を企画。ウィットに富み目立つ表現を心がけた。

Because they were close to completion, we did a presentation on the early summer proposals only. For the snorkeling ad it was hard to tell the fish were piranhas, so we did a similar ad using sharks, and also a more visually attractive one with tropical fish.

仕上がりの完成度を考慮し、夏の先取り方向案のみプレゼンテーション。シュノーケル案に関しては、ピラニアでは見た目にわかりにくいため、意味合いの近いサメ案とビジュアル的に楽しい熱帯魚案を用意した。

The outcome of the presentation was to work up the soap bubbles idea for the early summer, and the tropical fish idea for mid summer, separately. A crisp finish to tantalizing ads that incorporated a 'pop' look. The same campaign logo was used for both ads.

プレゼンテーションの結果、初夏にシャボン案、夏に熱帯魚案と分けて展開することに決定。ポップでどこか面白味のあるテイストを生かした、すっきりした仕上がりとなっている。2点のキャンペーンロゴも統一。

■ DF: ㈱レマン　Les Mains Inc.　Japan (1996)
■ CD, AD, D: 大橋清一　Seichi Ohashi　■ D: 相良多恵子　Taeko Sagara
■ P: 鶴田直樹　Naoki Tsuruta　■ CW: 西原直美　Naomi Nishihara

T. M. D. Co., Ltd. / Fashion Mall Promotion ■ ㈱ティー・エム・ディー／ファッションビル プロモーション

Ads for autumn at 109 to follow on from the summer campaign. Our starting point was the client's requirement of something appropriate for autumn which incorporated the 109-style lively image. The suggestion was to work on two ideas, for early autumn and autumn-winter, like the earlier summer campaign. Compared with summer, autumn is a season for dressing up, and people were looking out for the new twists in the season's fashion trends so we worked on the themes of sporty, casual and playful. For 109-style, as before, we were asked for a pop design with a fun-loving spirit. ■■■ 夏のキャンペーン表現を受けた、秋の109の企画。109らしい元気さを取り入れた秋らしいものを、というオーダーからスタートする。これも前回の夏のキャンペーンと同様に、初秋と秋〜冬の2案での展開も考えられるとのこと。夏に比べて秋は思いきりおしゃれを楽しめる季節でもあり、今期のファッショントレンドも加味したものが期待されているので、スポーティカジュアルやゲーム的なテイストを軸に企画をすすめる。「109らしさ」としては前回同様、遊びごころの感じられるポップな表現を求められた。

ROUGH SKETCHES

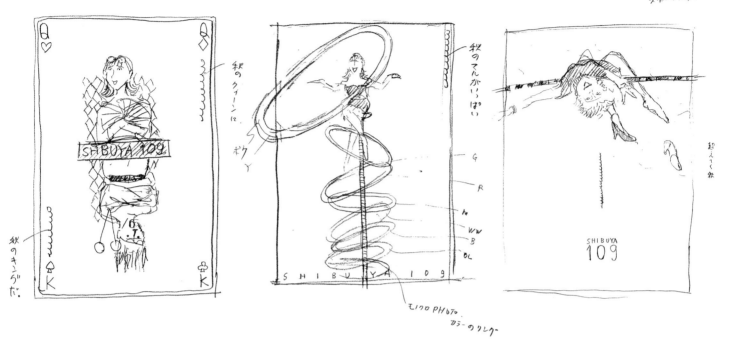

COLOR COMPS

世の中には、まだまだ ⊕ がたりません。 **Nice Shot! 109**

On the theme of fun in autumn, we planned proposals with a simple background, as in the summer campaign. One used high-jumping to stress sport, one used hoop-la to stress play, and as a new, innovative idea we used a playing card with different boy/girl visuals and copy.

秋の遊びごころをテーマに、夏のキャンペーンとの連動性が高いシンプルバックを使ったスポーツ感覚の高飛び案と、ゲーム感覚の輪投げ案の他、斬新な印象のトランプ案を男女のビジュアル／コピー違いで企画。

Of the 4 rough sketches, the playing card with girls top and bottom and the other two ideas were selected, and we produced color comps. We suggested using color to put over an autumn flavor in these lively posters.

数点のラフのうち、トランプ案は上下とも女性のビジュアルのものを選択、その他の2点とともに合計3点をカラーカンプで制作。色使いなど、元気な中にも秋を感じさせる工夫を施した表現を提案した。

The outcome of the presentation was to use the high-jump proposal for early autumn and the hoop-la idea for autumn-winter. We revised the copy to suit. We combined photography and computor graphics to create the same image as in the rough sketches. The finished work had some resemblance to the summer campaign but was more mature.

プレゼンテーションの結果、初秋に高飛び案、秋〜冬に輪投げ案という展開に決定し、合わせてコピーを再提案。ラフのイメージ通りの写真とCG合成で、夏のキャンペーンに連動しながらも大人っぽい仕上がりとなった。

■ DF: ㈱レマン　Les Mains Inc.　Japan (1996)
■ CD, AD, D: 大橋清一　Seichi Ohashi　■ D: 相良多恵子　Taeko Sagara
■ P: 武内俊明　Toshiaki Takeuchi　■ CW: 西原直美　Naomi Nishihara

世の中には、まだまだ ⊕ がたりません。 **Nice Shot! 109**

'Shonan Tokyu Shopping Center' in Shonan Life Town was due to open on Thursday 28 March 1996. Next to it was a household multi-store and nearby various sports and leisure facilities including a bowling alley. With all needs--clothing, food, housing, leisure and interests--supplied, Shonan would soon be the perfect place for a comfortable, convenient and enjoyable lifestyle. The client wanted to get the message out quickly to local residents. Something that would be easy to grasp so that everyone got to hear about it. They decided on a poster campaign. What sort of visuals and copy? Concept

development? Don't worry. Leave it all to the people at Green.
■■■■ 1996年、3月28日（木）、湘南ライフタウンに『湘南とうきゅうショッピングセンター』がオープン。隣にはホームセンターもあるし、ボーリング場をはじめとするレジャースポットも併設。衣・食・住・遊・趣、すべてそろった、快適で、便利で、楽しい生活が、もうすぐ湘南にやってくる。早く地元に住む人たちに教えてあげなければ。どうすれば、わかりやすいかな。どうすれば、みんなに伝わるかな。とにかく、ポスターを作って知らせよう。じゃあ、ポスターのビジュアルは？コピーは？展開方法は？みんなまとめて、グリーンにおまかせ。

FIRST PRESENTATION

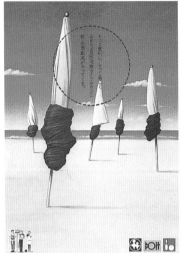

FINAL PRESENTATION

We wanted to make a pre-opening announcement. A 3-poster series has impact and we could possibly use a cartoon character. The visuals need to be interesting and attractive. And it's also important that people feel they can identify with it.

オープンの前に予告をしたいな。3連貼りもインパクトがあるし、キャラクターを作るっていうのもありだよね…。ビジュアルは、面白いものがいいかな、キレイなものがいいかな、親しみやすさっていうのも大切だしな…。

We were going to link the pre-opening and opening ads, so it needed a little more thought. We worked up the copy, buffed up visuals and narrowed it down to three proposals: the parasol, the graphic, and the character ideas. Once we'd got that far it was just one more step.

プレ告知とオープン告知を連動させることに決まったけれど、もう一考。コピーを練って、ビジュアルを揉んで、パラソル案、グラフィック案、キャラクター案の3案に絞り込み。ここまでくれば、決定までもうひといき。

In the end the parasol idea we had favored from the beginning won the day. We took some location shots down by the sea on a windy day. The production involved tough work putting together 20 or so shots to create the posters, but once they were done we delivered them back to the people of Shonan. The opening day was a great success, drawing crowds of customers.

最後まで残ったのは始めからイチ押しのパラソル案。強風に見まわれた海でのロケ、数十点にも及ぶ合成というハードな実制作を経たポスターは湘南に住む人たちのもとへ。オープン初日を大盛況で迎えることができました。

■ DF: ㈱グリーン Green Co., Ltd. Japan (1996)
■ CD: 平野元浩 Motohiro Hirano ■ AD: 幸田栄一 Eiichi Koda ■ D: 水渓文子 Ayako Mizutani
■ P: 増田英明 Hideaki Masuda ■ CW: 佐藤尚生 Takao Sato

Parché / Fashion Mall Anniversary Promotion ■ パルシェ／駅ビル　15周年プロモーション

To commemorate its 15th anniversary, the Parché shopping arcade in the Shizuoka JR station building wanted to revamp its image, highlighting the new and unique experience to be discovered in its shops. The communication concept at the center of the sales promotion campaign was 'Parché FIRST'. Parché, always enjoyable, whenever you go you find something new, a nice place to be any time. Parché, where customers come FIRST, for shopping that comes FIRST with customers. To mark the 15th anniversary with the concept 'Parché FIRST' we

suggested key visuals that would communicate the message clearly and strongly to the target group. ▬▬▬▬ JR静岡駅ビル『パルシェ』が開業15周年を迎えるにあたり、これまでに感じたことがない新しい魅力を発見できるお店を目指してイメージを一新。セールスプロモーション計画の背骨となるコミュニケーションコンセプトは「パルシェ・ファースト」。いつ訪れても楽しい。訪れるたびに新しい発見がある。どんな時でも心地よさを感じる。そして、いつでもお客様のはじまり（first）になる。お客様にとって一番のお店、パルシェ。15周年を「パルシェ・ファースト」で立ち上げるため、ターゲットに明快に、強力にアピールするキー・ビジュアルを提案。

ROUGH SKETCHES AND VISUAL

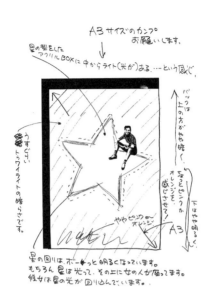

FIRST PRESENTATION

The initial idea we had to convey the 'Parché FIRST' message in a way easy to understand was the evening star. We added a model to it and finished it up nicely but it didn't have enough punch. We needed something with more impact. Suddenly I had the idea of a bright red apple.

「パルシェ・ファースト」を伝えるために…。わかりやすいところで、一番星。モデルをからめて、キレイに仕上げて。でも、力強さが足りない。もっとインパクトのあるものを…。そこでピン！と閃いたのが、真っ赤なリンゴ。

Love at FIRST bite. I recalled this Dracula punchline from my stay in the US. An apple with a chunk bitten out of it, and the word FIRST printed across it. I was convinced this was it and went straight to the photography.

Love at FIRST bite（最初のひと嚙みから愛が始まる。＝ハロウィンでのドラキュラの決めゼリフ）。長いアメリカ生活からヒントを得て、リンゴをガブッ！かじった跡にFIRST。もうこれしかない！と、いきなり撮影。

Adam and Eve, Newton, William Tell... The visual concept was nicely fleshed out, and was readily accepted. As the visual for the start-up campaign, it was used not only for posters but also developed into a commercial film and used for store decoration.

アダムとイブの物語、万有引力の発見、ウイリアムテルの逸話…と、ビジュアルコンセプトにしっかりと肉付けをして、すんなりとOK。立ち上がりのビジュアルとして、ポスターだけでなく、CFから店内装飾にまで展開。

■ DF: ㈱グリーン Green Co., Ltd. Japan (1996)
■ CD, AD: 幸田栄一 Eiichi Koda ■ D: 水渓文子 Ayako Mizutani
■ P: 増田英明 Hideaki Masuda ■ CW: 佐藤尚生 Takao Sato

Laforet Harajuku Co., Ltd. / Exhibit Announcement ■ ㈱ラフォーレ原宿／個展開催告知

An exhibition was to be held at Laforet Harajuku to mark the 40th year in the professional career of the renowned illustrator, Kazuo Umezu. We were really anxious to design the sort of poster that would draw in young people strolling through Harajuku who might never have come across Kazuo Umezu's work. ■ 鬼才楳図かずお氏のデビュー40周年を記念する展覧会をラフォーレ原宿で開催するにあたり、原宿を歩いている、楳図氏の作品を知らない若い人達も、引きずり込んでしまうような告知ポスターを作ろうと、気合いを込めて企画しました。

R O U G H   C O M P S

 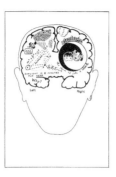 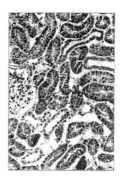  

  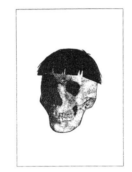 

D O L L   D E V E L O P M E N T

L O G O   C O M P S

We were thinking along two separate lines: to have Kazuo Umezu himself appear in the posters, or to use one or more of the cartoon characters, such as Makoto-chan, that he's famous for.

楳図かずお氏本人に登場していただくアイデアと、氏の生み出したキャラクター（まことちゃん等）をメインにしたアイデアの、大きく2方向で企画しました。

After a lot of consideration, we decided on a proposal that would use both the main ideas: Mr. Umezu's face mounted on a muscular black body to portray 'Macho Mr. Umezu', against a background filled with lots of his cartoon characters.

色々と検討した結果、黒人のカラダに楳図氏の顔を合成した"マッチョ楳図さん"のバックに、氏の生みだした作品の数々を敷き詰めるという当初考えていた2方向の折衷案に決定!!

What we most wanted to express was Mr. Umezu's remarkable originality and the intense energy that his works generate. We changed the body to a plastic model and for the background of the poster we used brilliant yellow and red to leave an incisive impression on the minds of people who saw it.

一番表現したかったのは楳図氏の不思議な存在感と、氏の作品が発している濃密なエネルギー。氏のカラダも黒人から人形へと変更し、バックの作品も黄色と赤でより強烈に見る人の脳裏に焼きつくように仕上げました。

■ DF: ㈱アイ アンド エス I & S Corp. Japan (1995)
■ CD: 浅野幸彦 Yukihiko Asano   ■ AD, D: 秋山具義 Gugi Akiyama   ■ P: ホンマタカシ Takashi Homma
■ CW: 山口哲一 Norikazu Yamaguchi   ©楳図プロダクション ／ 小学館

FM Japan Saison Corp. ／ Radio Program Promotion ■ エフエムジャパン　セゾングループ／ラジオ番組　プロモーション

This was a poster for a new program based on Japanese pops for J-Wave radio sponsored by the Saison Group. The client wanted the ad to emphasize that it was a Japanese pops program. As there was a lot of information to include, we were careful to ensure that the overall *effect did not look uncoordinated.* ■ セゾングループ提供、J-WAVE の邦楽中心の新番組告知ポスターです。その "邦楽" ということを特に強調して広告して欲しい、というオーダーが、クライアントからありました。伝えたい情報もたくさんあるので、とにかく全体の見え方が散漫にならないように気をつけて企画しました。

THUMBNAIL SKETCHES

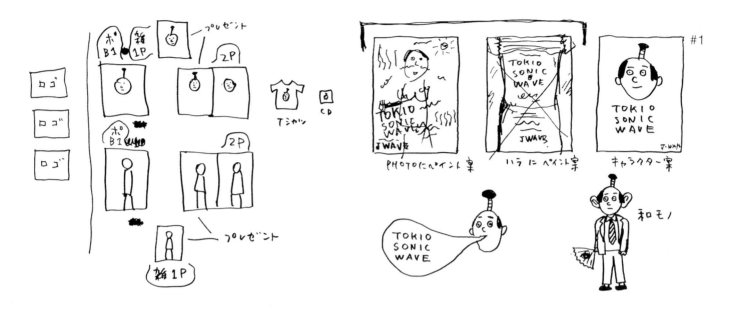

CHARACTER IDEAS

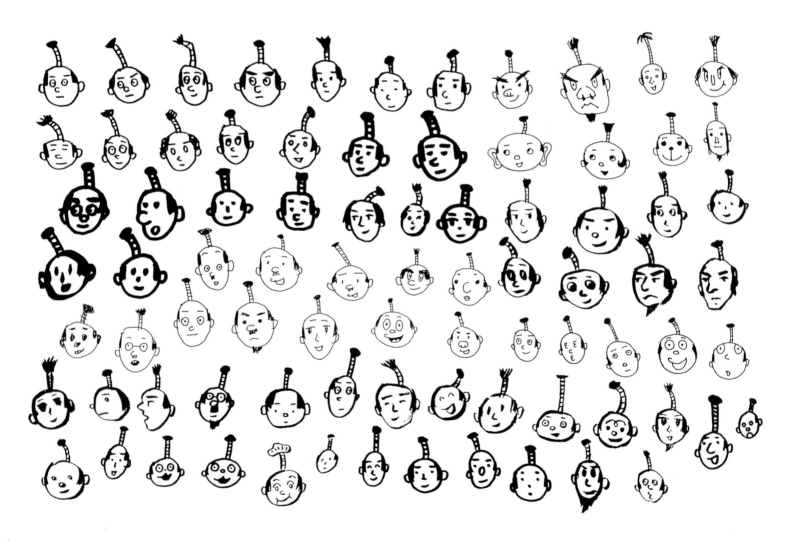

At our first in-house meeting, I didn't really listen to what people were saying. I was doodling some ideas in pen: Japanese pops → Japan → old-fashioned Japanese style → top knots. I thought this was the way to go.

邦楽 → 日本 → 和モノ → 殿さま…かなぁと、最初の社内打ち合わせの時に他の人の話も聞かず、アイデア（らくがき？）をサインペンで描いている時に、何となくこんな感じでやりたいなと思っていました。

Having decided I would do the illustration, I drew hundreds of heads with top knots using pens of different thickness, but when it came to the meeting, the very first one I'd drawn looked the most witless and seemed the best, so I changed his top knot a bit, and started the production process.

自分のイラストでいこうと決めたその後は、何百人もの殿さまを様々な線の太さで描いたのですが、結局打ち合わせの時に一番初めに描いた殿さまがぬけていていいなぁと、チョンマゲ等を修正して、彼で制作を始めました。

I wanted to convey all the elements in a neat, tidy way, so I used the program information as his body, and made a sword out of the copy. To ensure it didn't look too lightweight because it was in only one color, we used rubber thermography instead of ordinary printing to give a heavy-quality finish.

多くの要素をスッキリと見せたかったので、番組情報をカラダ、コピーを刀にして、見せたいものを一つにまとめて表現し、1色でもちゃちくならないよう、ラバーバーコ（ゴムのようなインク）で印刷しました。

■ DF: ㈱アイ アンド エス I & S Corp. Japan (1995)
■ CD: 浅野幸彦 Yukihiko Asano ■ AD, D, I: 秋山具義 Gugi Akiyama ■ CW: 関一行 Ikkoh Seki

For this event, the Geopolis underground area within the Korakuen amusement park was to be completely transformed into a disco hosted by famous Japanese DJs. To advertise the event the client wanted to use another illustration by Katsuhiro Otomo, who had provided illustrations for the ads promoting the new Tower Hacker and Lunar Park rides.

■■■ 後楽園ゆうえんちの地下にある、遊園地"ジオポリス"がイベント期間中、日本の有名なDJがやって来て、CLUBに大変身するとのこと。その告知ポスターを、以前"タワーハッカー""ルナパーク"の広告でお願いした、大友克洋氏のイラストレーションでいきたいとクライアントから要望がありました。

TYPOGRAPHIC CONCEPT

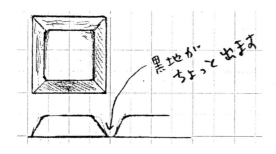

FIRST COMPS

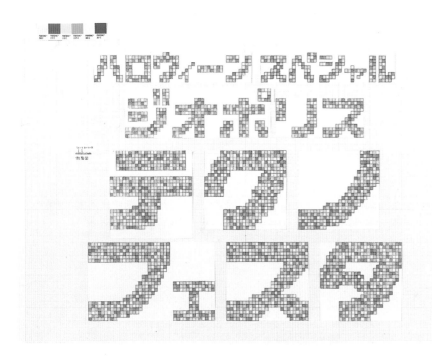

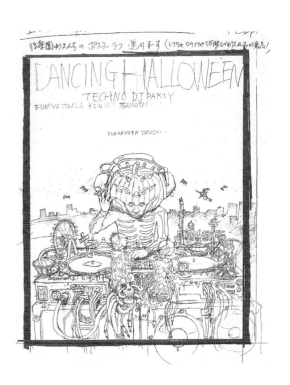

While waiting for the illustration we worked on the Techno Festa logo. We used graph paper and filled in squares with fluorescent pens, to give a slightly dated 'Techno' look.

大友氏からのイラストレーションを待つ間に、"テクノフェスタ"のロゴを同時進行で、方眼紙を蛍光ペンで塗りつぶし、ちょっと昔のテクノなイメージで制作していきました。

The rough sketches that Mr. Otomo faxed us included everything: Halloween, the DJs, the rides at Korakuen... So we just had to put some effort into designing attractive layouts and making posters that really throbbed with the beat of the music.

大友氏からのＦＡＸラフに、ハロウィーン、ＤＪ、後楽園ゆうえんちの乗物と、伝えたいことの全てが表現されていたので、後はレイアウトをきれいに、音楽が聴こえてくるようなポスターに仕上げるよう努力しました。

■ DF: ㈱アイ アンド エス I&S Corp. Japan (1996)
■ AD, D: 秋山具義 Gugi Akiyama ■ D: 野田凪 Nagi Noda ■ CW: 関 一行 Ikkoh Seki
■ PR: 石原正敏 Masatoshi Ishihara / 山下信一 Shinichi Yamashita / 田中栄子 Eiko Tanaka
■ Artist: 大友克洋 Katsuhiro Otomo © 1996 MASHROOM / BEYONDC.

Rover Cars / Mini Product Ad ■ ローバーカーズ／ミニ 商品広告

The Mini, one of the world's best known and best loved cars, has been around for 37 years. Spanning the swinging years of Kings Road chic, pop art patronage and films such as The Italian Job, its cult status has transformed it into what may be the ultimate '60s icon. The Mini enjoys a wide target market and is as much a statement of personality as a mode of transport. Its audience is, in essence, those who dare to be different and are bored with conventional run-of-the-mill cars. In 1996 Rover produced a limited edition Mini called the Equinox. With a wacky interior trim of black and purple Sun-and-moon fabric, and body colours in vivid purple or charcoal grey or silver, the car, like many limited edition models, appealed predominantly to the female market. Equinox provided the Agency an opportunity to push the brand in an innovative, unconventional and exciting manner - individual, fashionable, thrilling and desirable. This was summed up in the proposition The Mini Equinox: Proud to be Loud. As a result of the brief from Rover, the Agency produced a direct mail campaign to 25,000 exisiting Mini owners, a national magazine campaign and postcard run of 50, 000 for fashionable bars, restaurants and clubs. The tone of the advertising is feminine (although not 'girlie'), cheeky and irreverent, deliberately targeting women and empowering them to be assertive in their choice of car. These executions are designed to stand out amid the clutter of fashion pages in such women's magazines as Vogue, Cosmopolitan, Marie Claire, the weekend reviews and so on.

ミニが発売されて37年が経ちます。世界で最も有名な愛すべき車の一つという地位を不動のものにしました。ミニは「ミニミニ大作戦」などの映画、キングスロードの若い女性たち、ポップスや映画好きな人たちを通じて、カルト的なステータスが1960年代に確立されており、60年代最高の偶像といえるのかもしれません。ミニはターゲットとなる市場が広く、単なる移動の手段ではなく、持ち主のパーソナリティーを表現する役割を持っています。ミニを支持する人々は本質的に、あえて他人との違いを作ろうとする人たちであり、市場に出回る型どおりの平凡な車に飽きた人たちなのです。1996年、ローバー社はイクウェノクスと呼ばれるミニの限定車を発表しました。限定車は女性に人気がありますが、特にイクウェノクスは内装シートが風変わりで、生地には名前の由来でもある黒と紫の太陽と月があしらわれており、エクステリアのカラーには生き生きとしたパープル、チャコールグレー、シルバーがあり、その傾向が一層強い車といえます。イクウェノクスは、ミニを、個性的でファッショナブルで、魅力的な車として革新的な型にはまらない形でプロモートする絶好の機会でした。この考え方は「ミニ・イクウェノクス：目立つことの誇り」という言葉に集約されています。ローバー社からの要望を検討した結果、私達は現在のミニ・オーナー25,000人に対するダイレクトメール、雑誌媒体での宣伝、ファッショナブルなバー、レストラン、クラブへ50,000通のハガキ郵送というキャンペーンを行いました。広告のトーンは女性的（ただし「少女趣味」ではない）で、生意気もしくは大胆な感じで、女性をターゲットにするように熟慮されており、女性の積極的な車選びを可能にしています。こうした広告は、「ヴォーグ」、「コスモポリタン」、「マリー・クレール」、「ウィークエンド・レビュー」といった女性雑誌の華やかなファッションページの中でも際立つようにデザインされています。

THUMBNAIL SKETCH

FIRST PRESENTATION

The colour press ad had to reinforce the vital energy that the Mini brand is known and loved for. We needed to capture the individual and distinct personality of the Mini Equinox and its driver. We were very much aware that the environment the ads were to appear in was very pictorial and loud, as this suited the brand, but we had to ensure that our press ad was even brighter to guarantee standout. The link between the fashion interest of the publications we had chosen and the obvious style element of the Mini Equinox Special Edition naturally led us to the idea of a 'Mini Skirt.' This was originally briefed as a single page execution, but we felt if we could expand to three pages it would be more in tune with normal editorial and look like a fashion piece, each page featuring a different girl and 'skirt'. However, budget constraints wouldn't allow this for all of the proposed schedule so we decided to make a centrepiece for one publication, Vogue.

The cars were shot separately from the girls and the outfits were designed to enable us to bring both shots together on computer with a minimum of fuss. We chose bright coloured backgrounds to increase the standout of the models. We felt that a single line of small type would be enough copy to say what we needed and pan it horizontally up the ad as is normal in fashion spreads. When first roughs were presented to the client side, they virtually instantaneously accepted the campaign. They were supportive throughout the production process and delighted with the final results. The campaign has been effective in terms of sales and won a Silver Lion at Cannes in the International Press and Poster Awards.

カラーの雑誌広告で、ミニが有名かつ愛されている理由である、活気あふれるエネルギーを強調しなければなりませんでした。ミニ・イクウェノクスとそのドライバーが持つ個性的で明確なパーソナリティーを表現する必要があったのです。この広告が掲載される環境は、視覚に訴える要素が多い派手な場所です。これはミニのブランドに良く馴染む環境ですが、同時にこの雑誌広告をさらに鮮やかで間違いなく目立つものにしなければなりません。広告を載せる出版物のファッション性の高さと、限定車ミニ・イクウェノクスの特徴的なスタイルとの関連性から、「ミニスカート」というアイデアが自然に生まれました。最初は1ページの広告として考えられていましたが、もし3ページに増やせば通常の雑誌の内容とうまく同調させられると思いました。それぞれのページに違う女性と「スカート」を使って、ファッションページのように見せるのです。しかし予算の制約があり、掲載予定の雑誌すべてでこれを行うのは無理だったので、私たちは中心となる雑誌を「ヴォーグ」に決定しました。

車と女性は別に撮影し、背景は両方の写真をコンピューターで合成するときに、デザインしました。モデルがより際立つように背景には鮮やかな色を選びました。小さな活字一行のコピーで、言いたいことは十分に伝わると考え、ファッション記事の通常の見出しと同じく水平にパン・アップしました。クライアントに最初のラフスケッチをプレゼンテーションするとすぐにこのキャンペーンを認めてくれました。制作過程全体を通じて支持をいただき、最終的な作品も心から喜んでもらえました。キャンペーンは売上の点でも効果を上げ、カンヌの"インターナショナル・プレス・アンド・ポスター・アワード"で銀獅子賞を受賞しました。

The 'Mini Girls' outfits were designed to be an extension of the car as well as each girl's personality. It was imperative the shots weren't obviously car shots and the Mini blended subtly into each outfit. It was also very important the girls looked 'in control', with lots of spirit and attitude. Our intention was to create shots that looked immediately stylish and fashion-like but, after sparking the reader's curiosity, would reveal themselves on further inspection as Mini Equinox car ads.

「ミニ・ガールズ」の衣装は、それぞれの女性のパーソナリティーを表すと同時に車の延長になるようデザインしました。明らかに車だけの写真になるのは絶対に避けて、ミニをそれぞれの衣装にそれとなく調和させました。また、強い精神と態度を持った冷静な女性に見せることも重要でしたし、スタイリッシュでファッショナブルであることも大切でした。そして進めていくうちにミニ・イクウェノクスの広告のあるべき姿がわかってきました。

■ DF: Ammirati Puris Lintas UK (1996)
■ CD: A. Cracknell ■ AD: M. Forster ■ P: Frank Herholdt ■ CW: M. Stewart

At the annual UK Motorshow in October 1996, Rover chose to generate interest in the new 1997 Mini by highlighting the unique options available with the car. For instance, customers can now have a Mini that comes complete with sports accessories such as wide wheels, bucket seats, spotlights etc., or fashion options such as various interior colour schemes - or indeed a combination of both. As a result of this, the Agency produced four double-page spreads to be included in the Motorshow programme, based on the four anticipated areas of customisation of the Mini, i. e., classic, fashion, sports and luxury. These areas were encapsulated in the proposition Express Yourself. The ads were made to appeal to all visitors to the Motorshow, from those in the trade - manufacturers and retailers — to domestic customers who just love cars. They were designed to promote the Mini as a uniquely characterful small car which is dynamic and exciting, and can make you smile. The tone of the advertising is light, bright and easy, and comparable to tiny poster sites. The ads are

also cheeky, irreverent and unexpected. ■■■ 1996年10月、年に一度のイギリス・モーターショーが開催されます。ローバー社はこのイベントで、ミニの1997ニューモデルに対する関心を高めたいと考えていました。例えばワイドホイール、バケットシート、スポットライトなどのスポーツ・アクセサリーを装備したミニや、自分の好みに合わせて内装や色をコーディネイトしたファッション・アクセサリー仕上げのミニ、さらにこの両方を組み合わせたミニを持つこともできるのです。このためエージェンシーは、モーターショーのプログラムに入れる4種類の見開き広告を作りました。広告は予定される4種類のカスタマイズ、つまりクラシック、ファッション、スポーティー、ラグジュリーに基づいて作り、「自分を表現せよ」という言葉でまとめました。取引相手、メーカーの人間、販売業者、自動車が好きな国内の顧客など、モーターショーの来場者全員に訴える広告が必要でした。ミニをユニークなキャラクターを持つダイナミックでエキサイティングな小型車として、また人々を微笑ませる車としてプロモートできるようにデザインしました。広告のトーンは軽快で明るく分かりやすいもので、小さなポスターが貼られているような感じです。同時に生意気、大胆、意外さといった印象を与える広告になっています。

C O L O R   P R E S E N T A T I O N

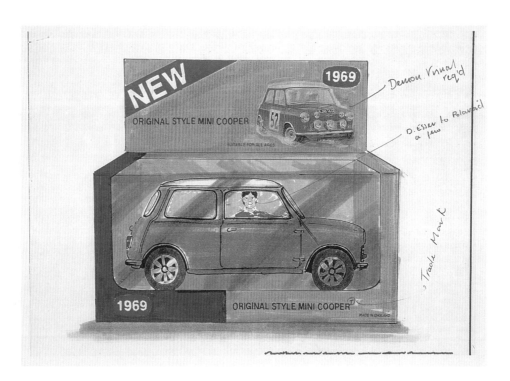

Taking the proposition Express Yourself as a starting point we developed the idea that the Mini is often an extension of the owner's personality and is therefore bought for various reasons - of which we chose four: the Mini is fun, fashionable, sporty and even luxurious. Our general theme covered the styles in which the Mini is often customised. There were four executions using the car in a modelled environment - a toy box to emphasize fun, a shoe box for fashion, a sports bag to reflect its sporting nature and a ring box to highlight its luxury appeal.

私たちは「自分を表現せよ」という言葉をスタート地点にして、ミニが往々にしてオーナーのパーソナリティーの延長になり、楽しさ、ファッション性、スポーツ性、さらには豪華さなど、さまざまな理由で購入されるというアイデアを発展させました。全体のテーマは、ミニがカスタマイズされるスタイルを集約することです。模型で作った４種類のシチュエーションに車を置いて、おもちゃ箱で楽しさを強調し、靴の箱でファッション性をアピールし、スポーツバッグでスポーツ性を反映させ、指輪の箱で豪華な買い物というステータスを際立たせました。

Upon Client approval we commissioned a photographer to work in conjunction with a model maker to produce high quality shots that portrayed the various 'styles' of the Mini in the relevant modelled environments. The overriding consideration was to make sure that the cars looked real and not like the models they were partnered with. The images were accompanied purely by the stand number where the Mini was being exhibited, the intention being to express the uniqueness of the car without the need for any further copy.

クライアントの承認を得て、私たちはカメラマンに模型製作者と共同で作業を進めるよう依頼しました。ミニのいろいろな「スタイル」を適切な環境の中で表現し、質の高い写真を製作するためです。最も考慮したのは、車を確実にリアルに見せ、一緒に組ませる模型と同じように見せないことでした。画像に付け加えるのは、ミニが展示されている場所のスタンドナンバーだけです。そのため、コピーを一切追加せずに車のユニークさを表現できる写真が必要でした。

The car shots were done separately from the models and were composed to enable us to combine both shots on computer. The vibrant backgrounds were designed to emphasize the standout of the finished shots and complement the 'loud' and individualistic character of the car. Special attention was paid to highlights and reflections to emphasize the car's original design and shape and to make the models appear real. The Client was enthusiastic about the idea, from the original concepts through to the final executions. Upon completion of the final artwork the Client was genuinely delighted and impressed with the Agency's results. At press time the Motorshow had yet to take place, so no feedback had been received.

車は模型とは別に撮影し、両方の写真をコンピューターで合成しました。出来上がった写真をきわだたせ、この車の「派手」で個性的なキャラクターを引き立てるために、背景は刺激的なデザインにしました。コンピューターで車と模型の画像を合成するプロセスでは、ハイライトと反射に特に注意して、ミニ本来のデザインと形状を強調し、模型を実物に見せるようにしました。最初のコンセプトから最終的な作品ができるまで、クライアントはこのアイデアを熱狂的に支持してくれました。最後のアートワークが完成した際、クライアントは心から喜び、エージェンシーの仕事に強い感銘を受けてくれました。モーターショーは今月の後半に開催されるので、今のところ反響は受け取っていません。

■ DF: Ammirati Puris Lintas UK (1996)
■ CD: A. Cracknell ■ AD: G Harper ■ P: E. Lee ■ CW: G. Dodd

Tower Records / Corporate Promotion ■ タワーレコード㈱／企業広告

This was a graphic to make Tower Record's slogan 'No music, no life' sink in a little more deeply. The issue was designing a graphic ad that incorporated the slogan mark of a circular shape in the red and yellow corporate colors in a very natural way.　タワーレコードのスローガン

である「NO MUSIC NO LIFE」（音楽の無い生活なんて）をより浸透させるためのグラフィックである。まあるい形状、赤と黄色を基調としたコーポレートカラーのスローガンマークを、いかに自然な形でグラフィック広告の中で表現できるかが課題であった。

MONOCHROME COMPS

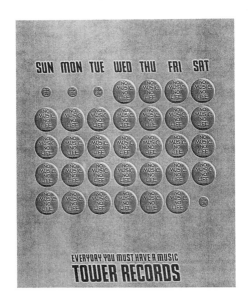

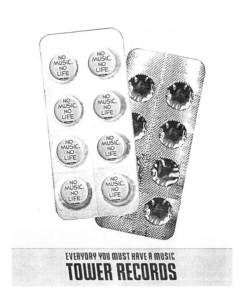

We tried putting the slogan in everyday things such as a fried egg, a tablet, a calendar, a badge and so on, to underscore the close link music has with daily life, and the ideas developed from there.

目玉焼き、薬、カレンダー、バッジなど普段の生活の中で見慣れたものにスローガンを入れ込み、いかに生活と音楽が密接に関連しているものなのかを表現することから、発想を展開させていった。

Music is taken for granted in our daily lives. We haven't perhaps thought about it, but life without music would surely be a boring succession of bland, colorless days. We are living on a planet where music is as important as air and water. This slogan ad that developed from single aspects of daily life ended up with this grand graphic.

私たちの生活の中に当たり前のように存在している音楽。普段気がつかないけれど、音楽の無い生活は無味乾燥とした味気のない毎日のはず。私たちは水や酸素と同じくらい大切な音楽惑星で暮らしている。日常の一コマから発想したスローガン広告は、このような壮大なグラフィックとなって結実した。

■ DF: ㈱博報堂　Hakuhodo Inc. / ㈱赤丸広告　Akamaru Advertising Office　Japan (1996)
■ CD, CW: 木村 透　Toru Kimura　■ AD, D: 箭内道彦　Michihiko Yanai
■ D: 杉山晴彦　Haruhiko Sugiyama　■ I: 木村さえ子　Saeko Kimura

We were commissioned to produce a visual idea that could be used not just once but again and again as a graphic for a new store opening. We were asked to produce something with a new, fresh look appropriate to a store opening, with an originality expected of the Tower Records image, and visuals that would be popular with a broad spectrum of people. ■■■ 新店舗用のグラフィックとして、一回限りではなく、今後続々とオープンする際に継続して使用できるビジュアルの開発を得意先より依頼された。店舗のオープンらしい新鮮さと、タワーらしいオリジナリティが感じられ、さらに多くの人に愛されるビジュアルに仕上げることが求められる用件である。

COLOR COMPS

FINAL PRESENTATION

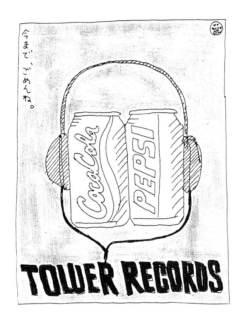

We worked on two approaches, one expressing the universal message 'Using music makes everything go smoothly', and one designed specifically on the theme of a Tower Records store opening.
「音楽を媒介にして、物事はスムーズになる」という普遍的なメッセージを表現したものと、タワーレコードの新規出店らしい「オープン感」を表現したものの2方向で表現を展開させた。

In the end, we went back to the original objective of a visual for a store opening. We produced a visual that communicated this message in a clearly understandable way.
最終的に、店舗のオープン用ビジュアルという目的に立ち戻って、分かりやすく、オープンらしさを伝えるビジュアルを制作することになった。

■ DF:㈱博報堂　Hakuhodo Inc. / ㈱赤丸広告　Akamaru Advertising Office　Japan (1996)
■ CD, CW:木村 透　Toru Kimura　■ AD, D:箭内道彦　Michihiko Yanai
■ D:杉山晴彦　Haruhiko Sugiyama　■ P:伊藤之一　Yukikazu Ito

Tower Records ／ Opening Announcement ■ タワーレコード㈱／オープン告知

The Oita store opened in August, 1996, and was the first real music store in the district. The concept for this campaign focussed on the idea of the long-awaited 'real thing' finally arriving. We began creative work for an ad that would appeal to teenagers, the core target, with a basic message of something unprecedented arriving, and a simple design with powerful impact, exploiting a bright, American, liberated feel in the red and yellow corporate colors. ■ タワーレコード大分店は、

大分地区に今までなかった本格的なミュージックストアとして、96年8月にオープンした。当キャンペーンのコンセプトは、「待ち望まれた、本物の到来」である。他に追随を許さない登場感をベースに、タワーレコードのコーポレートカラーであるレッド＆イエローを基調とした、アメリカっぽいイメージで明るい開放感、シンプルかつインパクトの強いクリエイティブを、コアターゲットであるティーンエージャーに向けて訴求できる広告づくりを目指してクリエイティブワークは始まった。

C O L O R　P R E S E N T A T I O N

えらいことだ。本物が来たぞ。

To convey the idea of something long-awaited, a first-time appearance in the region, we concentrated on ways of using a strong-impact visual as a motif. Specifically, we developed ideas around army tanks, missiles, the space shuttle, etc.

地域初の本物感、待望感を表現するため、インパクトの強いビジュアルをモチーフに切り口を収集。具体的には、戦車、爆弾、スペースシャトルなどからアイデアを構築していった。

We used parts of a jeep-like large vehicle to create a main visual that projected strong appearance and a sense of the future. To make it more apt for a music store we installed fog lamp-type speakers, and created a powerful announcement of the new store opening.

ジープなどの大きめのクルマをデフォルメして、登場感・未来感を伝えるメインビジュアルを制作。ミュージックストアらしく、ホグランプ型スピーカーを搭載して、新店舗オープンを力強くアナウンスする構図にした。

■ DF: ㈱博報堂 Hakuhodo Inc. / ㈱赤丸広告 Akamaru Advertising Office Japan (1996)
■ CD, CW: 木村 透 Toru Kimura ■ AD, D: 箭内道彦 Michihiko Yanai
■ D: 杉山晴彦 Haruhiko Sugiyama ■ CG: 谷田一郎 Ichiro Tanida

Mass Transit Railway, Hong Kong / Promotion ■ マス トランジット レイルウェイ／プロモーション

The purpose of the ads was to draw people's attention towards the depressing prospect of wildlife extinction. The ads were targetted towards the general public and strove to evoke a positive response towards the conservation activities sponsored by the World Wide Fund for Nature. The concept revolves around the fact that if wildlife is not protected today, future generations may have to use colour pictures to enjoy the beauty of mother nature's bounty. A printing press is used to symbolize the 'mother' of wild animals as they come into this world as pictures. ■■■■ 広告の目的は、人々の目を野生生物の絶滅に関する見通しが暗いことに向けさせることでした。ターゲットは一般大衆で、世界自然保護基金が支援する保護活動に、前向きな反応を引き出すためのものでした。広告のコンセプトは、いま野生生物を守らなければ、未来の人々は母なる自然の恵みを楽しむためにカラー写真を使わなければならなくなる、という事実が中心になっています。この世界に野生動物を写真として生み出す「母親」のシンボルとして印刷機を使いました。

THUMBNAIL SKETCHES

FIRST PRESENTATION

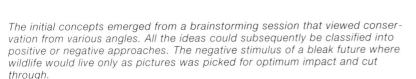

The initial concepts emerged from a brainstorming session that viewed conservation from various angles. All the ideas could subsequently be classified into positive or negative approaches. The negative stimulus of a bleak future where wildlife would live only as pictures was picked for optimum impact and cut through.

最初のコンセプトが生まれたのは、自然保護をさまざまな角度から検討したブレーンストーミングでした。その後、すべてのアイデアを有効な手法とそうでないものに分類しました。野生生物が写真でのみ存在する暗い未来という否定的な刺激が、望ましいインパクトを与えるアイデアとして選び出されました。

The negative scenario of a bleak future where wildlife thrived only as pictures was developed further. A printing press 'giving birth' to various forms of life became the key icon of the ads. The tone and mood of the final visual had to reflect a gloomy aura without compromising on its impact. The decision to use photography instead of illustrations was aimed at adding credibility to the whole concept.

野生生物が写真としてのみ繁栄する、暗い未来の否定的なシナリオをさらに発展させました。さまざまな生物を「誕生」させる印刷機が広告の重要なシンボルになり、最終的なビジュアルのトーンやムードは、インパクトを減らさずに陰鬱な雰囲気を表現する必要がありました。コンセプト全体に信憑性を与えるために、イラストではなく写真を使用することに決めました。

In the final stages of the production, the client, especially MTR's Advertising & Publicity Manager Ms. Nancy Pang, encouraged the creative team to push the concept further. The result shows in the details. The type face for the Chinese and English versions is actual metal type used by printing presses. The borders are the typesetter's tray and the type mounting boards for the Chinese and English ads respectively. And the final composition of the press and floating pages is dramatic yet sepulchral.

制作の最終段階で制作チームは、クライアント側、特にMTRの宣伝広告部長からコンセプトをさらに前面に出すよう奨められました。成果はディテールに現れました。中国語版と英語版の書体は、印刷機で使用する本物の金属活字にし、縁取りには中国語版では植字機のトレー、英語版では植字台を使いました。印刷物や浮かんでいるページの最終的な構図は、ドラマチックかつ重苦しい雰囲気に仕上げました。

■ DF: J. Walter Thompson Hong Kong (1995)
■ CD: Iris Lo / Chan Man-Chung ■ AD, D: Kelvin Hung
■ P: Stephen Cheung ■ I: Simon Lam ■ CW: Ronnie Yeung / Francis Cleetus

The brief was to highlight the most popular dishes on the menu and portray the restaurant as an exciting, fun and lively place to eat.

■■ メニューの中でいちばん人気の高い料理を強調し、このレストランをエキサイティングで楽しくいきいきとした食事ができる場所として表現すること。

ROUGH SKETCHES

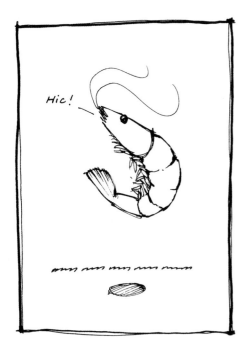
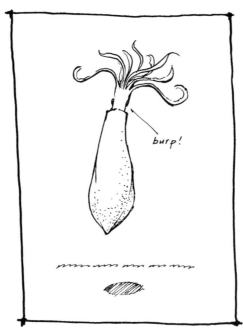
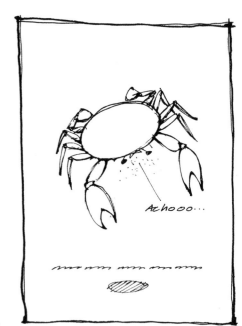

FINAL PRESENTATION

Come, taste the freshest drucken prawns in Singapore. So fresh, indeed, you might even hear it's famous last words. CELEBRITY ORIENTAL RESTAURANT

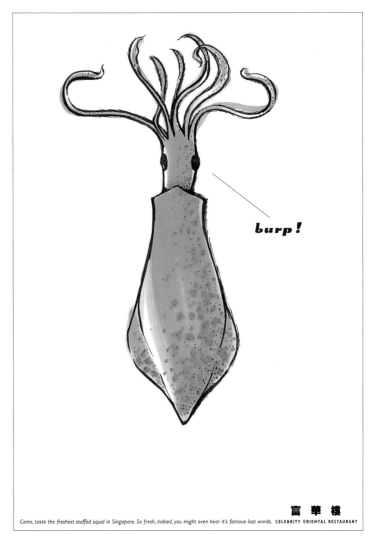

Come, taste the freshest stuffed squid in Singapore. So fresh, indeed, you might even hear it's famous last words. CELEBRITY ORIENTAL RESTAURANT

achooo!

Come, taste the freshest pepper crab in Singapore. So fresh, indeed, you might even hear it's famous last words. **CELEBRITY ORIENTAL RESTAURANT**

achooo!

Item #23:
PEPPER CRAB
NO. 1 MARITIME SQUARE, #02-138
HARBOUR PROMENADE, WTC. TEL: 273 9158
CELEBRITY ORIENTAL RESTAURANT   富 華 樓

burp!

Item #24:
STUFFED SQUID
NO. 1 MARITIME SQUARE, #02-138
HARBOUR PROMENADE, WTC. TEL: 273 9158
CELEBRITY ORIENTAL RESTAURANT   富 華 樓

hic!

hic!

Item #36:
DRUNKEN PRAWNS
NO. 1 MARITIME SQUARE, #02-138
HARBOUR PROMENADE, WTC. TEL: 273 9158
CELEBRITY ORIENTAL RESTAURANT   富 華 樓

This was the first idea. We were discussing the brief over a few drinks at a pub. One of us mentioned 'Pepper Crab' and a story about sneezing while eating it. Achoooo!!... The rest was easy.

最初のアイデアで決まりました。クライアントの指示について、何度かパブで飲みながら話し合いました。一人が「ペッパークラブ（コショウ蟹）」のことに触れて....食べてるときにクシャミをする話をしました。ハーックション！！....あとは簡単でした。

The design is minimalistic yet modern - just like the restaurant's decor and image. Apart from appetising shots, there's an element of quirkiness that appeals to the younger audience.

デザインはミニマリズム風に....ただしモダンに —— レストランの装飾やイメージと同じです。食欲をそそる写真は別ですが、若い人たちにアピールする奇抜な要素を使っています。

The photographer played a vital role in the final stages. Although everything is clean and graphic, it's not 'cold'. There's a friendly feeling to the whole communication. The client is thrilled. Now, you need to make reservations at least a day in advance.

最終段階では写真家が重要な役割を果たしました。すべてさっぱりしていて写実的ですが、「冷たい」感じはありません。フレンドリーな雰囲気が広告全体にただよっています。クライアントも感激していました。今では、少なくとも前日までに予約が必要な状態です。

■ DF: Ogilvy & Mather Singapore (1995)
■ CD: Steve Elrick / Sau Hoong ■ AD, D: Yeo Yeow Thong. Yang ■ AD: Kate Saarinen
■ P: Sebastian Tan / The Shooting Gallery ■ CW: Jackie Hathiramani

Volvo Cars Japan Corp. / Promotion (Safety) ■ ボルボ・カーズ・ジャパン／プロモーション（安全）

The main consideration was that Volvo has already established a reputation and position in the market because of its safety features, so the ad should demonstrate the company's confidence and pride. I thought if we could put across the message: Volvo = Safety just in visuals, we'd achieve deeper level understanding than with a pronouncement in words, so I decided not to have any copy. The open safety pin implied the further message that however safe the equipment, *it's dangerous unless used correctly.* ■ 制作するときに注意した点は、ボルボはすでに安全性で確かな実績と評価を得ているので、自信と余裕のある堂々とした広告表現でなければならないと考えました。ビジュアルを見ただけで「ボルボ＝安全」というメッセージに（読者が一瞬、考え）気づいてもらえたら、一方的な言葉による説明より、もっと深いコミュニケーションが成立するのでは…、と考え、ノン・コピー表現にしました。そして、安全ピンが開いたままになっているのは、「どんなに安全な道具でも、正しく使わないと危険ですよ。」というメッセージも込められています。(AD: 沢 正一)

THUMBNAIL SKETCHES

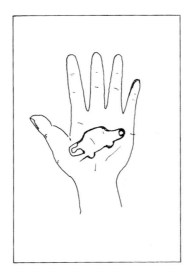 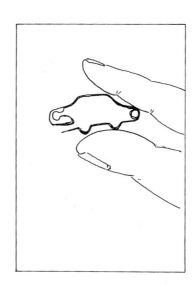

FIRST PRESENTATION

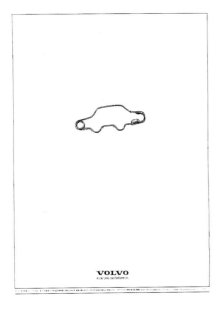 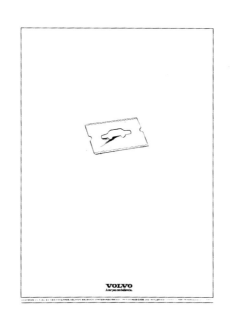 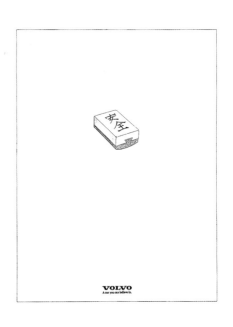

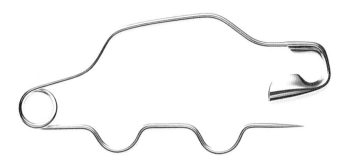

VOLVO
A car you can believe in.

43rd CANNES International Advertising Festival 〈Press & Poster〉 GRAND PRIX Award. ／ 第43回カンヌ国際広告祭〈プレス＆ポスター部門〉グランプリ受賞

I was just thinking we could create a new type of ad by expressing the message of a 'safe car' symbolically, with no words, only visuals, when suddenly the safety pin idea flashed into my mind.

アイデアは、"安全な車"というメッセージを、言葉を使わず、ビジュアルだけで記号化できれば、新しいタイプの広告ができるのでは…、と考えている時、安全ピンが"ピン"とひらめきました。

Safety razor, closed safety pin.. tried out all sorts of ideas, but we did a presentation only on the open safety pin idea. I thought this was best suited to Volvo.

安全カミソリ、安全パイ？、閉じた安全ピンなど、いろいろなアイデアを作ったが、結局、開いた安全ピンのみプレゼンテーションしました。ボルボにとって最もふさわしいアイデアは、安全ピンだと考えたからです。

To get a newspaper ad that would stand out among all the other information, we decided on a layout making lavish use of the white background. And the tire parts of the pin were made flat to the ground.

情報が多く盛り込まれた新聞の中で、とにかく目立つ新聞広告にするために、白地を思いっきり贅沢に生かしたレイアウトにしました。そして、ピンのタイヤの部分が、地面に対して水平になるようにしています。

■ DF: 電通ヤング＆ルビカム㈱ Dentsu, Young & Rubicam Inc. Japan (1996)
■ CD: 川瀬 稔 Minoru Kawase ■ AD, D: 沢 正一 Masakazu Sawa ■ P: 和田 恵 Megumu Wada

The message was 'We're not hiding anything about the polluting effect of cars on the environment. The company pledges to direct efforts to do something about this, and report its progress.' To convey the message suitably, I thought the ad would best be direct, sincere and without embellishment. The design should be quiet, in muted tones, with the copy printed small. I did a basic layout that would never date, so that the ad would remain in the memory as an image associated with Volvo. ■■■■ 「環境に対する車の公害問題を、包み隠さず公開した上で、それに対する企業の努力の方向を約束し、さらに、その経過を報告します。」というメッセージです。そのメッセージが正しく伝わる広告にするためには、正直で飾らない誠実な広告でなければならないと考えました。そして表現的にも、静かで控え目なトーンがふさわしいと思い、キャッチフレーズを小さく扱いました。この広告が、いつまでもボルボのブランド・イメージとして、記憶に残るように、何年たっても古く感じない様な、ベーシックなレイアウトにしました。（AD: 沢 正一）

ROUGH SKETCHES

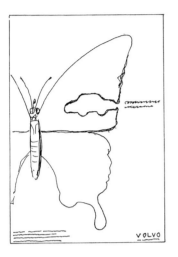 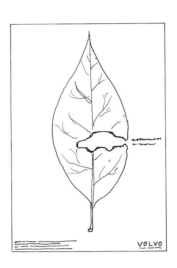 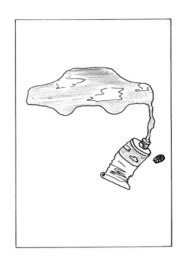 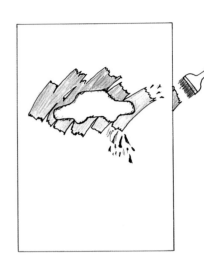

FIRST PRESENTATION

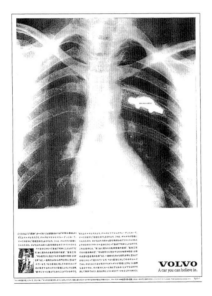 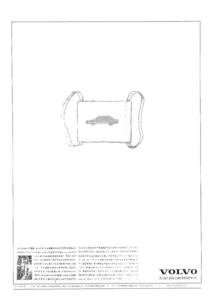

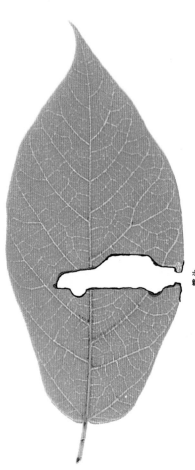

ボルボは「環境破壊データ」を公開します。
新車の1台1台について――。

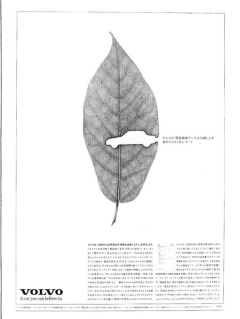

Had the idea that the pollution problem caused by cars could be thought of as 'cars eating away at nature'. I turned this into a visual, with the image of 'eating away' symbolized in a leaf that had been eaten away by a caterpillar. This was the start of the idea.

車の公害問題とは、"車が自然を蝕む"という事だと考えました。そして"蝕む"という言葉を、そのまま虫食いの葉で、蝕む（文字通り？）様子を、シンボリックにビジュアル化したのが、アイデアのきっかけです。

One other theme: that the Volvo paintshop does not pollute the air. Tried to illustrate the relationship between the car and the air by using X-ray photos, masks, etc. and the outline of a car.

他にもう1つ「ボルボの塗装工場は空気を汚しません」というテーマがあります。レントゲン写真やマスクなどと、車のシルエットを使って、車と空気との関係を表現してみました。

The reason we used the outline of a car was that even though the theme was environmental pollution, I thought it should be clearly a car-maker's ad. I want to make the outline a Volvo trade-mark by using it again in the future.

車のシルエットを使用したのは、環境問題がテーマとはいえ、車メーカーの広告である事が明快でなければならないと考えたからです。そして、そのシルエットを使い続ける事で、それをボルボのトレード・マークにしたいと思っています。

■ DF: 電通 ヤング＆ルビカム㈱ Dentsu, Young & Rubicam Inc. Japan (1995)
■ CD: 川瀬 稔 Minoru Kawase ■ AD, D, I: 沢 正一 Masakazu Sawa ■ CW: 天畠良光 Yoshimitsu Tenbata

The special feature of this brand is that it tastes good despite being low tar. We worked on this, using an intelligent and humorous design to raise the brand image of the cigarette. We followed two guiding principles: as far as possible not to use anything except the packaging, and to create a clean-looking ad with a layout exploiting the white ground of the paper, and using only the blue of the packaging and the surrounding white. By sticking to these two points I thought we would put over a light, clean concept suited to a low tar cigarette, as well as building intelligence and humor into the brand image. ■■■■■ "低タールなのに味がある"という商品特性を、知的でユーモアのある広告表現により、ブランド・イメージを高める事を目的に展開しました。表現上の注意として、①商品パッケージ以外の余計な要素は、できる限り使わない。(ケイ線などのグラフィック要素にとどめる。) ②紙の白地を生かしたレイアウトで、パッケージのブルーと、余白のホワイトだけの清潔な紙面にする。この2つの点を守る事により、低タールタバコらしいライトな清潔感と、知的でユーモアのあるブランド・イメージを、つくる事が可能ではないかと考えました。(AD: 沢 正一)

ROUGH SKETCHES

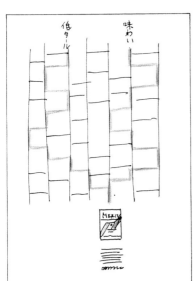

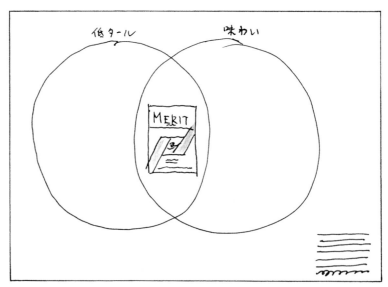

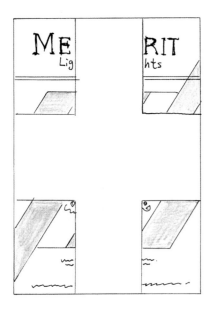

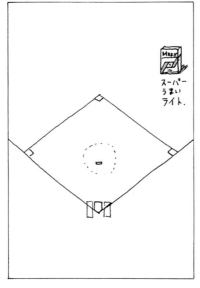

How far could we go with the simple strategy of 'low tar but great taste'? We started off trying out all sorts of angles very freely, aiming for simple ideas that were intelligent, humorous and easy to grasp.

"低タールなのに味がある"というシンプルなストラテジーを、どこまで飛躍したアイデアで表現できるのか。そして、知的でユーモアのある、解りやすいシンプルなアイデアを目標に、いろいろな方向で、最初は自由に考えてみました。

Did the presentation on the 'open taste' idea. This expression has a double meaning in Japanese as it's also the name of a popular fish dish.

"味のひらき"という作品は、アメリカ人クライアントには、"Open Taste"という和訳に(魚を開いた日本で有名な食べ物の名称と同じ発音で、Double Meaning になっている。)という説明をつけて、プレゼンテーションしました。

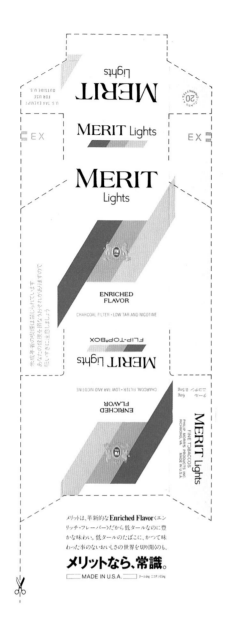

Leo Burnett-Kyodo Co., Ltd.

味のひらき。

低タールでは、味で並ぶものがない。

低タールを求めても、味わいにたどりつく。

味のある 低タール

メリットなら、常識。

■ DF：レオ・バーネット協同　Leo Burnett - Kyodo Co., Ltd.　Japan (1991)
■ AD, D, CW：沢 正一　Masakazu Sawa　■ D：市村真悟　Shingo Ichimura
■ P：大久保歩　Ayumi Okubo　■ CW：松村修司　Shuji Matsumura

Cutty Sark Scots Whisky / Cutty Sark Product Ad ■ カティーサーク スコッチ ウイスキー／カティーサーク　商品広告

Cutty Sark is projected as a Scots whisky aimed at young people with a different approach to life. They want to be original as an expression of their uniqueness. But originality does not mean extravagance. It is just being different in a clever way. Cutty Sark advertising must be modern, up-to-date, intelligent, with a fresh look. It should be seductive rather than imperative, allowing free interpretation. It must also be dynamic and interactive, and committed to social concerns. Neither a picture of the bottle nor copy is necessary to get the

message across.. ■ カティーサークを、人とは違ったライフスタイルを求める若者向けのスコッチウイスキーとして宣伝する、というプロジェクトがくまれました。こうした若者は、彼らのユニークな所が、オリジナリティであると感じています。しかし、オリジナリティが贅沢を意味するわけではありません。賢いやり方で、他人との違いを示すことを意味するのです。カティーサークの広告は、次の条件を満たす必要がありました。── 現代的、最先端、見た目が新鮮、知的。── 誘惑的、ただし押し付けがましくはない。── 自由な解釈ができる。── 力強く、相互作用を生む。── 社会の関心事に結びつく。メッセージを伝える上で、ボトルやコピーは必ずしも必要ではありませんでした。

THUMBNAIL SKETCHES

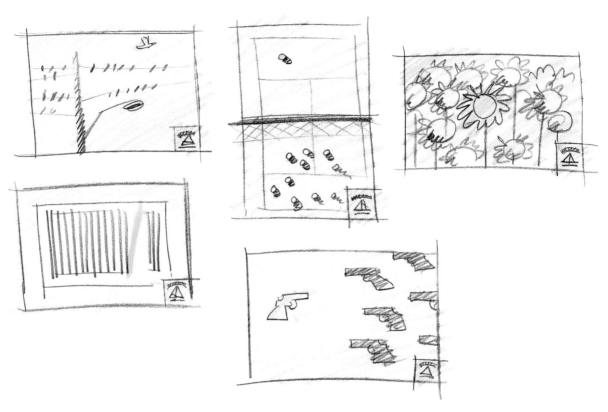

FINAL PRESENTATION

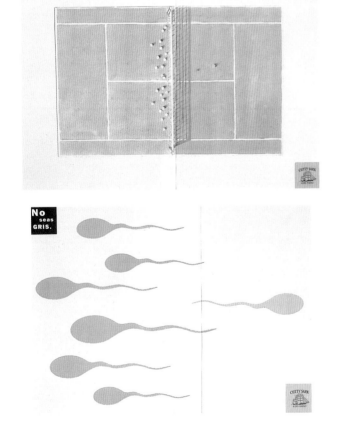

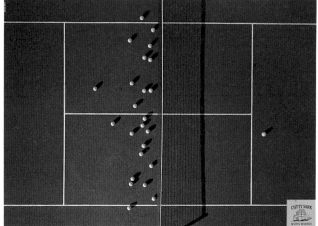

As the client wanted to change the image of the advertising, focussing on a teenage audience, we thought of different ways to approach this target. The brainstorming session ended up with a very simple line: Cutty Sark thinks for himself and consequently acts by himself. It means don't be grey, don't be like others. From that point we started to look for situations.

クライアントは広告のイメージを変え、若い人たち、つまり10代の人たちを狙ったものにしたがっており、このターゲットの人たちの言葉に近づくような新しいやり方を練りました。ブレーンストーミングの結果、カティーサークは自分で考える、そして自分で行動する、というシンプルな考え方がまとまりました。どっちつかずはやめよう、他人と同じはやめよう、といった感じです。この点から、広告のシチュエーションを考えました。

Once we had the situations we tried to define the look. We knew what our audience liked about design. We did different tries with colors and with B/W + yellow, and finally we saw that the combination of this blue/grey with the yellow, as an expression of freedom, fitted perfectly with the message we were trying to put across.

シチュエーションが決まった後、見せ方を明確にしました。ターゲットの人たちがどんなデザインが好きかはよくわかっています。白黒＋黄色をもとに、違った配色を試し、最終的に青／灰色と黄色のコンビネーションが自由の表現に適していて、伝えようとしていたメッセージにぴったりでした。

Some of the ideas were easier to finish than others. Many hours with the paintbox, then the client, and... But once we saw the result we loved it, and so did the client and the target audience. Since this campaign has been running, the name Cutty Sark is more on the spot than it's ever been. And that's something to be pleased about.

アイデアによっては仕上げるのがもっと簡単なものもあります。何時間も絵の具箱と格闘し、クライアントと打ち合わせをし、そして最終的には、出来上がりを見て私たちは満足しました。クライアントもターゲットの人たちも同じでした。このキャンペーンが始まってから、カティーサークの名前は今までになかったほど身近になりました。これはたいへん喜ばしいことです。

■ DF: Delvico Bates, S. A. Spain (1995)
■ CD: Pedro Soler / Enrique Astuy
■ AD: Angel Villalba / Jorge Herrera / Sandra Garcia
■ P: Carlos Navajas / Miguel Martinez ■ I: Fernando Bayona

Announcement of a new service program making maintenance charges free for the first 3 years after purchase. In Japan there is a persistent belief that imported cars may be very expensive to maintain, which discourages people from switching from domestic to imported cars. Hence this program. The timing was just after the economic bubble when car importers were all rushing to lower prices, so advertising was all focussed on prices. The Hosokawa cabinet was being pressed to take strong measures to revive the economy, and economic topics dominated the news. The client requested something that would have a lot of impact in these circumstances. ■■■■ 購入後3年間のメインテナンス費用を無料にする新サービス・プログラムの発表広告。日本では一般的に「輸入車は維持費が不安だ」という意識が根強く、国産車から輸入車に乗り換える際の大きな障害となっていた。そこで開発されたのが、このプログラムである。当時はバブル経済が崩壊した直後であり、輸入各社は値下げに走り、広告も価格訴求一色。社会全体も、細川内閣が強力な経済対策を国民から強く求められるなど、経済をめぐる話題が沸騰していた。このような環境の下、とにかくインパクトがあるものをというのが顧客の要望であった。

R O U G H   S K E T C H E S

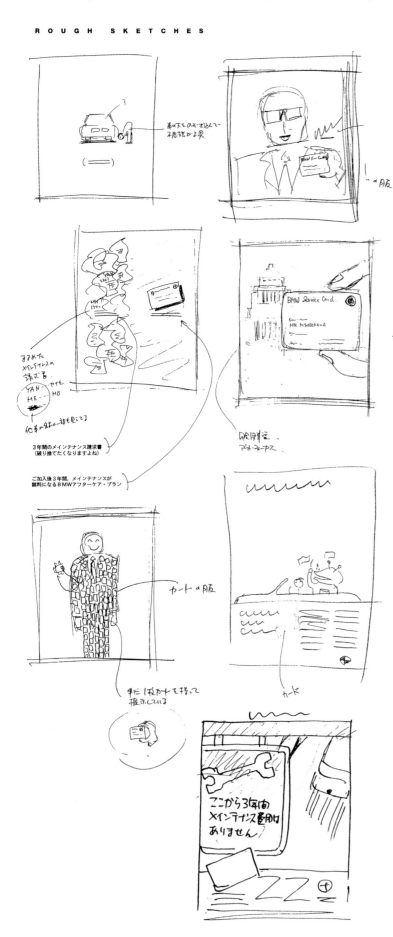

F I R S T   P R E S E N T A T I O N

WHICH WOULD YOU CHOOSE?

Three-years of maintenance bills you'd rather throw away.

Three years of maintenance absolutely free, after entering the BMW After Care Plus program.

NO MAINTENANCE COSTS NEXT 3 YEARS.

BMW HAS CHANGED IN A MAJOR WAY. BUT WHERE?

(After you enter the BMW After Care Plus program, you get three years of maintenance absolutely free.)

NEXT TIME, WHY NOT CHANGE TO AN IMPORT CAR THAT DOESN'T CARRY A *KANEGON* [MONEY EATING MONSTER].

"BMW HAS ALWAYS PUT THE INTERESTS OF THE CUSTOMER FIRST. FOR EXAMPLE, HOLDERS OF THIS CARD WON'T PAY A SINGLE YEN FOR CAR MAINTENANCE FOR THREE YEARS."

IT'S ALL BECAUSE OF THAT CARD.

BMW After Care Plus
Three years of maintenance absolutely free, after entering the program.

Ideas exploiting various approaches were examined: aiming at novelty interest, putting forward the benefits of the service, showing it as representative of company policy. We were also asked to supply a name for the program, so we considered ideas related to a name, too.

話題性を狙ったもの、サービスの便益を前面に出すもの、企業姿勢として打ち出すものなど、様々な切り口でアイデアを検討。また、プログラムのネーミングも依頼の一つであり、それと連動したアイデアも考慮した。

In considering the angle of the car, the way to show the service card, etc., we were thinking how we would later do the photography and put it all together. The schedule was tight so we skipped comps and did a presentation with rough sketches.

車のアングル、サービス・カードの見え方など、決定後の撮影や写真合成を念頭に置きながら仕上げた。スケジュール上の制約から、この時はカンプを作成せず、ラフスケッチによるプレゼンテーションとした。

Finally, we made an introductory ad on the theme 'Message to Prime Minister Hosokawa', and a follow-up with the 'Free-Way' motif. This arrangement aimed to stir novelty interest and to put over the name and the merits of the program in a straightforward way.

最終的に、「細川首相へのメッセージ」を導入広告とし、「フリーウェイ」をモチーフとしたものをフォローアップ広告とした。話題性を狙ったものと、商品名およびメリットを直接的に訴求したものの組み合わせである。

■ DF: ㈱コーブ・イトウ広告社　Cove - Ito Advertising Ltd.　Japan (1993)
■ CD, CW: 山本修靖　Nobuyasu Yamamoto　■ AD: 佐藤昌己　Masami Sato
■ P: ㈱クラッカースタジオ　Cracker Studio

Announcement of a nation-wide sales event intended to introduce a 'face-lift' model to the market. The model had a newly developed engine, and its major improvements were a big saving in weight through the use of aluminum, and increased torque to reduce turning circle. But in appearance it's indistinguishable from earlier models, so the differences can only be appreciated in the driving seat. This was the crucial point. Also, the purpose of the ad was not to promote the product but to announce the showroom event. Bearing this in mind,

we proposed a campaign revolving around test driving. ■■■■ フェイスリフト製品の市場導入を目的とした全国展開のセールス・イベント告知広告。新開発のエンジンを採用した製品であり、主な改良点は、アルミブロックの採用による大幅な軽量化と低回転域でのトルクの増大である。しかし、外観は前モデルと見分けがつかない。つまり、実際に走らせてはじめて違いが分かる製品である。これが最も重要なポイントであった。また、広告の役割は、プロダクト広告ではなく、あくまでもショールーム・イベントの告知広告である。このような観点から、試乗促進を軸とするキャンペーンとして立案した。

ROUGH SKETCHES

WHEN THE DAY COMES, DON'T FORGET YOUR DRIVER'S LICENSE.

当日は、免許証をお忘れなく。

Back to the future.

GET YOUR TEST DRIVE TICKET THIS WEEKEND AT THE SHOWROOM

WE MADE A DRAMATIC CHANGE. BUT YOU HAVE TO DRIVE IT TO UNDERSTAND.

大胆に変えました。走らせると分かります。

FROM PRO DRIVER TO BEGINNER, EVERYONE CAN ENJOY IT: INTRODUCING THE NEW BMW 328i.

プロ・ドライバーから若葉マークまで。
みんなに愉しいニューＢＭＷ３２８ｉ、デビュー。

THE NEW BMW 328i

当日は、免許証をお忘れなく。

The New BMW 328i

New BMW 328i ￡,800,000円

The New BMW328iデビュー・フェア
8月26日(Sat.)・27日(Sun.) 10:00AM～6:00PM

We started examining two possible directions: emphasizing the improved product performance resulting from the new engine, or stressing the showroom event. These rough ideas illustrate this process.

新エンジンの搭載によりパフォーマンスを高めた製品特性の訴求に力点を置くか、あるいはイベントの告知効果に比重を置くか、大きく2方向で検討を始めた。ここに掲載したものは、そのプロセスを示すラフアイデア。

In the end we decided on the showroom event, rather than going into details on the product features. The visuals focussed not the car itself but on a driving license, and for the background we decided to use a showroom where the sales event would be based.

最終的に、製品の特性を詳細に伝えることより、イベントの告知効果に比重をおくこととした。このため、ビジュアルの中心を車ではなく「免許証」に置き、また、イベント会場であるショールームを背景として設定した。

The completed work is based on the comp, as you can see. The same driving license design was used for a 'test drive ticket' that was included in a direct mail shot to promote the sales event. A lottery was also held to pick prizewinning (real) license numbers.

ご覧のように、カンプ通りの仕上りとなった。補足ではあるが、イベント集客用のDMには、この広告と同じデザインの運転免許証を試乗券として封入し、また本物の免許証番号で賞品が当たる抽選会を実施した。

■ DF: ㈱コーブ・イトウ広告社　Cove - Ito Advertising Ltd.　Japan (1995)
■ CD, CW: 黒田雅也　Masaya Kuroda　■ AD: 三村嘉浩　Yoshihiro Mimura
■ D: 田中規隆　Noritaka Tanaka　■ P: 越谷喜隆　Yoshitaka Koshiya

Air Pacific operates the only direct flight between Japan and Fiji, so the campaign was planned to focus on the attractions of Fiji, the destination, rather than the airline's cabin service etc. It was geared to three different targets: honeymoon couples, young women office workers and additionally, family groups. Family groups were added because, judging from Hawaii's experience, the market potential of families is very high, even though the proportion of families among current travellers to Fiji is low. The basic concept 'Paradise of Smiles' was intended to single out Fiji as a friendly, unsophisticated place rich

in untouched natural beauty hard to find in other resort destinations.
　■───　エア・パシフィック航空は、日本 - フィジー間で唯一の直行便である。このため、広告は旅客サービスの差別化ではなく、目的地の魅力を訴求するものとして企画された。ターゲットはハネムーナー、ＯＬ、そして新たにファミリーを加え３つの層を設定。これは、ハワイに見られるようにファミリーのマーケット・ポテンシャルは非常に高い一方、フィジーへの旅客に占める家族の割合が低いことによる。基本コンセプトは“笑顔の楽園”とし、他のリゾート地にはない手付かずの大自然、素朴で親しみのあるフィジアンのイメージで差別化を狙った。

MONOCHROME COMPS

FINAL PRESENTATION

We followed up two ideas, one showing typical target group visitors enjoying Fiji, and one using Fijians to build an image of Fiji as an unsophisticated, friendly place. The key lay in choosing the best visuals to represent Fiji.

フィジーを楽しむターゲットの姿を表現するか、フィジアンを主役として素朴で親しみのあるフィジーのイメージを形成するか。この２方向でアイデアを模索。この土地ならではのビジュアル要素の選択がキーであった。

It was finally decided to feature Fijians, although honeymoon couples were also included to appeal specifically to this target group. We concluded that photo tones and finish would be very important, and proposed using a photographer from a non-commercial background.

最終的にフィジアンを主役とする方向としたが、ハネムーナーのみはターゲットの心理を考え本人達を登場させた。また、写真のトーン、仕上がりが極めて重要であると判断し、商業系ではない写真家の起用を提案した。

Kazuyoshi Miyoshi was commissioned for the photography. His work is particularly strong in color and creating a real sense of being there. We ensured that Fiji was portrayed very naturally, without anything contrived, and worked hard to show Fijian smiling faces without any affectation.

色彩や臨場感に卓越したスタイルを持つ写真家、三好和義氏に撮影を依頼した。作為的でなくフィジーの素顔が自然に伝わるよう留意、特にフィジアンの笑顔がケレン味なくストレートに表現されるようこだわった。

■ DF: ㈱コーブ・イトウ広告社　Cove - Ito Advertising Ltd.　Japan (1996)
■ CD, AD: 宮本道人　Michihito Miyamoto　■ P: 三好和義　Kazuyoshi Miyoshi
■ CW: 上田佳弘　Yoshihiro Ueda

Mycal Honmoku ／ Fashion Mall　Re-Opening Announcement　■　マイカル本牧／ファッションビル　リニューアルオープン告知

The design aimed to use the idea of a black and white documentary-type film to put over the modern image of Yokohama Honmoku. By achieving balance with the powerful color used for the word OPEN, the focus of the message, we created a sense of expectation for the re-opening of the store. We used a European style type face that would work when overlaid on the photography. The models appear in the style fashionable at the start of the Showa Era (1925), that symbolized 'Western style' and 'the height of fashion', to convey a chicness appropriate to Yokohama. We used MYCAL Honmoku facilities for the location photography and gave it an intimate feel by using scenes that would appear familiar. At MYCAL Honmoku customers are very relaxed, often bringing their pet dogs and calling out to each other.

Into such every day scenes we introduced a humorous dog character to subtly express a comfortable familiarity.　■■■■■　横浜・本牧のモダンなイメージをドキュメンタリータッチのモノクロ映画風に表現しました。さらに訴求の核となる「OPEN」の文字などにインパクトのあるカラーバランスを配し、リニューアルの期待感を訴求しています。書体については蓄積イメージを活かすヨーロッパ風を踏襲しました。モデルのスタイルは「モボ・モガ風」で演出。ファッショナブルな昭和の幕開けを告げたスタイルは、「西洋風」と「流行の先端」を象徴し、お洒落な横浜らしさを訴求しました。写真は、マイカル本牧内の施設をロケーション地とし、どこかで見たことのある風景を出すことにより、身近な印象をあたえています。マイカル本牧では、愛犬を連れたお客様同士が、気軽に声を掛け合う情景をよく見かけます。こうした日常シーンを背景に、「擬人化したイヌ」をユーモラスに登場させ、親しみやすさをさりげなく表現しました。

F I N A L　　P R E S E N T A T I O N

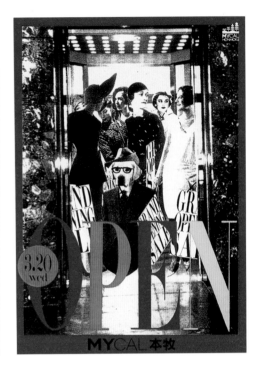

Pedestrian bridge: With the dog character at their head, happy, lively people gather on the bridge that connects the separate shopping areas, to generate a sense of expectation for the Grand Opening.
歩専橋編：各番街をつなぐ橋を舞台に、勢い良く集う人々、その先頭をいく擬人化したイヌで、グランド・オープンの期待感を演出。

Escalator: People coming to the new MYCAL on an escalator. Discreetly placed among them is the dog character. The customers all carry shopping bags with a SALE slogan to achieve a stronger advertising effect.
エスカレーター編：新しいマイカル本牧に連なる人々を、エスカレーターを使って表現。その中に、さりげなく擬人化したイヌが存在。また、セールタイトルの書かれたショッピンバッグを持たせ、より一層の広告効果を狙います。

Elevator: An unusual design using an elevator to stimulate the sense of expectation. We made it more entertaining with a touch of parody.
エレベーター編：新しいマイカル本牧の期待感をエレベーターを舞台にユニークに表現。パロディタッチのイメージ作りで楽しさを演出。

Slogan: The details of the Sale are highlighted against a background of European flavor typography. By putting this together with the three different opening announcements we conveyed symbolically both messages of Opening and Sale.
タイトル：ヨーロッパタイプの欧文の文字組（タイポグラフィ）を背景に、セールタイトル、セール期間を浮き立たせました。オープン告知のバリエーション3種類との組み合わせにより、オープンとセールを象徴的に表現。

■ DF: ㈱アルト・カンポ・カンパニー　Alto Campo Company　Japan (1995)
■ CD, AD: 高畑小百合　Sayuri Takahata　■ D: 松井 薫　Kaoru Matsui　■ P: 山田純子　Junko Yamada
■ Stylist: 高畑三穂　Miho Takahata　■ Hair & Make-up: 水島裕作　Yusaku Mizushima

Street fashion is a powerful motor driving present-day youth culture. The client wanted to establish a new brand allied to street fashion. Our work started from looking at the design of the watch. We narrowed down the target audience to 'cross-boarders' (skate- and snow-boarders) because a marketing analysis showed that information directed to this group would spread to those around them. The creative team then started making promotional material according only to whether or not it would communicate to this group. Keeping the tone of our final goal always in mind, we tried to make it quite cute but also aggressive. We were particularly careful that it didn't turn into the sort of ad that was obviously adult-designed. Because if the snow-boarders ridicule it, then that's the end of the campaign. ■　いまどきのヤングカルチャーをぐいぐい引っぱっているストリート系ファッション。そこに向けて新しいブランドを確立したい。クライアントからのオーダーがあり、デザイン画を見るというところからこの仕事は始まりました。まずターゲットをクロスボーダー（スケートボーダー、スノーボーダー）に絞りました。情報は彼らをコアにして、周辺の連中に波及するという分析がマーケッターから出されたからです。我々クリエイティブスタッフは彼らに受けるということだけ考えてすべての制作物をつくり始めました。ちょっとかわいいもの、ちょっとヴァイオレントなものなど、最終ゴールのトーンの部分を常に念頭に置きながら、「オトナが考えた若者向け広告」だけにはならないように気をつけました。スノーボーダー達にバカにされたところで、このキャンペーンはおしまいですから。

LOGO DEVELOPMENT

Logo: With some 200 name proposals we did a target survey and decided on the name SPOON. We aimed for something more than a straightforward logo by creating a 'world' for the product that the target audience could visualize.

約200のネーミング案の中から、ターゲット調査を経て「SPOON」に決定。単なるロゴタイプではなく、ヴィジュアライズすることで商品の世界観を視覚的にインプットさせることを狙いました。

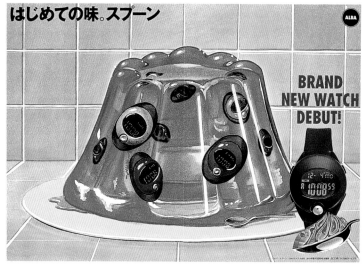

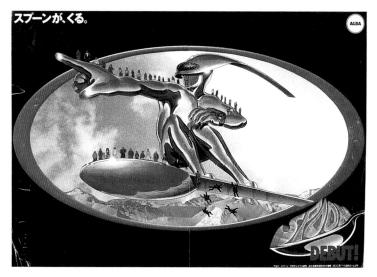

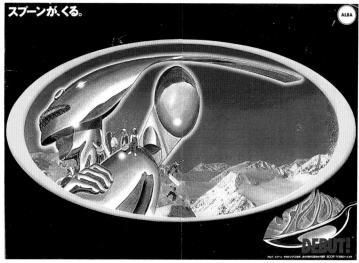

SIMPLE?

COOL?

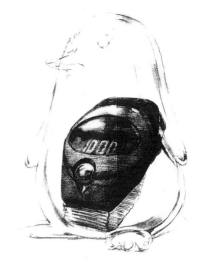

BRAND
NEW WATCH
DEBUT!

FRESH?

BRAND
NEW WATCH
DEBUT!

DELICIOUS?

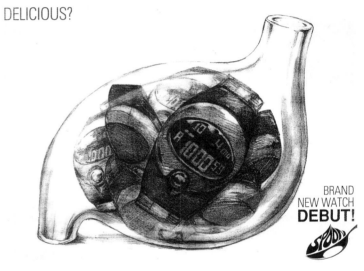

BRAND
NEW WATCH
DEBUT!

SHINING?

BRAND
NEW WATCH
DEBUT!

CUTE?

BRAND
NEW WATCH
DEBUT!

ENJOY?

BRAND
NEW WATCH
DEBUT!

HELLO!

BRAND NEW WATCH
DEBUT!

COOL?

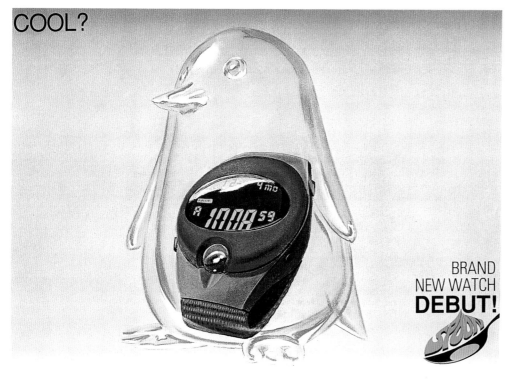

BRAND
NEW WATCH
DEBUT!

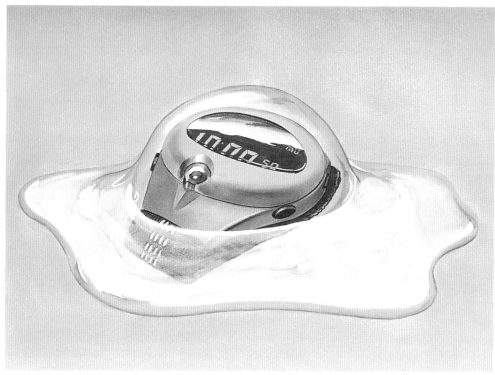

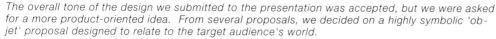

The overall tone of the design we submitted to the presentation was accepted, but we were asked for a more product-oriented idea. From several proposals, we decided on a highly symbolic 'objet' proposal designed to relate to the target audience's world.

プレゼンテーションで提出した表現全体を覆うトーンはOKだが、もっとプロダクトよりの案が欲しいとの返事。いくつかの案の中で、ターゲットの世界観をシンプルに表現した最も記号的なオブジェ案に決定。

SPOON watches are cool, and from that we got the penguin. SPOON watches are good quality, and from that we got the 'good!' sign. SPOON watches are the greatest, and from that we got the crown. We used these simple ideas in the design, making variations to the visuals and copy. We added charm and a sense of with-it-ness to the visuals by using strong colors and a shiny plastic look. All Seiko ads contain an address to write to for a catalogue, and we were surprised to hear that the response to the SPOON ads was the best ever.

スプーンはカッコイイからCOOL、だからペンギン。スプーンはいかしてるからEXCELLENT、だからグッドのサイン。スプーンはイチバンだからGREAT、だから王冠。スプーンを見て思う最も単純な感想を、ヴィジュアルとコピーで少しずらすことで表現しました。ビジュアルはイマっぽさとカワイサを出すため、プラスチックな素材感とカラーでポップにあらわしました。セイコーの広告には、すべてカタログ請求の宛先を入れるのですが、スプーンは空前の反響が集まり、我々も非常に驚きました。

■ **DF:** ㈱旭通信社 Asatsu Inc. Japan (1995)
■ **CD:** 横川 覚 Satoru Yokokawa ■ **AD:** 小松洋一 Yoichi Komatsu
■ **D:** 斎藤多聞 Tamon Saito ■ **P:** ホンマタカシ Takashi Honma ■ **CW:** 藤本英雄 Hideo Fujimoto

The debut campaign was a great success and sales were going extremely well, so what should we do for the second year? This was the starting point. The objective of this campaign was to boost the product image as a serious brand and not simply for cross-boarders. We proposed three possible approaches at the presentation. 1: The 'product hero' idea that followed on from the debut campaign and used copy to gain a response from the target audience. 2: Matching scenes the target audience could identify with to copy they could respond to. 3: To get an even closer reflection of the target audience in the SPOON brand, develop ads around a logomark that brought together

the message and logo. Of these, the third approach was chosen and we moved to production. ■■■■ デビューキャンペーンは大成功、売れ行きも絶好調、さて2年目はどうする？というところからスタート。クロスボーダー達だけにとどまらないメジャーブランド化へ向けてパワーアップすることがこのキャンペーンの目標です。プレゼンテーションには次の3方向を提案しました。①デビューキャンペーンを継承しつつ、コピーでターゲットの共感を得ることを考えたプロダクトヒーローの方向性。②ターゲットが共感するシーンにターゲットが共感するコピーを合わせた方向性。③ターゲットマインドをスプーンというブランドにより色濃く反映させるため、メッセージとロゴマークを一体化させたマークを中心に展開する方向性。この中で③の方向性が採用され制作に入りました。

THUMBNAIL SKETCHES

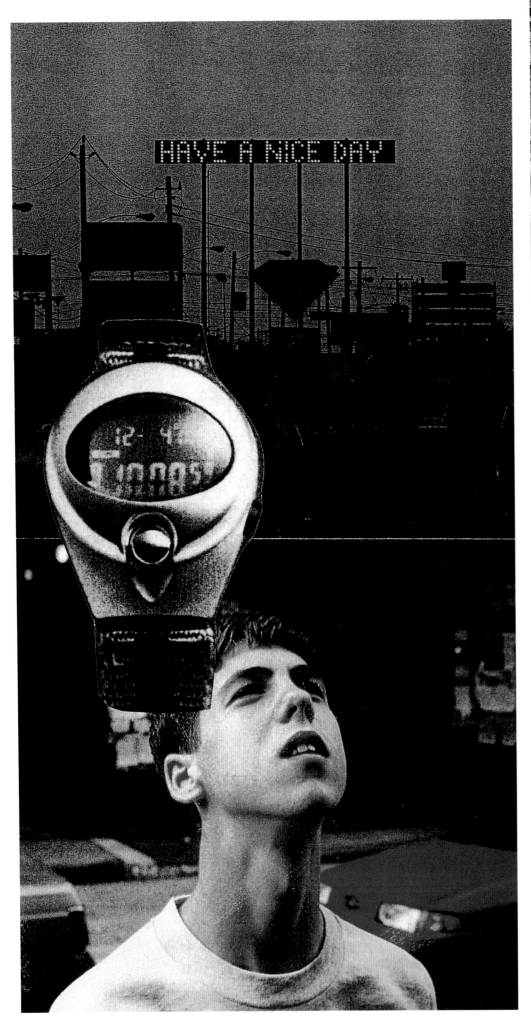

ラブマーク

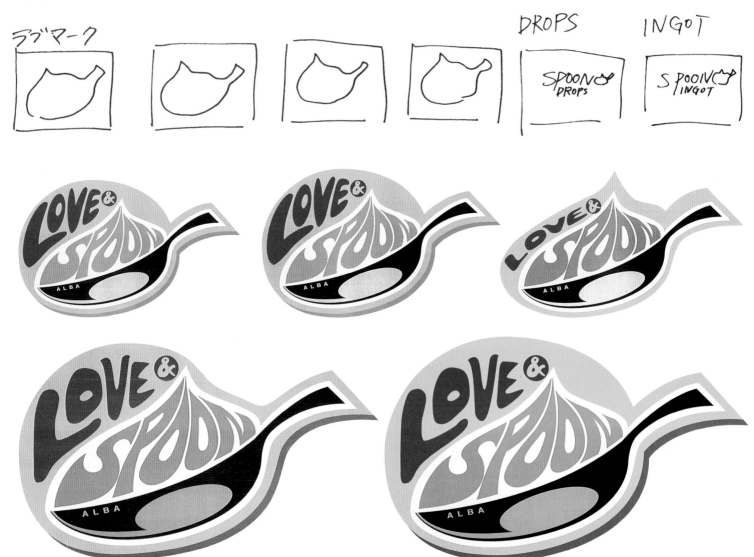

DROPS

SPOON DROPS

INGOT

SPOON INGOT

We isolated the words LOVE and SPOON as important for the target audience. We aimed for a response from the target generation by combining the slogan LOVE & PEACE with the 'must' watch SPOON.

ターゲットにとって大切なものは何か。それはラブとスプーン。ターゲット世代の中で、ある種キーワード的な合言葉
LOVE&PEACE と、マストウオッチSPOONをダブらせることで彼らの共感を得ようとしました。

We commissioned Robert Rosenheck for the photography. Models selected there and then on the street in New York were photographed holding the LOVE sign: the message in logomark form. We used non-Japanese models because we wanted to avoid Japanese associations and add a universal dimension to the message. We narrowed down the models we wanted from a pretty wide range and reduced the total to about 600 shots. Then we selected the photos that most symbolized our target, to make understanding from the target the biggest priority, and finally brought the number of shots down to 7. All through, we tried hard not to overlook the element of humor.

カメラマンにロバート・ローゼンヘック氏を起用。NYのストリートで直接ライブにキャスティングしたモデル達に、メッセージをマーク化した「LOVEサイン」を持たせて撮影しました。外国人にした理由は、「日本」という意味性を排除し、メッセージを普遍的なものにしたかったからです。かなり幅広いキャラクターの中からターゲットを選定し、合計600カットあまりを押さえました。そしてターゲットに対してのわかりやすさを優先させるため、象徴的にターゲットを写し出したフォトを選び、最終的には7カットまで厳選しました。全体を通じて忘れないように心掛けていたことは「ユーモア」でした。

■ DF: ㈱旭通信社 Asatsu Inc. Japan (1996)

■ CD: 横川 覚 Satoru Yokokawa ■ AD: 小松洋一 Yoichi Komatsu

■ D: 斎藤多聞 Tamon Saito ■ P: ロバート・ローゼンヘック Robert Rosenheck

■ CW: 藤本英雄 Hideo Fujimoto

Laforet Harajuku Co., Ltd. / Fashion Mall Promotion ■ ㈱ラフォーレ原宿／ファッションビル　プロモーション

The ad for the 1996 Laforet Grand Bazar started in the form of a contest between four firms. The client wanted something fresh and there were no other initial requests. The ad for the winter season Grand Bazar had been a parody of a cartoon character 'Virtua Fighter'. We had produced a 'Bazaar Fighter' using Ichiro Tanida's computer graphics. For the summer campaign we suggested a higher powered version and submitted our proposals. The concept was the same as before: Bargains have to be fought for. ■ 1996年ラフォーレグランバザールの広告は、4社競合の形で始まった。とにかく新鮮なものを求められていて、それ以外のリクエストは初めは無かったと思う。冬のグランバザールの広告は、バーチャファイターをもじって、谷田一郎氏のCGを起用し、バザールファイターを制作した。夏もさらにパワーアップしたものを、と考えて企画を出した。コンセプトについては、初回と同じで「バーゲンは勝負だ」というもので望むことになったのだが……。

SCHOOL GIRL DEVELOPMENT

TELEVISION COMMERCIAL ROUGHS

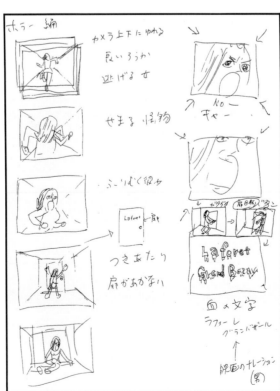

スパイ編

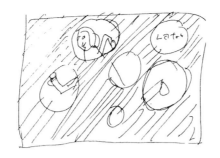

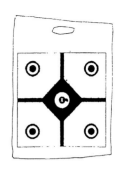

(30(40(50(70(X

Laforet
Grand
Bazar

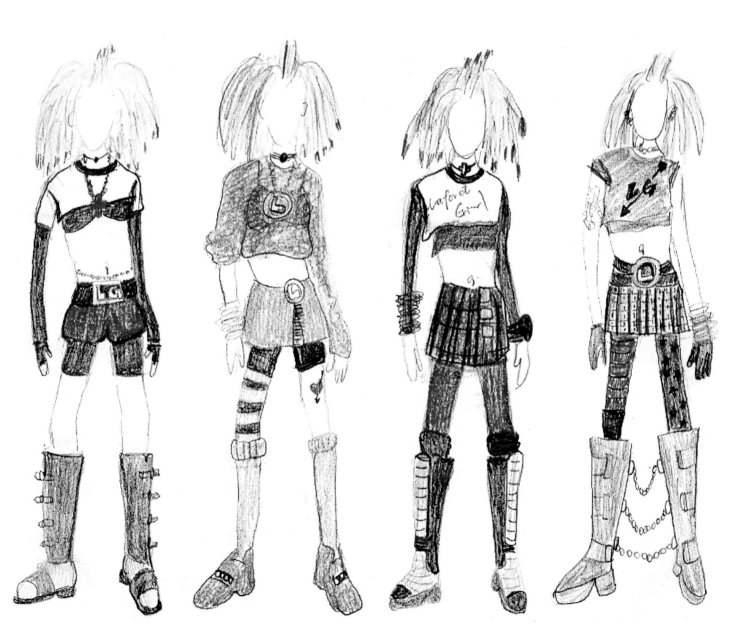

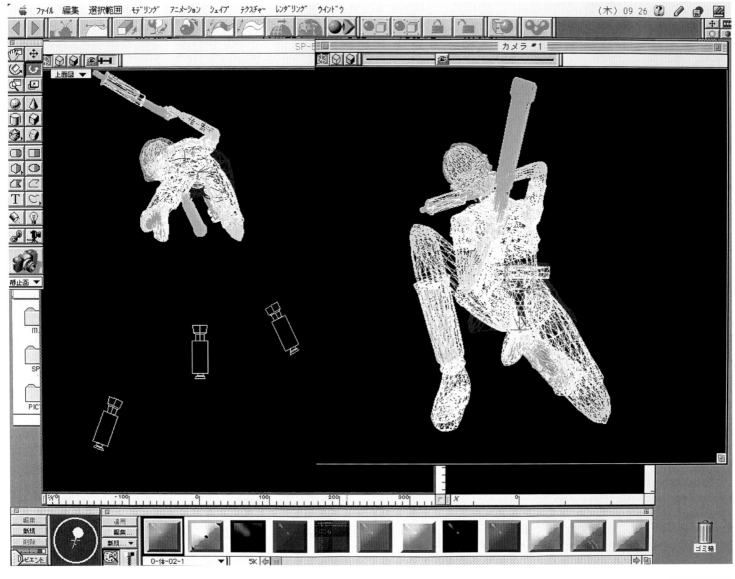

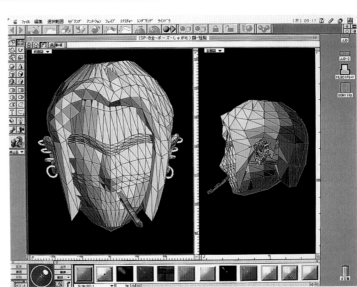

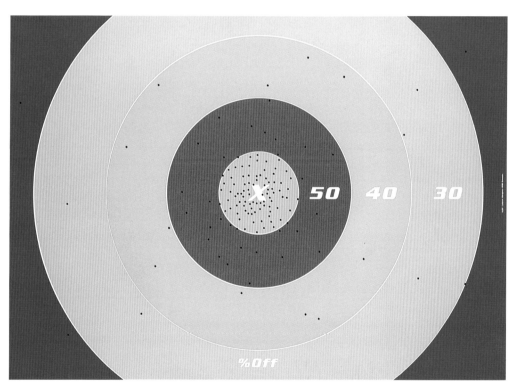

Messrs Tanida, Sakura and I joined forces and came up with about 30 to 40 ideas. Out of them all, I thought an idea that combined a now-outdated schoolgirl delinquent look with Namie Amuro as the main model would most appeal to young people, and could be done in an acceptable way. The graphic was soon close to its final form and everything in the copy was converted to Chinese characters. To clarify the meaning of the Chinese characters, we decided to add some little stickers to the poster, with LAFORET in Roman letters, etc. However the client was not keen to use high school girls, the target audience, in the ad, regardless of the content, so the whole idea fell flat. We started again and eventually came up with the idea of the girl shooting for what she wanted.

谷田氏、佐倉氏と3人でいろいろと持ち寄った企画は、ざっと30〜40位あったと思う。その中で、昔の不良＋アムラーリーダー案が今一番若者にオモシロク、またカッコヨク映り受け入れられると考えた。グラフィックは最終形に近い形ですぐにまとまり、コピーはすべて漢字となった。そのポスターには、漢字の意味を補うように、かわいらしいステッカーで、"LAFORET"とか数種類のものを貼ることにした。しかしラフォーレは、ターゲットである女子高生達を、案の内容に関わらず使用するということを以前より控えていたらしく、あっさりボツになった。そしてまたひたすら考えた上、欲しい物をねらい撃つ女の子案となったのだった。

■ DF: ㈱サン・アド Sun-Ad Co., Ltd. Japan (1996)

■ CD, AD, D: 青木克憲 Katsunori Aoki ■ CD, CW: 佐倉康彦 Yasuhiko Sakura ■ CG: 谷田一郎 Ichiro Tanida

Laforet Harajuku Co., Ltd. / Fashion Mall Promotion ■ ㈱ラフォーレ原宿／ファッションビル プロモーション

During February and March, branches outside Tokyo were to be renovated and we were asked to design a re-opening announcement together with a local TV commercial. The same visuals were to be used in Tokyo for the Spring Fair. As the production staff were the same as for the Laforet Grand Bazar ad, we needed a new character from Mr. Tanida. Production of the earlier Grand Bazar ad was delayed, so the new character design was not ready in time for the

presentation, which served only to explain the content of the ad. ■ 2月と3月に地方館がリニューアルオープンすることになり、地方用としてTV-CFも含めたものを企画することになった。東京は、そのヴィジュアルを流用してスプリングフェア用にするとのこと。ラフォーレグランバザールと同じスタッフで制作するため、谷田氏による新しいキャラクターが必要であった。前に出したグランバザールの制作が押したため、プレゼンテーションにはキャラクター制作が間に合わず、企画内容を理解してもらうまでにとどまった。

FIRST PRESENTATION

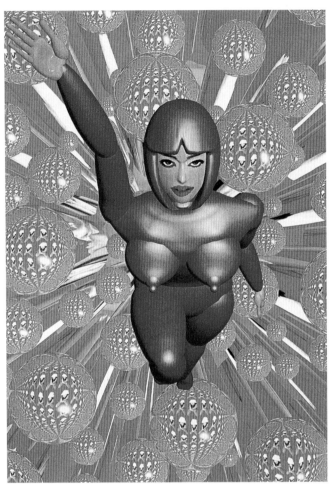

For the first presentation, the earlier 'Bazaar Fighter' visual was used with different coloring, to give an idea of the overall effect. /
初回プレゼンテーション、説明の為バザールファイターのビジュアルに色をつけたもの。

CHARACTER THUMBNAIL SKETCH

The proposal was quickly decided as something simple and clear, with the refurbishment conveyed in the message New Laforet. Against a glittering background familiar from the children's cartoon Sailor Moon, a cartoon figure in bright colors changes form. We had some difficulty choosing the second figure and Mr. Tanida thought up several resembling Gundam robot toys. Among them the most crazy was a girl with rippling muscles, and I thought her rather slovenly look was what we wanted, because it best portrayed a feeling of strength and energy. We didn't worry over much about the details. We used hot stamping, embossing and transparent thermography for the printing and the layout we made a bit chaotic. It was all a lot of fun.

企画は簡単で明確、新しくなります→新ラフォーレということですぐに決まる。内容もセーラームーンのようにキラキラとしたバックで、色鮮やかに変身するというもの。中でも選択に悩んだのが変身後のキャラクターイメージで、ガンダムぽいものなどいくつも谷田氏は考えてくれた。中でも一番バカバカしい筋肉娘が、少々悪い表現ではあるが、なげやりな感じで一方向でいいと思った。この感じが、元気なパワーを一番表現することができると思ったのだ。ディテールにはさほどこだわらず、ひたすらドカーンドカーンというのが自分の考えていた気持ちだった。印刷は箔押し＋カラ押し＋透明バーコと盛りだくさんで、レイアウトはハチャメチャにした。とても楽しかった。

■ DF: ㈱サン・アド Sun-Ad Co., Ltd. Japan (1996)

■ CD, AD, D: 青木克憲 Katsunori Aoki ■ CD, CW: 佐倉康彦 Yasuhiko Sakura ■ CG: 谷田一郎 Ichiro Tanida

Okamoto Industrial Inc. / Benetton Condoms Product Ad　■　オカモト㈱／ベネトン コンドーム　商品広告

We have been handling advertising of Okamoto 'Skinless' condoms since 1993.   Before that Okamoto had not often linked up to other brands, so this tie-up with Benetton to launch a new brand of condoms was the first for some time.   We were asked to continue to produce the advertising.   It was also the first time a TV commercial for a condom was to be made in Japan, so the emphasis at the presentation tended to be more on the TV commercial.　■　オカモトのコンドーム（スキンレス）の広告を1993年から手掛けていた。オカモトはそれまで、ブランドとライセンスを組んだものはあまりしてなく、久しぶりにベネトンと組みコンドームのニューブランドを出すことになった。その際、広告の制作を引き続き受けることになった。又、コンドームのキャンペーン広告としては、日本初のTV-CFをうつということもあり、どちらかというとTV-CFの企画を先行したプレゼンテーションだった。

M O N O C H R O M E　　C O M P S

F I N A L　　P R E S E N T A T I O N

Magazine Ad.

TV Commercial

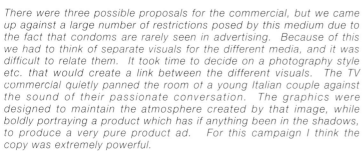

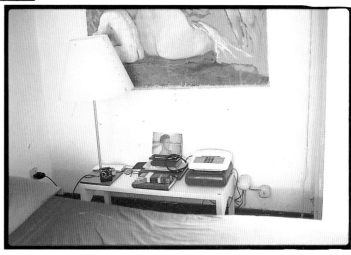

There were three possible proposals for the commercial, but we came up against a large number of restrictions posed by this medium due to the fact that condoms are rarely seen in advertising. Because of this we had to think of separate visuals for the different media, and it was difficult to relate them. It took time to decide on a photography style etc. that would create a link between the different visuals. The TV commercial quietly panned the room ot a young Italian couple against the sound of their passionate conversation. The graphics were designed to maintain the atmosphere created by that image, while boldly portraying a product which has if anything been in the shadows, to produce a very pure product ad. For this campaign I think the copy was extremely powerful.

TV-CF案は3案考えられたが、広告としてはあまり見かけないコンドームという商品のため、媒体からのいろいろな規制があった。そのため、媒体別にビジュアルを考えなければならず、統一感を出すことが難しかった。別々なビジュアルでありながら、どこか統一性を持たせるための写真の感じなどを決めるのに時間を取った。CFの案は、イタリアの若いカップルの部屋をただ淡々と映し、音はカップルの熱い会話が流れているものとなった。グラフィックはその映像の気持ちを残しつつ、どちらかというと今まで日陰にあった商品を堂々と出し、純粋な商品広告として出そうとした。この企画にこのコピーといってもいいぐらいコピーの力が強かったと思う。

べネトンの
いちばん
ちいさい服。

Poster

■ DF: ㈱サン・アド Sun-Ad Co., Ltd. Japan (1994)
■ CD: 花上憲司 Kenji Hanaue ■ AD, D: 青木克憲 Katsunori Aoki ■ P: 今泉好人 Yoshihito Imaizumi ■ CW: 長谷川宏 Hiroshi Hasegawa

Okamoto Industrial Inc. / Skinless Condoms Packaging ■ オカモト㈱／スキンレス コンドーム　パッケージ

The Benetton condom was a great success in 1994 and even now is still on the market. Independently of it, a new product involving a new production technique was to be launched under the original 'Skinless' brand name. All condoms are packed in the same type of box. There is no special packaging and distinctions are made simply through different coloring. The shape has nothing special about it, but condoms have come to be strongly associated with that size of box. It was not a question of a new shape of box, but what was wanted was a box that would stand out (like the Benetton brand) among all these special but ordinary boxes of condoms. ■ 1994年のベネトンコンドームは大成功に終わり、今現在も売れている。それとは別に、本体のスキンレスブランドに新しい技術の加わった商品を出すこととなった。コンドームというのは、みんな同じ形のハコに入っている。別に特別なパッケージのものはなく、カラーリングがそれぞれ違うだけである。形には個性はないが、その大きさイコールコンドームだということは浸透している。特に新しい形にするわけではないが、そういう特種かつ平凡なハコの中で、目立つもの（ベネトンのような）を求められた。

LOGO DEVELOPMENT

FIRST PRESENTATION

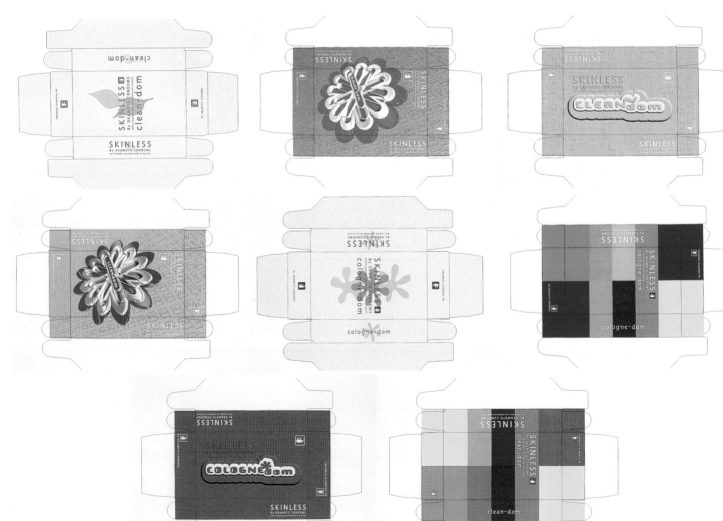

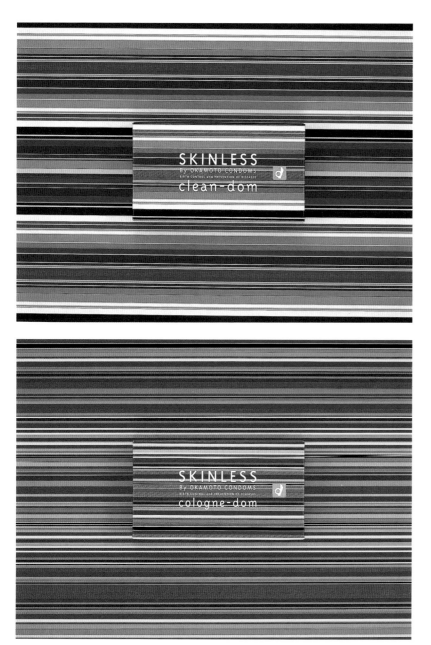

The Benetton package was certainly something different for condom boxes. We were asked to provide something like it, so while we kept the bright coloring just as it was, we sought a new look. It was just at the time everything was going digital, so I thought we should go that way. Making fine lines with four-color processing and adding different colors to each of them had not been possible with previous methods. I think this is a good example of a simple two-dimensional composition made possible through digital technology. We also showed some computer graphic-type ideas at the presentation, but in line with our strong positive feelings about it, the first proposal was selected. However for a digital production it is difficult to assess color on the monitor, and this remains an issue for the future.

ベネトンのパッケージは、コンドームにしては確かに新鮮で良かった。そのようなものというオーダーであったので、色とりどりなカラーリングをそのまま生かしつつ、新鮮な見え方を考えた。ちょうど、デジタル表現が定着してきた頃だったので、それを使ったものにしようと思った。4色で細かいラインを作りそれぞれに色を付けた、今までの版下の指示では、あまり考えられないことだ。デジタルならではのなせる平面構成の簡単ないい一例だと思う。他にもCGぽいもの等プレゼンテーションには出したが、これがやはりオススメという気持ちどおりに決定された。ただデジタル制作だと色を考える際、モニターではまだ自分は読み切ることが難しく、今後の課題となった。

■ DF: ㈱サン・アド Sun-Ad Co., Ltd. Japan (1996)
■ CD: 花上憲司 Kenji Hanaue ■ AD, D: 青木克憲 Katsunori Aoki
■ CW: 長谷川宏 Hiroshi Hasegawa

Hiromichi Nakano Design Office Co., Ltd. / Apparel Maker Mark

We have been handling the graphics, particularly licensed logos, for Hiromichi Nakano since 1992. The starting-off point here was a basic new look for Hiromichi Nakano, and we have been producing various images designed to match this new look. For the same reason we were also asked to produce illustrations (something that could also be used as a logo) for each season. We were given carte blanche as regards motifs, but as it was so vague, it was difficult to think up any motif.

■　㈱ヒロミチ・ナカノ デザインオフィス／アパレルメーカー　マーク

ヒロミチ・ナカノのグラフィック、特にそれぞれのライセンス先のロゴマークを1992年から手掛けている。本体のヒロミチ・ナカノをリニューアルしたのが始まりだ。それぞれすべて本体にあわせて統一したイメージで制作している。それと同じ考え方で、季節ごとの絵がら（マークにも使えるようなもの）を出すことになった。モチーフは花でも何でもOKということだったが、漠然としていたのでモチーフを考えるのは難しかった。

THUMBNAIL SKETCHES AND CHARACTER DEVELOPMENT

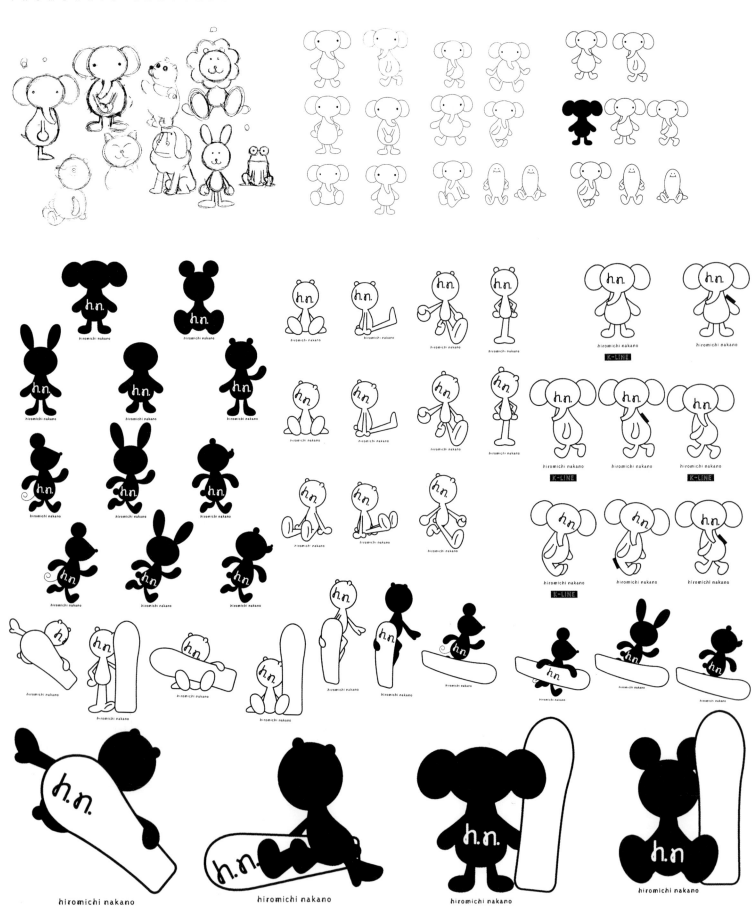

hiromichi nakano

After a lot of thought, I decided on doing a zoo series. Because we were going to need variations at very short intervals, we got Mr. Kubo in to help. First we got him to make some rough sketches of illustrations, and selected what we thought would be good. Then we asked him to do them on a Mac so that the thickness of the lines and so on could be finished relatively simply. We made a link between them by putting an 'h.n.' somewhere in all of them. Once again, we coordinated all the details of the finish such as the thickness of the lines. Mr. Kubo produced a number of different variations for us, and we planned to increase them further through the same sort of process.

いろいろ考えた末、ZOO シリーズでやることに決めた。さらに短期間である程度のバリエーションを必要とすることもあり、久保氏にも手伝ってもらうことにした。まずラフで久保氏にイラストをいくつか出してもらい、その中からいいと思われるものをチェックした。次にMAC上でおこしてもらって、ケイの太さなどつめの部分が比較的簡単に進むようにした。「h.n.」をどこかに入れることで、他との連動をはかった。これにあわせ、再度ケイの太さなどをつめ完成。いろいろなバリエーションを出してもらって、上記のようなやり方で増やしていった。

■ DF: ㈱サン・アド Sun-Ad Co., Ltd. Japan (1994)
■ CD: 中野裕通 Hiromichi Nakano ■ AD, D, I: 青木克憲 Katsunori Aoki
■ I: 久保誠二郎（動物） Seijiro Kubo (animals)

Sony Corp. / Audio Equipment Product Ad ■ ソニー㈱／オーディオ　商品広告

This was an ad to promote a new audio model, 5MD PIXY, and the target audience was music lovers and young people. The selling points of this particular model were the capability to load 5 CDs and select the required tracks freely, and what's called the 'jog dial', a function that lets you play around with the sound in various ways. This was the gist of the orientation. My reaction was: music! It sounds crazy but we need to make a 'musical' poster. That's the quickest way to reach the target audience. What's a 'musical' poster? One

that spills music. Right! So let's start spilling ideas! ■■■■ SONYの新しいオーディオ(5MD PIXY)の広告です。ターゲットは、音楽好き、そして若者、訴求ポイントは5枚のMD、5枚のCDが内蔵できて自由に聞ける。それとJOG DIALと言って、自分で色々音を遊べる機能がついている事です。オリエンテーションは、簡単に言うと以上の様な事だった。とは言え音楽だ、バカみたいだけど音楽ぽいポスターを作ろう、それが一番ターゲットへの近道だ！と思った。音楽ぽいポスターってどんなもの？うーん、なんか音楽がいっぱい！みたいなやつ、よーし、じゃあそれをいっぱい考えよう！

R O U G H   S K E T C H E S

F I R S T   P R E S E N T A T I O N

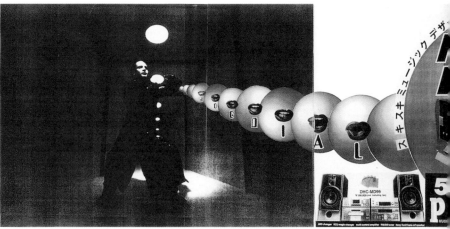

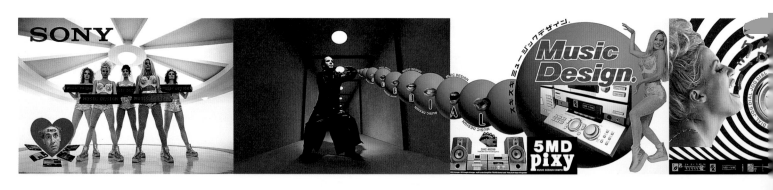

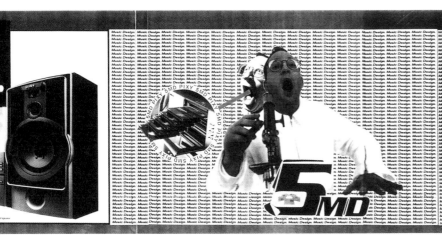

Knowing we wanted a musical poster I did masses of rough sketches, some punk, some rock and some jazz. But all the time something bothered me. Nothing seemed to come together. So what do we do now?

音楽ぽいポスターがつくりたい、ラフスケッチを重ねていくうちに、パンク風、ロック風、ジャズ風、そしてなんとなく気になるものがなんの脈絡もなく残った。しかし全くまとまりがない、どうしよう。

We tried bringing all sorts of visual elements into a single story line, which with luck would sound like music. The problem was that we would ruin it by over-organizing it. It's got to be a mixture that is nevertheless coherent. That was the point.

いろんなビジュアルの要素を、ひとつのストーリーの中に押し込もう。うまく行けば、いろんな音楽が聞こえてくる。問題は、まとまり過ぎるとダメな事だ。ごちゃごちゃしていながら、まとまっている。これがポイントだ。

We chose to use collage. We got an enormous pile of pieces and spent day after day cutting and pasting. And all the while I kept thinking, I really hope it'll look cool. Because music is cool!

デザインの手法は、コラージュを選んだ。そのためカット数は膨大な量になった。みんなで毎日、切ったり貼ったりした。そのあいだいつも思っていた事は、「カッコよくなればええなあ」「音楽ってカッコええからなあ」。

■ DF: ㈱電通　Dentsu Inc.　Japan (1996)
■ CD: 白土謙二　Kenji Shiratsuchi　■ AD: 沢田耕一　Koichi Sawada　■ D: 大藪厳太郎　Gentaro Oyabu　■ P: 半田也寸志　Yasushi Handa　■ CW: 大建直人　Naoto Odate

Matsuya Ladies is the name of a building of fashion boutiques in Hakata in Kyushu. The client wanted a promotional campaign for 4 seasons: spring, summer, autumn and Christmas, targeting young people. The orientation was extremely simple. So we matched that with a simple slogan in English 'Let's go to Matsuya Ladies'. I didn't want to do anything very fashion-oriented, or anything sweet and sentimental. A chic 'Let's go to Matsuya Ladies' with a touch of standard humor. ■■■■■ マツヤレディースは、九州の博多にあるファッションビルです。広告の目的は企業広告。春・夏・秋・クリスマスの年4回。ターゲットは若者、オリエンテーションはすごくシンプル。それじゃこっちもシンプルにLet's go to Matsuya Ladies.こまかなファッションの事や、恋や愛の事はちょっと恥ずかしいし、カッコワルイと思った。マツヤレディースが思ってる、若者達への気持ちをハッキリ言った方がいい。「マツヤレディースに行こう！」と。ちょっとだけオシャレして「Let's go to Matsuya Ladies.」出来上がりのイメージは、誰でも見たことのあるギャグ。

ROUGH SKETCHES

I wanted to do something very simple and easygoing. The basic idea was of girls responding to 'Let's go' in crazy poses. Thought up lots of ideas, like doodling during class.

すごくシンプルなものにしたかった。そして気楽なものに、Let's go と言われて、みんながちょっとふざけてイメージするものを、アイデアの元にした。授業中のラク書きみたいなものを、たくさん考えた。

Because the idea was so simple, the balance was extremely important. One small thing could easily spoil it. The size of the cannon, the amount of smoke, the faces of the girls, the number of feet, how to put it all together... that really worried me.

アイデアがシンプルなので、デザインのバランスがすごく重要になってきた。ちょっとした事で、すごくカッコワルクなる。大砲の長さも煙の量も女の子の顔も足の数も、合成のやり方も、すっごく気になってきた。

I was concerned all along about color. Eventually, I decided on monochrome as the base for the cannon poster to give it old-fashioned authenticity. For the poster with all the feet, unashamed bright colors.

デザインも決まり入稿、でもデザインの途中から気になっていた色彩が難しい。いろいろ悩んで、大砲のポスターは昔のギャグの感じを出すため基本をモノクロに。足バタバタのポスターはアッケラカンと派手なカラーに。

■ DF: ㈱電通　Dentsu Inc. Japan (1995)
■ AD: 沢田耕一　Koichi Sawada　■ D: 高橋秀明　Syumei Takahashi
■ P: 瀬尾隆　Takashi Seo　■ CW: 大建直人　Naoto Odate

Tipness Ltd. / Fitness Club Opening Announcement ■ ㈱ティップネス／スポーツクラブ オープン告知 　　 D e n t s u I n c .

The Tipness Fitness Club was opening a new venue in Shinjuku to complement its five other branches in Tokyo. They wanted to advertise the opening and attract new members. The campaign was to include poster ads for stations, flyers to be delivered with newspapers and flyers to be handed out in streets around Shinjuku. The station posters were a big responsibility. On the way back from the orientation I thought 'An opening, and in Shinjuku of all places. Shinjuku station is so big and the Tipness poster is to display here.. It will have to be really conspicuous or it will be swamped..'

■■■■ スポーツクラブ「ティップネス」が、渋谷・赤坂・吉祥寺・五反田・中野につづき、新宿にオープンする。広告の目的は、そのオープン告知と会員の募集です。広告媒体は、駅貼りポスターと新聞のオリコミ、そして新宿で配られるビラなどである。駅貼りポスターの責任は重大である。オリエンテーションの帰り道、ボクはこんな風に思った。「まずはオープンやな、それも新宿に、新宿の駅ってすごいなぁグチャグチャで、ここに貼られるんかぁティップネスのポスター.....。これは目立つのやらんと埋もれてしまうなぁ.....」

R O U G H S K E T C H

C O L O R C O M P

Thought something really dramatic and forceful would be good. Making the sense of 'opening' outrageously loud. Like parting the waves and opening a path through the sea for everybody to go through.

「ティップネス新宿オープンみんな行けー！って感じの強引で強烈なやつがええなー。オープンて感じも目茶苦茶派手なやつ。あっあの海が割れて人がドドーッて行くやつ。オープンって感じで行けーって感じ。」どうかな？

Began to get concerned about the actual production. Decided to put together a photo of people walking across the sea bed. 30 people. We'll use stock photos for the sea, the sky and the path across the sea bed. It began to fall into place. Wondered whether it would really turn out spectacular.

実際の制作の事が気になってくる。さあどうする。海底を歩く人々は合成。人数は３０名。海、空、海底の道はレンタルフォト、どんどん具体的になってくる。これで本当に大スペクタクルが出来るのだろうか。

Time to calm down. 'Tipness has opened in Shinjuku'. This is to advertise this fact. So the message should be bold. The visuals should convey an opening and a great flow of people all going to Shinjuku. Let's get it right and let's make it flamboyant.

冷静になりましょう。「ティップネスが新宿にオープンした。」この事を伝えるための広告です。と言う事は、告知は堂々と！ビジュアルは、オープン感！新宿に行く人々の動き！これを徹底させましょう。勿論、大袈裟に。

■ DF: ㈱電通 Dentsu Inc. Japan (1996) ■ AD: 沢田耕一 Koichi Sawada ■ D: 池田博範 Hironori Ikeda ■ P: 瀬尾隆 Takashi Seo ■ CW: 佐藤澄子 Sumiko Sato

Fuji Television Network Inc. / TV Station Promotion ■ ㈱フジテレビジョン／テレビ局　プロモーション

Fuji Television has been guided by the watchword 'If it's not interesting it's not television', and they wanted an ad that would advocate that sentiment. This was the orientation. I thought it would certainly be challenging. We couldn't think how to approach it until shortly before the presentation when we came up with the idea PUSH, an incredibly positive word. But what sort of ad could we build round it? We needed something unusual, so we aimed to make it way-out. Like, can we really do something like this? For the sake of Fuji TV. ■

「面白くなくっちゃテレビじゃない。」と言って全力で走って来たフジテレビ。それに拍車をかける広告にしたい、と言うオリエンテーション。「おもろいやんか、一丁やってみるかー！」と思ったのも束の間、結構難しい。うーんと悩んでプレゼンテーションのギリギリで出てきたアイデアが「PUSH」、無茶苦茶ポジティブな言葉だ。しかしどんな広告になるんだ？普通にやればちょっと恥ずかしい前向きのものになるんとちゃうか。変なものにしよう、変なものに。こんなやり方もあったのか！って感じの、それがフジテレビのためなのだ。

ROUGH SKETCHES

MONOCHROME COMP

At this stage we were still wondering whether to go with PUSH. Thought for ages whether to do straightforward gags, or something clever that was total nonsense. The only thing that never changed throughout was the feeling of wanting to do something way-out.

この頃はまだ「PUSH」で行くかどうか悩んでいた。シンプルなギャグで行くか、訳のわからないナンセンスでカッコよく行くか、とにかくいっぱい考えた。ずっと変わらなかった事は「変なもの」にしたい気持ちだった。

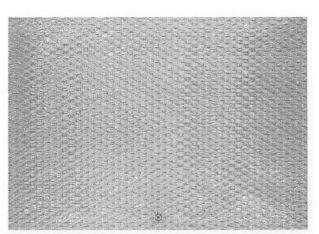

Decided on PUSH! We'd have PUSH in English and a symbolic finger-man. But it was a bit too trite. We changed the balance by making the finger-man younger: son of finger-man. But still it wasn't interesting. And it wasn't way-out.

「PUSH」に決定！キャラクターは、「指男」。英文でPUSHそしてシンボリックな指男。ちょっとカッコよすぎる、そして気持ち悪い。指男のバランスを変えよう。「指男の子」にした。でもこれだけじゃ面白くない。変じゃない。

Right before the presentation, I thought of something really way-out: making a poster you actually can PUSH by sticking some of that bubble wrap onto it. We went and bought some of the wrap and tried sticking it on a 2B-size poster. It was pretty way-out so I was pleased.

プレゼンテーション、ギリギリに変な事を思いついた。「PUSH」出来るポスターにしよう。ポスターにエアーキャップ（プチプチ）を貼りつけよう。実際にエアーキャップを買って来てB倍サイズの紙に貼ってみた。「なかなか変だ。よかった。」と思った。

■ DF: ㈱電通　Dentsu Inc. Japan (1995)
■ CD: 佐々木宏　Hiroshi Sasaki ■ AD: 沢田耕一　Koichi Sawada
■ D: 徳田祐司　Yuji Tokuda ■ P: 坂田栄一郎　Eiichiro Sakata ■ CW: 大建直人　Naoto Odate

Namco Wonder EGGg / Amusement Park Opening Announcement ■ ナムコワンダーエッグ／アミューズメントパーク オープン告知　　　D e n t s u　I n c .

This ad was to announce the opening of a small amusement park, Namco Wonder EGGg, in Futako Tamagawa, a suburb of Tokyo. The parent company, Namco, is one of Japan's largest suppliers of game machines, and some experimental games were installed in Wonder EGGg, including the latest total-experience machines, shooting games, *etc. It is targeted at young couples.* ■■■■ 東京郊外の二子玉川に新設される小規模アミューズメントパーク、ナムコワンダーエッグのオープン告知広告である。母体のナムコは、ゲーム機器の最大手であり、ワンダーエッグ内には最新の体感マシーン、シューティングゲーム他かなり実験的なものが設置される。ターゲットはカップル。

ROUGH SKETCHES

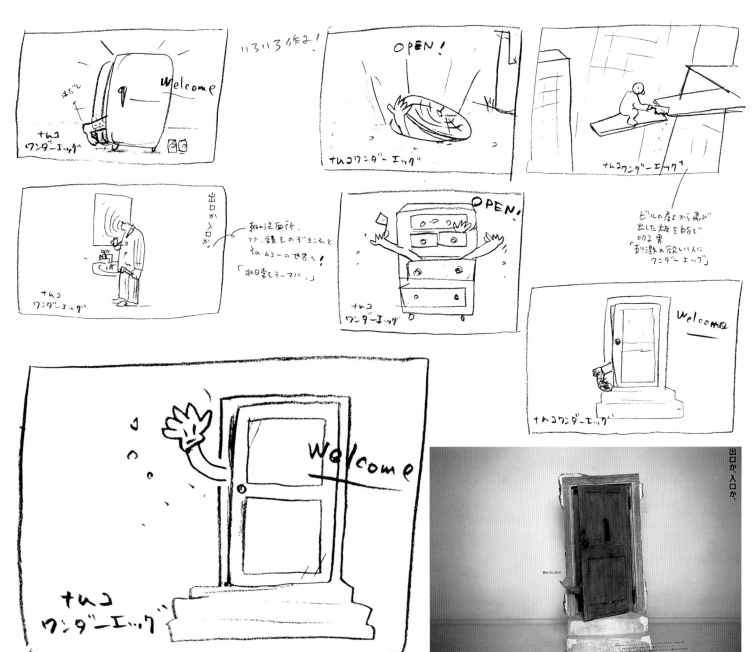

出口か、入口か。

Futako Tamagawa, where Wonder EGGg is located, has in recent years become a popular place for dating couples. To have Wonder EGGg suddenly appear in an area surrounded by quiet residential streets was sure to create surprise and expectation. Rather than putting over information about the amusement park itself, for this ad we focussed on stirring up excited expectation. As the slogan 'Way In? Way Out?' suggests, Wonder EGGg is intended to build a bridge between the every-day and the non-every-day. A few hours spent inside will open up an unknown world full of surprises and excitement. I thought that if we could create an ad that put over this feeling, it would be a success.

ナムコワンダーエッグの位置する二子玉川は、近年人気を集めるデートスポット。周りは閑静な住宅街である。その中に突然現われたワンダーエッグは驚きと期待を持って受け入れられるに違いない。広告展開は、テーマパークの内容そのものを伝えるよりも、オープンの期待感を盛り上げることを念頭に制作された。キャッチフレーズ「出口か、入口か。」が示すようにワンダーエッグは日常と非日常の懸け橋。その中で過ごす数時間は驚きと楽しさに満ちた未体験世界。そんな気分が広告から届けば成功だと思った。

■ DF: ㈱電通　Dentsu Inc.　Japan (1993)
■ AD: 阪口正太郎　Shotaro Sakaguchi　■ D: 藤岡貞二　Teiji Fujioka
■ P: 上田義彦　Yoshihiko Ueda　■ CW: 山本高志　Takashi Yamamoto

The Calpis Food Industry Co., Ltd. / Algin Super X Product Ad

Algin Super X is a health and energy drink that was launched several years ago. The label shows a roaring lion. The energy drinks market is highly active, and this time the advertising agency suggested narrowing down the target audience to office workers and producing an ad to encourage consumption at station kiosks.

■■■■■　アルギン・スーパーXは、発売数年を経た栄養ドリンクである。ラベルには吠えるライオンが大きくある。活性化するドリンク市場の中で、今回はターゲットをサラリーマンに絞り込み、駅のキヨスクでの飲用促進を目的として広告展開をはかろうと企画が進められた。

FIRST PRESENTATION

Having narrowed down the concept to 'an energy drink for office workers to consume at stations', we worked on ideas that would be witty and produce the appropriate impact.

「サラリーマンが駅で飲む。」とコンセプトが絞り込まれている以上、その中でどれだけインパクトとウィットを盛り込めるかを考えてアイデアを探した。

The final proposal was to have the professional wrestler Atsushi Onita as an office worker proceeding unfazed through an exploding ball of flame. At the client's request we photographed the wrestler as himself and not as an office worker.

最終決定案は「サラリーマンになったプロレスラー大仁田厚が、爆発する火の中をものともせずに進む姿。」であったが、クライアントの要望により、サラリーマンではなくレスラーそのままの姿で撮影された。

■ DF: ㈱電通 Dentsu Inc. Japan (1993)
■ CD: 鎮目彰夫 Akio Shizume ■ AD: 阪口正太郎 Shotaro Sakaguchi
■ D: 大石恵美子 Emiko Oishi ■ P: 白鳥真太郎 Shintaro Shiratori ■ CW: 関根昭博 Akihiro Sekine

International Wool Secretariat ／ Wool Promotion ■ 国際羊毛事務局／ウール プロモーション

The IWS is a non-government body that is funded by a number of wool growing countries. Its aim is to develop the global wool market by encouraging fabric makers and fashion houses to use wool, and promote the wearing of wool to the general public. Since the 1960s, the IWS has promoted its logo, the Woolmark, as a guarantee of authenticity and quality, but two years ago, the association decided to change its promotional approach from a country-by-country strategy to an international advertising campaign. Wool has something of an old fashioned image and despite remarkable product advances in recent years it is still often associated with bulky, shapeless knitwear. Our task was to create a campaign to run in fashion magazines around the world with the aim of attacking wool's old image. We wanted to make wool more modern, more exciting and more fashionable. ■■■■■ IWS （国際羊毛事務局）は数多くの羊毛産出国が資金を提供する非政府団体です。この団体の役割は世界中の羊毛市場を発展させることであり、繊維製造業者やファッション関連企業にウールの使用を奨励したり、一般の人たちにウールの衣類を利用するよう勧めています。1960年以来、IWSはみずからのロゴであるウールマークを信頼と品質の証明としてプロモートしています。2年前までウールマークの宣伝は国ごとで別々に行われていましたが、国際的な宣伝キャンペーンを行ったほうが効率も効率も良いと判断されたのです。ウールには何となく古くさいイメージがあり、最近の製品が著しく進歩しているにもかかわらず、いまだに不格好でかさばる毛糸編みの衣類を連想させます。私たちの仕事は、この過去のイメージを打破するために世界中のファッション雑誌でキャンペーンを行うことでした。私たちはウールをモダンで刺激的でファッショナブルなものにしたいと考えました。

M O N O C H R O M E   C O M P S

We believed the clothes needed to be portrayed in an active role - not, as in most fashion campaigns, 'catalogue' type ads. The line, You Can Trust the Wool That Wears the Woolmark came first. It was a case of deciding how best we could echo this visually, and our first concept showed the product being tested in some way: stretched, creased or otherwise put under stress. However, it proved difficult to make the clothes look fashionable and attractive in such situations. Our next thought was Your Eyes May Deceive You, But You Can Trust the Wool That Wears the Woolmark, and it was this that led us to the trompe l'oeil visuals. The bar stool was one of our first concepts. These stools actually exist in a London bar called Ny-lon. The rest of the ideas flowed from there.

ありきたりのファッションキャンペーンと差をつけるため、単純に「カタログ風」の広告を作るのは避けました。広告の中で衣服が積極的な役割を果たす必要があると考えたのです。「ウールマークのついたウールなら信じられる」という言葉が最初に浮かびました。問題は、このアイデアを視覚的に表現する最善の方法を決めることです。最初のコンセプトは何らかの方法で製品をテストするというもの。例えば衣類が引っ張られたり、しわにされている、もしくは負荷がかかっている状態といったようなものです。しかし、こうした状況で衣服をファッショナブルで魅力的に見せるのは難しい事です。次のアイデアは「眼はあなたをだますかもしれない、でもウールマークのついたウールなら信じられる....」というもので、このアイデアから私たちは「だまし絵（トロンプルイユ）」に到達しました。バーのスツールは最初のコンセプトの一つです。このスツールは「NY-LON」というロンドンのバーに実在するもので、残りのアイデアはここから発展させました。

We developed many different visual ideas, some of which proved too compli-
cated. We needed to show a fair amount of each garment, so ideas that involved closeups were rejected. It would have been easier to copy existing images from the world of photography and painting, but we decided to create
new ones as we felt they would have more impact. The copy was 'compart-
mentalised' so as to give emphasis to key words in what is quite a long headline. The design also allowed us to be consistent with the look of the ads when
translated into 20 languages.

さまざまなビジュアルのアイデアを数多く練り、中には複雑すぎるものもありました。一つ一つの
衣服を大量に見せる必要があったので、クローズアップを含むアイデアも排除しました。写真や
絵画の世界に存在する画像を模写すれば簡単だったでしょうが、私たちは新しい画像を作ることに
しました。そのほうがインパクトがあると感じたからです。コピーは「区分した」フォーマットに
なるようデザインし、非常に長い見出しの中でキーワードを強調しました。さらに、20ヶ国語に
翻訳された場合も広告の外観が共通するデザインになっています。

The Client bravely bought the concept and it ran totally uncompromised. The
pictures were painstakingly executed by Nadav on location and were composed entirely in the camera, without the aid of any electronic image manipula-
tion or any post production. The campaign was well received in all the markets
throughout the world and the translations were carefully vetted to ensure we
retained the integrity of the ideas to make it a truly international campaign.

クライアントはこのコンセプトを積極的に受け入れ、まったく妥協せずに作業が進みました。写真は
Nadav により現場で入念に制作され、カメラに収めた画像全体を構成しています。コンピューターを
利用した画像処理や撮影後の編集などは、一切行っていません。キャンペーンは世界中の市場で
好評を得ました。翻訳もアイデアを完全に伝えるために慎重に吟味されており、国際的なキャン
ペーンと呼ぶにふさわしいものが仕上がっています。

■ DF: Abbott Mead Vickers BBDO Ltd. UK (1995)

■ AD, D: Peter Gausis ■ P: Nadav Kander ■ CW: Alfredo Marcantonio

DUO's advertising throughout the year consists mostly of B size posters (seasonal posters), 'F' flyers for fashion and 'G' flyers for goods. Ads in these three formats are produced four times a year. Additionally, posters and in-store decorations are produced twice a year for the anniversary of the opening and for Xmas.

DUOの年間の広告制作物は主に、B全ポスター（シーズンポスター）、チラシ〈F〉〈ファッション〉〈G〉〈グッズ〉の3本立ての年4回。その他に年2回、アニバーサリーとX'masに伴うB3Wのポスターや館内の装飾等があります。

F I N A L   P R E S E N T A T I O N

As the mall is located some distance from the center of Sapporo, the approach used focusses on the immediate locality. Instead of TV and transportation ads, flyers and posters in the building are used to convey DUO's message in a seasonal format. They target women in the 20-35 age-group who enjoy being fashionable in their own way. So for the B size posters we establish a concept that appeals both to their fashion sense and feelings, and during production we focus on getting an emotional response. The twice-a-year advertising stresses a festive feel and is as playful, loud and expansive as possible. It's designed to portray a different image of DUO from the seasonal posters.

札幌中心部よりも立地が離れている為、広告のアプローチとしては地場中心型。TV・交通よりもチラシと館内のポスターで、季節のイメージにデュオが発信するメッセージを盛り込みながら広告物を展開しています。ターゲットは20〜30代前半のオシャレを自分なりに楽しんでいる女性。だからB全のポスターも、ファッション性＋マインドにメッセージするコンセプトを立てて、内面へのアプローチをポイントに作成しています。又、年2回の特宣に伴う広告物は、お祭り性重視で、できるだけ楽しく、目立って、どっかスコーンとぬけているような物で→季節のポスターとは違うデュオの一面を表現しています。

■ **DF:** ㈱東急エージェンシー 北海道支社　**Tokyu Agency Inc. Hokkaido Branch**
／ ㈱マーケティング・コミュニケーション・エルグ　**Marketing Communication ERG　Japan (1996)**
■ **CD, AD:** 吉村紀子　**Noriko Yoshimura** ■ **AD, D:** 佐藤誉樹　**Takaki Sato**
■ **P:** 藤原晋也　**Shinya Fujiwara** ■ **CW:** 土肥晴美　**Harumi Doi**
■ **PR:** 引地幸生　**Yukio Hikichi** ■ **Stylist:** 橋場綾子　**Ayako Hashiba** ■ **Hair & Make-up:** 新井昭久　**Akihisa Arai**

■ ㈱4丁目プラザ／ファッションビル　プロモーション

4 Chome Plaza is a fashion mall celebrating its 25th anniversary this year. For the spring campaign ad the client wanted to put over the message 'above all else, we aim to be our customers' favorite shopping venue', and to use the popular shortened name, 4 Pura, as a new logo. The design of the posters, the mainstay of the campaign, was based on the idea 'the best shopping for individual style', conveying the message that 4 Pura was not just fashionable but also provided for individual tastes. We worked on two visuals with the slogan 'Not so much the best one (venue) as the only one'. ████ 今年25周年を迎えるファッションビル「4丁目プラザ」。スプリングキャンペーン広告におけるクライアントの要望は、「何事においても、お客様にとっての一番店を目指す。」という指針をどのように発信していくか。また、ビルの愛称である「4プラ」のコミュニケーションマーク・リニューアルである。キャンペーン広告のメインであるポスターの表現は、「個性、一番店」を目指し、流行をふまえながらも独自の個性を確立する4プラ、をメッセージ。「ベスト・ワンよりオンリー・ワン」をキーワードに、2つのビジュアル表現を検討した。

THUMBNAIL SKETCHES

FIRST PRESENTATION: B

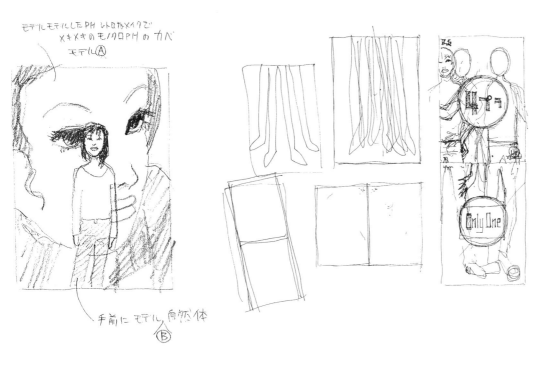

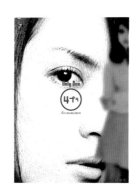

FINAL PRESENTATION: B

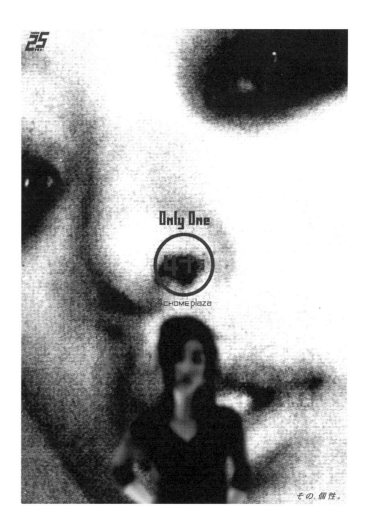

We offered two proposals that put over a powerful message through the faces of models expressing their own style unaffected by fashion trends. Proposal A matched two girls the same size in as straightforward a design as possible. Proposal B aimed to generate interest by showing a girl first without make-up and then having used make-up to create a new personality.

流行に左右されない、自分のスタイルを持ったモデルの素顔に力強いメッセージを感じ、A案では等身大の彼女たちを出来る限りストレートに表現する方向に。B案では素顔の自分と、メイクで作られた自分との対比に面白さを・・・。

At the B/W comps stage, we found that for Proposal B, the strong makeup of the model at the back gave her a conventional fashionable look rather than her own individual look. So for the color comps we had the model at the back without makeup too. For proposal A we kept the photo B/W to bring out the models and the logo separately. At this stage we did a presentation.

モノクロカンプ作成時、B案ではバックのモデルのメイクが強調されすぎ、「自分のスタイル」というより「流行のスタイル」に見えてしまう。カラーではバックの方をノーメイクに作り直して完成。A案ではモデルとマークをそれぞれに強調するため、写真をモノクロに。この段階で、いざ、プレゼンテーション。

The client appreciated that the design for proposal B generated interest and had impact, but selected proposal A for its straightforward handling of the message. The project was completed through a process of trial and error: auditioning models, running B/W plate tests, choosing paper, changing the printing of the logo to silk printing, and so on. We produced three types of posters in different shapes and sizes.

B案での表現方法の面白さ、インパクトの強さは高く評価されたが、メッセージがストレートに表現されたA案に決定。モデルオーディションに始まり、モノクロ製版テスト、紙の選定、マーク部分の印刷をシルク印刷に変更するなど、試行錯誤のすえ完成。B全単体・B倍横2連・B倍縦2連の3タイプの組み合わせで掲出された。

■ DF: ㈱東急エージェンシー北海道支社 Tokyu Agency Inc. Hokkaido Branch / ㈲ナウ Now Japan (1996)
■ CD, AD: 工藤良平 Ryohei Kudo ■ AD, D: 中西一志 Kazushi Nakanishi
■ D: 田中寛樹 Hiroki Tanaka ■ P: 田坂義章 Yoshiaki Tasaka ■ Stylist: 畠谷真奈美 Manami Hataya

MTV Music Television do Brasil / TV Station Promotion ■ エムティービー　ブラジル／テレビ局　プロモーション

MTV asked us to create a single ad to announce the winner of a promotion MTV did with a manufacturer of fashionable, 70s-style women's shoes and the most popular Brazilian youth magazine: 'MTV, Melissa and Capricho in search of a new MTV-VJ'. We were asked to introduce the look and face of this winner, so that she would be remembered when seen later on TV. MTV sent us 2 pictures of this 20-year-old girl, chosen from 3,000 applicants, and two logotypes we had to use: the promotion logotype and the regular one for MTV.

■　MTVからプロモーションの優勝者を告知する広告を1枚制作して欲しいという依頼がありました。このプロモーションは、MTVが個性的な70年代風の女性用シューズ会社とブラジルで最も人気の高い若者向け雑誌と一緒に行ったもので、「MTV、メリッサ、カプリチョ、新人MTV-VJ募集」というタイトルでした。私たちへの要望は、このプロモーションの優勝者の容姿を紹介して、後にテレビで彼女を見るときのために覚えてもらうことでした。MTVからは3,000人の候補者から選ばれた優勝者である20歳の女性の写真が2枚と、使用するロゴ2種類が送られてきました。ロゴはプロモーション用のものと、告知者であるMTVの通常のロゴの2種類です。

THUMBNAIL, VISUAL MATERIALS AND VISUAL CONCEPT PRESENTATION

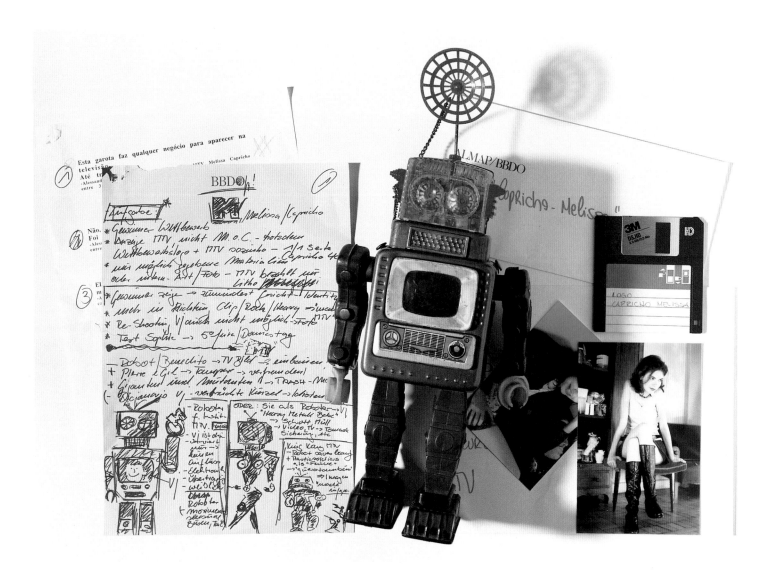

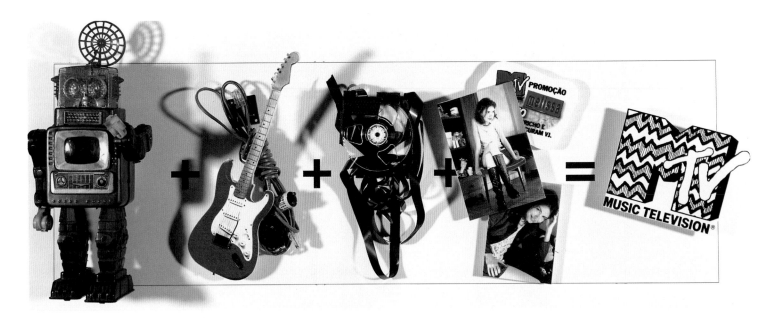

The problem was that the mood of the photos was completely different from the visual language MTV normally uses for its communication. Because there was no money to remake the pictures and the 'New Face' wasn't available at that time, we had to focus on an in-house solution, a graphical, artificial interpretation of the 'new VJ at MTV'. We came up first with some ideas for manipulating the photos, and then considered going the 'wired' way of photo-collage.

問題は、送られてきた写真の雰囲気とMTVがいつもの宣伝で使っているビジュアルの表現形態が、まったく異なっていたことです。写真を撮り直す予算もなく、その時点では新人のスケジュールもあわなかったため、今ある素材で解決するよう「MTVの新人VJ」のグラフィックに手を加えて表現する、という方法しかありませんでした。最初に、写真を操作して、有名なフランスの「ピエール・エ・ジル」のようにしたり、奇妙なフォトコラージュを施すアイデアをいくつか思いつきました。

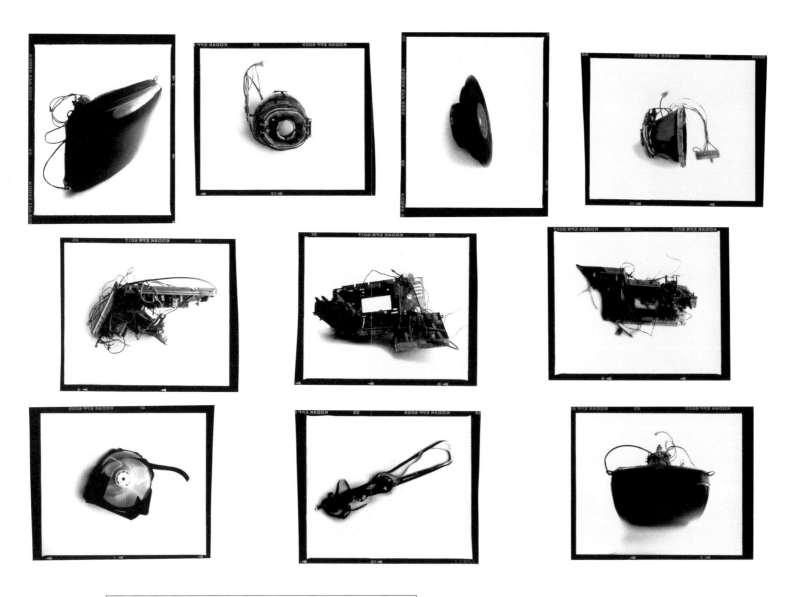

While thinking about other MTV ads we had done, we came to the conclusion that the idea of manipulating did not fit the communication line that normally uses just one object or detail to convey an idea. Looking for this metaphorical object, we remembered the Japanese television-robot toys of the 60s. The concept behind this was that MTV is seen by the consumer as a high-tech TV station, with a great human touch. The work the VJ does is to give MTV a face, to make it a 'person' to identify with while presenting the newest clips. So we thought of constructing a wild metal female MTV television-robot and let the VJ present herself on its monitor.

すでに手がけたことのあるMTVの他の広告について考えてみると、写真を操作するアイデアはMTVの宣伝手法に合わないという結論に達しました。これまでの手法は、通常1種類だけの物や装飾によってアイデアを伝えていたのです。こうした「象徴的な物」を探すうちに、60年代の日本のおもちゃ「テレビ・ロボット」を思い出しました。このコンセプトの裏にあるのは、消費者がMTVのことをハイテク設備を持ちながら非常に人間味のあるテレビ局として見ている事実です。VJの仕事は最新のビデオクリップを紹介しながら、MTVの「顔」となり共鳴する「人」となることなのです。そこで私たちは「ワイルドでメタリックな女性のMTVテレビ・ロボット」を組み立てて、そのモニターで新人VJに彼女自身を披露させるというアイデアを思いつきました。

After presenting an idea-board to our client, showing all the ingredients we thought of using to build our robot, we collected broken televisions, stereo systems, and wire from shops round the agency and broke them up some more to take chromes of every single part. These photos we used for a first 'construction' at the lightbox to have the main characteristics of the robot approved by the client before starting on the high-resolution fusion in Photoshop. In consideration of Melissa, we wanted to keep the robot and the colors light and female. We also aimed to make the layout like a futuristic magazine cover, thinking of Capricho. MTV was more than happy with the result and even called it one of the craziest ads they ever had. Later the image was used for posters and printed on T shirts.

アイデア・ボードをクライアントに提示して、ロボットを作るのに必要と思われる材料を見せた後、私たちは近くの店で壊れたテレビ、ステレオ、ワイヤーなどをいくつか集めました。これらをさらに壊して、あらゆるパーツのクロムめっきを剥がしました。ロボットの特徴を決めるためにライトボックス上で最初の「組み立て」を行い、そこで使用した写真をクライアントに承認してもらった後、フォトショップによる高解像度での合成を始めました。「メリッサ」を考慮して、ロボットと色は明るく女性的にするよう心がけました。また「カプリチョ」に関して言えば、レイアウトを未来的な雑誌のカバーのようにしています。MTVは出来上がりを非常に喜び、いままでの広告でいちばんクレージーな広告だとさえ言ってくれました。後にMTVはこのビジュアルを、会社のポスターやTシャツに使用することを決めています。

■ DF: ALMAP / BBDO Comunicações Ltda. Brazil (1996)
■ CD: Marcello Serpa   ■ AD, D, I: Oliver Zion Fuchs   ■ P: Mario Fontes   ■ CW: Sophie Schönburg

Part of the work we do for our client MTV, besides the image campaign and event/ program announcements, is to develop so-called 'special day ads' or 'MTV news'. These ads in general communicate topics like birthdays of musicians, band news, international celebrations, political events, etc. The thematic suggestions for these ads are offered by the agency. There is no real request from the client side. One week before the birth of Madonna's daughter, the newspapers were spreading the news of this forthcoming 'pop event'. So we wanted to use Madonna's baby for an 'MTV news' topic, as we had announced her pregnancy some months earlier. ■■■ クライアントであるMTVのために行った仕事のうち、イメージキャンペーンやイベント／番組の告知以外で行った1つが「スペシャルデー広告」もしくは「MTVニュース」と呼ばれるものの制作でした。これは、ミュージシャンの誕生日や死亡、バンドの情報、国際的な記念日、政治状況などのさまざまな情報を知らせる広告です。こうしたテーマの広告はエージェンシー側がたまたま提案したもので、クライアント側から実際に要求があったわけではありません。マドンナの子供が生まれる1週間前、この目前に迫った「ポップス界の事件」について新聞でも報じられていました。マドンナの妊娠については私たちも9ヶ月ほど前にニュースとして知らせていたので、「マドンナの赤ちゃん」を「MTVニュース」に使いたいと考えました。

B R A I N S T O R M I N G

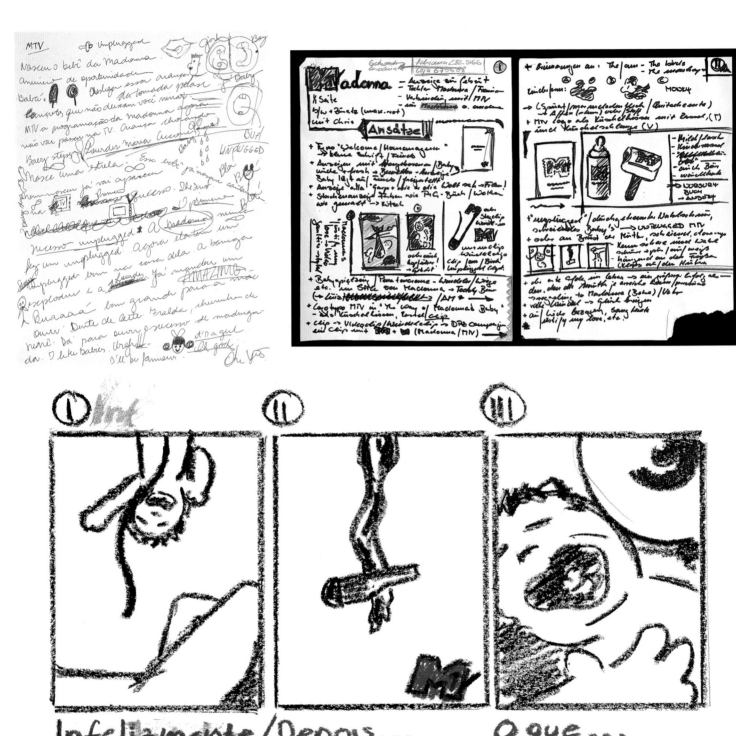

In the first brainstorming process we came up with some ideas we did not finalize. This was because they turned out as normal 'Happy Birthday Welcome' ads, and a real link between the birth and MTV was missing. Keeping in mind MTV's simple visual communication strategy using just one 'object' to convey an idea, and the fact that we used a 'sado/maso-styled' (Justify my Love) teddy bear to announce Madonna's pregnancy, we thought about styling baby or nursery products in an 'MTV/Madonna' way.

最初のブレーンストーミングでは、いくつかのアイデアが浮かびましたが結局使用しませんでした。ごく普通の「誕生お祝い広告」にしかならないと分かったからです。また、子供の誕生とMTVをつなぐものが欠けていました。1つだけの「物」を使ってアイデアを伝えるMTVのシンプルな映像スタイルと、以前「SMスタイル」（「ジャスティファイ・マイ・ラブ」）のテディベアを使ってマドンナの妊娠を伝えた事実を念頭に置いて、赤ちゃんや子供を表すためのMTV／マドンナらしいスタイルについてさらに考えることにしました。

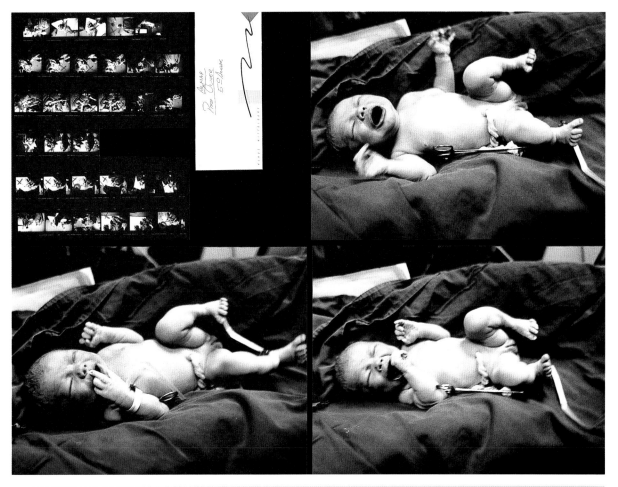

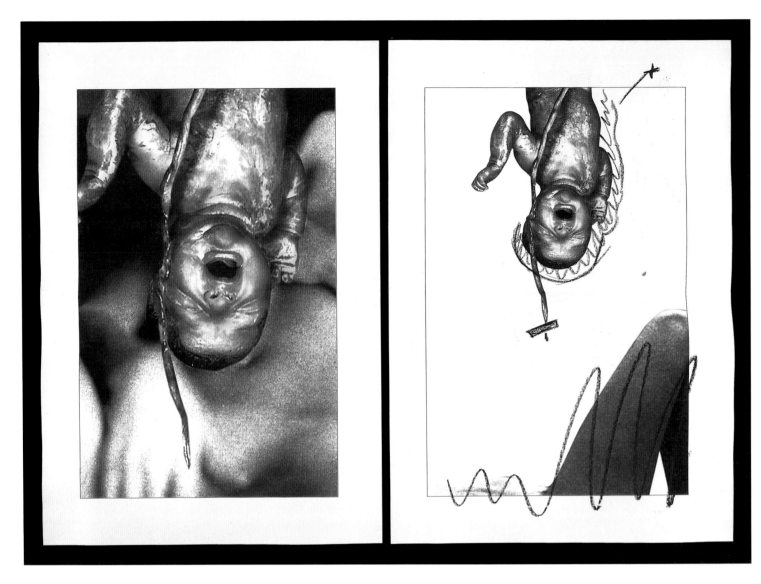

T H I R D   P R E S E N T A T I O N

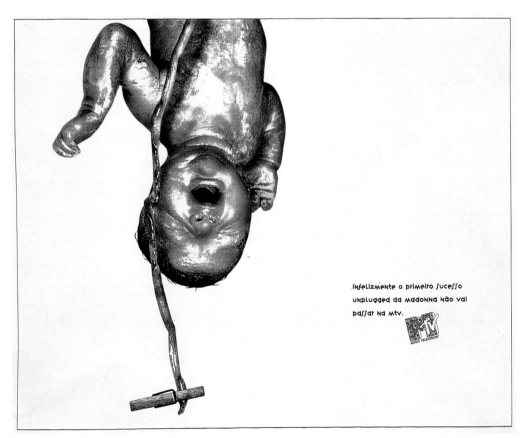

iNfelizmeNte o primeiro sucesso
unplugged da madonna Não vai
passar Na mtv.

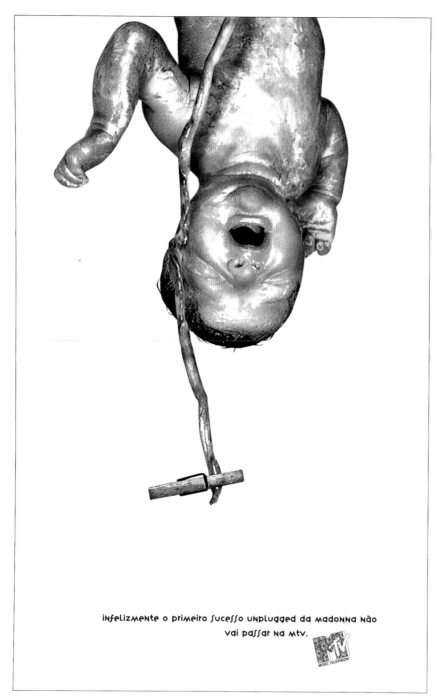

Looking at the images we collected from magazines showing the moment of birth and new-born babies, upside-down, receiving the famous first slap, and also realizing the dominant presence of the umbilical cord in these pictures, we ended up seeing the baby's first cry after the cord is cut as the 'biggest unplugged success in life' for both the child and mother. In connection with MTV's 'Unplugged' series we remembered that MTV had never shown a 'Madonna Unplugged' acoustical concert, though millions of viewers were desperately waiting for one. So we finally had the link between the birth of Madonna's daughter and MTV, while playing with viewers' expectations. We decided simply to show a 'freshly un-plugged' baby, upside-down and crying, with the message that 'unfortunately Madonna's first unplugged success won't be shown on MTV'.

誕生の瞬間や、生まれたばかりの赤ちゃんが頭を下にして、有名な最初の「平手打ち」を受けている様子の写真を雑誌から集めて見ているうちに、写真の中でへその緒 が目立っていることに気がつきました。そして、へその緒を切った直後の赤ちゃんの 泣き声を、子供と母親にとっての「人生最大のアンプラグド（つながりを断つの意味）が成功した様子」として捉えるアイデアが生まれました。MTVの「アンプラグド」シリーズに関しては、数多くの視聴者が待ち望んでいるにもかかわらず「マドンナのアンプラグド」アコースティック・コンサートがMTVで放送されていないことも思い出しました。これでついにマドンナの子供の誕生とMTVをつなげるものができたわけです。視聴者の期待をもてあそぶことにもなりますが、このアイデアを使うことに 決めました。「新しくアンプラグド」された赤ちゃんが、頭を下げて泣きながら、「残念ながらマドンナ最初のアンプラグド大成功の様子はMTVで放送されません」と言っている姿を使うアイデアです。

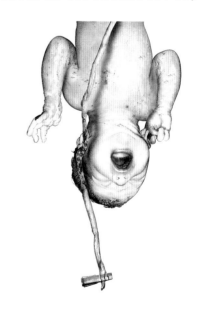

The birth came sooner than expected and we had to look for archive or magazine images for our ad. But no photo of a new born baby was available, and bringing one from the US or elsewhere would have taken too long. So we decided to take live photos in several hospitals at the moment of birth, with the permission of the parents who first saw the layout. Because the light in delivery rooms is not designed for photography and we did not want to use spotlights or flashes, the photos were good in part--hand, face, body or umbilical cord-- but none of them was perfect all over. So we made a high resolution fusion of many different images in Photoshop, recreating the light and skin structures. On the day of the birth the ad ran in Brazil's evening paper 'Jounal a Tarde'. It was very successful and our client was happy to receive a lot of response to the ad. It was even discussed among religious and more traditional circles in Brazil who are not MTV viewers. Later, the baby image was used for the MTV Internet page, opening the News section.

出産は予定より早くなり、ストックしてあるビジュアルや雑誌のビジュアルから広告で使うものを探すことになりました。しかし利用できる新生児の写真はありませんでした。アメリカや他の場所から調達するには時間が足りません。知り合いで子供が産まれたばかりの人全員に頼んで写真を借りてみましたが、探している写真は見つかりませんでした。そこで、いくつかの病院で誕生の瞬間の写真を「生で」撮影することに決めました。撮影はまず両親にレイアウトを見せ、許可を取った上で行いました。しかし分娩室の光の状態は撮影に向いておらず、スポットライトやフラッシュも使いたくなかったため、手、顔、身体、へその緒など一部分だけが使える写真ばかりで、全体として完全な写真は一枚もありませんでした。私たちはフォトショップで異なるたくさんの画像を高解像度により合成し、同時に光と肌の構成を修正することにしました。広告は出 産と同じ日にブラジルの夕刊紙「Jounal a Tarde」に掲載されました。結果は大成功で、クライアントも広告に関するさまざまな意見が集まり喜んでいました。掲載されて以来、MTVの視聴者ではない信仰の厚い伝統的なブラジル人の間でも盛んに話題にのぼりました。その後、この赤ちゃんの画像はMTVホームページ、ニュースセクションの冒頭部分に使われました。

■ DF: ALMAP / BBDO Comunicações Ltda. Brazil (1996)
■ CD: Marcello Serpa ■ AD, D, CW: Oliver Zion Fuchs ■ P: Fernanda Tricoli ■ I: Roger Sakamoto ■ CW: Christiane Lastoria Parede

Kraft Suchard do Brasil / Kibon Icecream Product Ad ■ クラフト スシャー／キボンアイスクリーム　商品広告

The agency was asked to develop a new campaign for the 1996 summer communication for Kibon's Fruttare, following a communication strategy and positioning that - now for many years - has brought Fruttare to a leading position in Brazil's market for fruit-icecream: the fruit on a stick. Fruttare already is synonymous with 'frozen fruit' in consumers' minds, so it was our task to find a creative form that would put more focus on 'fruit on a stick'. Thus we decided to let the wooden Kibon icecream stick play the main character in the

1996 campaign.　■■■■■　エージェンシーへの依頼は、キボン・フルターレの1996年夏に行う新しいキャンペーンを考えることでした。「スティックについたフルーツ」のキャッチフレーズで、フルターレをブラジルのフルーツアイスクリーム市場をリードする地位に何年もの間つかせた。宣伝の戦略や方法に従ったキャンペーンが求められました。消費者の頭の中では、事実上フルターレが「凍った果物」と同じ意味の言葉になっています。私たちの仕事は「スティックについたフルーツ」を新しい視点でとらえたクリエイティブの形を見つけることでした。そこで私たちは木製キボン・アイスクリームスティックを1996年のキャンペーンメインキャラクターに選びました。

THUMBNAIL SKETCHES

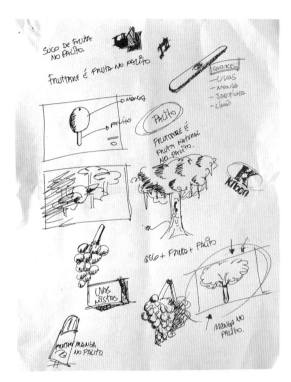
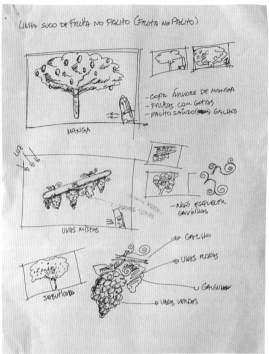

FINAL PRESENTATION

In the first brainstorming process we came up with around ten ideas for communicating 'fruit on a stick'. We kept in mind that the visual communication of Fruttare in recent years was perfectly simple, but some of our ideas turned out to be too abstract in trying to find similar simple language to announce the product's positioning.

最初のブレーンストーミングでは、この「スティックについたフルーツ」宣伝するため10アイデアほど思いつきました。フルターレの昨年の広告ビジュアルは、完璧なまでのシンプルさを持っていました。私たちのアイデアのいくつかも、ストレートでシンプルな手段を目指したため、抽象的になりすぎたものもありました。

Based on its capacity for impact, its adequate handing of the positioning of the product and the consumer, its differentiation from last year's campaign, simplicity and memorability, we chose just one idea to present to the client: Fruttare's wooden icecream stick as a branch or trunk of fruit plants or trees, announcing that all fruit wants to be Fruttare fruit.

インパクトの大きさ、製品や消費者を考慮した宣伝としての妥当性、昨年のキャンペーンとの差別化、シンプルさ、印象の強さなどに基づいて、クライアントに提示するアイデアを一つに絞りました。木でできたキボンのフルターレ・アイスクリームスティックを、果物の生る植物や樹木から伸びた根や幹とし、果物はみんなフルターレ・フルーツになりたがっている、と表現するのです。

As the concept required the wooden stick to be a natural part of all Fruttare fruit trees, the artwork had to be a perfect fusion of these two elements different in color, size and structure, to avoid an artificial look in the final illustration. The art direction work was very intense. All the parts: sticks, fruit, trunks and leaves, had to be photographed separately and brought together digitally in Photoshop. Then another fusion took place: 'fruit on a stick' and 'frozen fruit' finally came together in this campaign. The copy says: In summer, all mangoes and grapes want to be Fruttare fruit. Fruttare. Fruit at the right temperature.

コンセプトは、木でできたアイススティックが果物のなる植物や樹木の自然の一部になるというものでした。そのためアートワークでは色、サイズ、構造の異なるこの二つの要素を完全に融合して、最終的なイラストレーションが人工的に見えないようにしなければなりませんでした。アート・ディレクションの作業は非常に入念に行いました。あらゆる部分、スティック、果物、幹、木の葉を別々に撮影し、後からフォトショップでデジタル処理により合成しました。そしてもう一つ、ついにこのキャンペーンでは「スティックについたフルーツ」と「凍った果物」が一つになったのです。「夏になると、マンゴーもブドウもみんなフルターレになりたがります。フルターレは良く冷えたフルーツです」。

■ DF: ALMAP / BBDO Comunicações Ltda. Brazil (1996)
■ CD: Marcello Serpa ■ AD: Luiz Sanches Jr. ■ P: Studio Freitas / Freitas
■ I: Marco César ■ CW: Ricardo Chester / Atila Francucci

Japan Racing Association / Race Meet Announcement ■ 日本中央競馬会／競馬開催告知

This ad appeared in '95, which was a year of bad news, with the Kobe earthquake, the subway gas attack and so on. Events at the Hanshin race track were temporarily suspended and the local racing community was subdued, but sport was the one bright topic in the news, particularly the success of the Japanese baseball star, Hideo Nomo, playing in the US. At such a time, we judged there wasn't much point in trying something trivial, so for '95-'96 we decided to take advantage of Nomo's gutsiness. It was also something of a gamble,

because the fate of the ad turned on Nomo's performance...

この広告が出た '95年というのは、地震・地下鉄サリン事件、他暗いニュースが多い年でした。阪神競馬場もしばらくの間休場、関西競馬界もシュンとしていた中、明るい話題はスポーツ、その中でも特に野茂投手の活躍でした。こんな年にチマチマした事をしてもあまり効果はないと（独断で）判断、野茂投手の度胸の良さに乗っかって '95年度はこれでいこうという事になりました。（ただし、野茂投手の成績いかんでこの広告の評価が決まるだろうという、コワーイ賭けでもありました。）

ROUGH SKETCHES

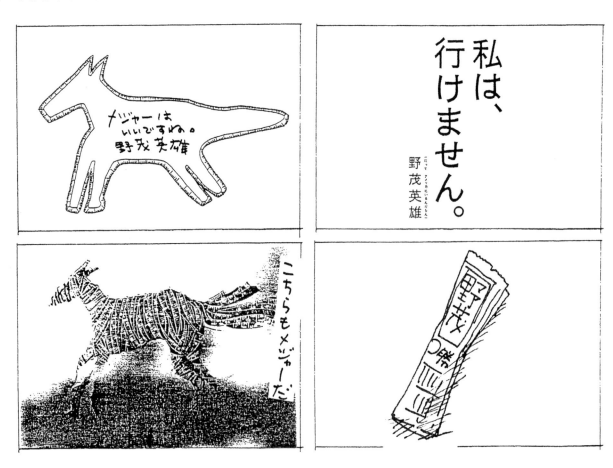

FIRST PRESENTATION

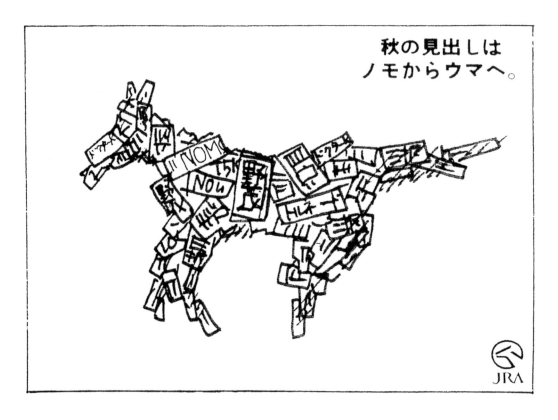

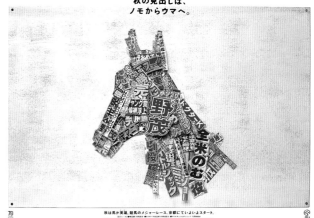

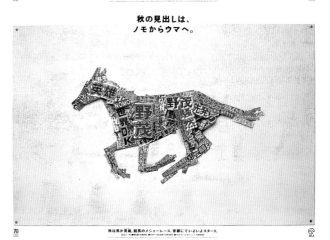

We struggled hard to think of an entirely original way of using Nomo, and as it was for horse-racing, we'd virtually decided to go with the idea of using the sports (and racing) papers, but were just a bit concerned that it would lack abrasiveness and impact, so we went on struggling a bit longer.

他社とは違う、野茂投手の出し方に四苦八苦、競馬だからスポーツ新聞でいこうかと何となく決まりかけてはいたものの、もうひとつ、ヌケと強さがないと、引き続き四苦八苦していました。

We suddenly decided to switch to a straightforward design of a horse created out of sports paper headlines. The copy was decided there and then as a straight pitch that readers couldn't fail to catch. (It was less than two days before the presentation)

急に「見だしで馬を作る」というストレートな表現に変更、見てる人にすぐに伝わる直球勝負でいきましょう、とコピーもこの時点でこれになりました。（プレゼンテーション2日前の夜でした）

Okay, so it was a bit of a clumsy idea. To make sure it had impact, so people didn't dismiss it too quickly ('Oh no! Not Nomo again!' 'It's only horse-racing') we were very careful about the details, the arrangement of the headlines (all real ones) and so on. I think we achieved our aim of making a star-quality ad with a star-quality personality.

言ってしまえばオモチャの様なアイデアですが、「あぁまた野茂？」「ハイハイ、競馬ね」で終わらない様に、見る人に印象的になる様に、ディテールや記事（全て本物）の配置他、細かい所に気を使いまくりました。結果、「華のある人」を使った「華のある広告」にしたかった、という狙いは成功してると思います。

■ DF: ㈲中野直樹広告事務所　Nakano Naoki Advertising Office Inc.　Japan (1995)
■ CD: 荒木 宏　Hiroshi Araki　■ CD, CW: 山崎隆明　Takaaki Yamazaki
■ AD: 中野直樹　Naoki Nakano　■ AD, Art: 宮本庄二　Shoji Miyamoto
■ D: 安村厚子　Atsuko Yasumura　■ D, Art: 古谷智彦　Tomohiko Furutani
■ P: 大山栄泰　Eitai Oyama　■ CW: 石松かおり　Kaori Ishimatsu / 直川隆久　Takahisa Naokawa

Matsushita Electric Industrial Co., Ltd. / Corporate Promotion   ■ 松下電器産業㈱／企業広告

The process this 'documentary' type ad involved was very unusual. It started off from a tiny newspaper article spotted by our AD, about people in Kobe affected by the Hanshin Earthquake being cheered by lights. Straight off, we called the agency and the client to discuss the idea. Once they'd checked that Matsushita light bulbs were used for this 'encouragement in lights', we got the go-ahead. Six of us immediately set off for Kobe. ▬▬▬ まったくのドキュメンタリーであるこの広告にかかったプロセスは、従来とは大きく異なるものです。"阪神大震災の被災地で、あかりが人々を励ます力になっている"出発点は、ＡＤがふと目にとめた小さな新聞記事でした。さっそく電話で、代理店と松下電器に企画意図を打診。光のエールに使用されている電球が松下電器のものであることを確認してもらい、即ＧＯサインをいただきました。そして急いでスタッフ6人、ロケハンに向かったのです。

V I S U A L S

F I R S T   P R E S E N T A T I O N

Because the earthquake had disrupted transportation, the journey to Kobe took two and a half hours instead of the usual 30 minutes. We had to wear masks to protect ourselves from the dust of the demolition work. We decided on locations which would give representative views of the illuminated word FIGHT! , and split up into three groups: one each bound for the waterfront, the city center and the mountain side. Keeping in touch by transceiver, we took several hundred shots. We raced back to the Osaka office, compared the shots and narrowed the locations down to two. The following day we went back to Kobe, this time with a photographer. Two of the positives were blown up, and full size comps were done straight off. We didn't bother with rough sketches or mini comps, and it was unusual to use the actual positive film for the comps. When we did a presentation of two proposals the following day, the one selected was the one that gave the view shared by thousands of ordinary people in Kobe. We only had to finish it off. We were rather apprehensive about making an ad out of a catastrophe still fresh in people's minds, but the end result was something that I believe people affected by the earthquake were happy to see.

当時は鉄道も完全に復旧していなかったため、普段なら30分で行けるところを2時間半もかけて到着。全員マスクをかけ（ビルの解体による粉塵がすごかったのです）「ファイト」のあかりが象徴的に見える位置を求め、海沿い、街中、山の中腹と3グループに分散しました。トランシーバーで連絡を取り合いながら、数百カットの写真を撮影。すぐ大阪のオフィスに戻ってプリントを並べ、ロケのポイントを2ヶ所に絞りました。翌日から、今度はカメラマンを同行して再び神戸へ。撮影した2点のポジを引き伸ばし、いきなり原寸カンプを作成しました。つまり通常の手書きラフやミニカンプの工程をすっかり飛ばしたわけです。本番ポジでカンプを作る、というのも異例なことでした。後日2案をプレゼンテーションしたところ、被災された方々と同じ視点で捉えているという理由で、上の案に決定。そのままフィニッシュ作業へと向かったのです。記憶も生々しい大惨事をテーマにするため、さまざまな不安もありましたが、結果としては被災地の方々にも元気を届けられるような広告ができたと思います。

■ DF: ㈲中野直樹広告事務所 Nakano Naoki Advertising Office Inc. Japan (1995)
■ CD: 高田 務 Tsutomu Takada / 岡野誠二 Seiji Okano
■ AD: 奥浪嘉彦 Yoshihiko Okunami / 中野直樹 Naoki Nakano
■ D: 江上直樹 Naoki Egami / 稲葉光昭 Mitsuaki Inaba / 三好能順 Yoshiyuki Miyoshi
■ P: 荒井英一 Eiichi Arai ■ CW: 塩出芳樹 Yoshiki Shiode / 納健太郎 Kentaro Osame

Alfred Dunhill Ltd. / Luxury Label Promotion ■ アルフレッドダンヒル／プロモーション

Alfred Dunhill, the English name in luxury specialising in accessories and clothing for men, was founded in 1893. There is a strong English heritage and commitment to superb quality and style. The task was to launch and highlight Alfred Dunhill's range of products from the Autumn / Winter 1996 range. ▆▆▆ ダンヒルは紳士服、アクセサリーを専門とするイギリスのブランドで、1893年に創立しました。イギリスの伝統が色濃く残り、一流の品質とスタイルを貫いているブランドです。クライアントの要望はダンヒルの1996秋冬商品を売り出し、強調することでした。

ROUGH SKETCHES

The Alfred Dunhill Centenary Watch. Indispensable whatever the angle.

The Alfred Dunhill Tie collection. Indispensable in the Tropics.

FINAL PRESENTATION

ALFRED DUNHILL   The Centenary Watch. Indispensable whatever the angle.

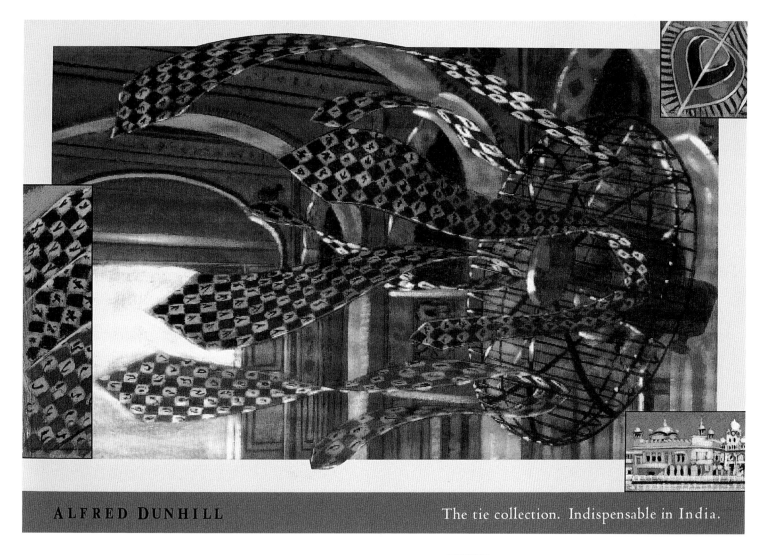

ALFRED DUNHILL   The tie collection. Indispensable in India.

The Alfred Dunhill Tie Collection. Indispensable for keeping cool.

The Alfred Dunhill Centenary Watch. Indispensable whatever the angle.

The initial sketches were drawn up and agreed. Marker pen colour boards were then produced to further define the composition final plan for the photographer.
最初のアイデアスケッチは、すぐ認められました。その後マーカーペンでカラーボードを作成し、カメラマンのために最終構図プランをはっきりさせました。

The beautifully shot executions are by John Offenbach, who previously worked with renowned photographer Nadav Kander.
美しい写真は、有名な写真家Nadav Kanderと一緒に仕事をしていたことがあるJohn Offenbachが撮影しました。

■ DF: Bartle Bogle Hegarty UK (1996)
■ CD: Dennis Lewis ■ AD, CW: Dennis Lewis (fragrance/menswear)
■ AD: Rosie Arnold (watches/ties) ■ P: John Offenbach ■ CW: Will Awdry (watches/ties)

Murphy's Irish Stout was launched in the UK by Whitbread Beer company in 1987. It had achieved marginal success up to 1992 with about a 10% brand share. The dominant brand in the sector is Guinness. The task was to develop a long term brand positioning to create a consumer need for an alternative stout, to develop a taste positioning for Murphy's distinct from that of Guinness and give credible 'stout' credentials to the brand. The difference in taste of Murphy's is that it is a smooth stout. Scenarios for both TV and press executions featuring Irish people in tricky or potentially hazardous situations were developed with the endline: 'Like the Murphy's, I'm not bitter'. This 'not bitter' theme works on three levels: the taste is not bitter, its represents a laid-back, typically Irish attitude, and Murphy's as a stout is superior to bitter (which in the UK is another word for

beer). Now the Murphy's brand commands 32% of the market: (MRSL Oct 95). ▭　マーフィーズ・アイリッシュ・スタウトはイギリスでウィットブレッド・ビール・カンパニーから1987年に発売されました。1992年までにある程度の成功を収め、ブランドのシェアは10%となっています。この分野でのトップブランドはギネスです。新しいスタウト（黒ビール）に対する消費者の需要を作り出し、長期に渡るブランドの地位を向上させること。ギネスとは違うマーフィーズ独自の味を高く位置づけて、信頼できる「スタウト」として証明すること。マーフィーの味の違いは、口当たりの良いスタウトであるという点にあります。TVと出版物の宣伝用に、困難な状況や危険を伴う状況にあるアイルランドの人々を使ったシナリオを作り、「マーフィーと同じ、私はビターじゃない」というエンドラインをつけました。この「ビターじゃない」というテーマは3種類の意味を持っています。――苦みのない味 ――落ち着いた、アイルランド的な態度 ――マーフィーズがビターより上質なスタウトだということ。（イギリスでビターはビールと同義語）現在、マーフィーズのブランドは市場の32%を占めています。

FINAL PRESENTATION

Bernadettes blind date didn't measure up to expectations but like the Murphys she wasnt bitter

Maria's blind date didn't measure up to expectations but like the Murphy's she wasn't bitter.

Eugene inherited his Uncle Clancy's estate, but like the Murphy's he wasn't bitter.

These draft pencil sketches were drawn by the artist, Sara Hodge, in conjunction with a verbal or visual brief from the agency creative art director and copywriter.

下絵となった鉛筆スケッチは、エージェンシーで創作を担当したアートディレクターとコピーライターからの言葉とビジュアルによる指示を受けて、アーティストのSara Hodgeが描きました。

Once the individual concepts and pencil sketches were agreed, the artist made the models for each advertisement execution by hand with approvals by the BBH creative team during development. Sara was the artist responsible for the latest three ads in this campaign, and it took five weeks to complete from initial briefing.

コンセプトが認められた後、アーティストがそれぞれの広告用に手製の模型を作成しました。Saraはこの商品のキャンペーン中もっとも新しい3つの広告を担当したアーティストです。最初の打ち合わせから完成までは5週間かかっています。

■ DF: Bartle Bogle Hegarty UK (1996)

■ CD: John Hegarty ■ AD: Graham Watson ■ P: Mike Parsons ■ I: Sara Hodge ■ CW: Bruce Crouch

Boddingtons Beer has been brewed in Manchester, UK since 1778. When Whitbread took over the brand and decided to launch it throughout the UK, there was the need to both grow the brand outside its heartland region and to preserve and retain its appeal in the North West of England. The task was to launch Boddingtons nationally in the UK. Its key product points: its creamy head and particularly smooth taste.

います。ウィットブレッド社がこのブラ
なった際、このブランドを地元以外にも広めなが
アピールをそのまま維持しなければなりませんでした。バディン
的に売り出す際、製品のセールスポイントは、一売りであるクリーミーな
ななめらかさでした。

COLOR COMP

A very distinctive idea for the press work was developed early on in the campaign. The original art director, Mike Wells, knew he wanted something very graphic and clean, something very like pop art. The styling included using a 'poster' format 'The striking image uses the colours of the beer itself - - a very rich golden colour and creamy white frothy 'head' - - against a stark, black background. The sign-off strip, in the packaging colour (yellow) and type-face, has the same end-line 'The Cream of Manchester'. Early executions established the 'cream' theme and in-cluded a cone 'ice-cream' and a slice of a beer glass 'cream cake', and have now become more surreal with 'hand cream'. The titles of the executions are not printed in the ad, the visual pun should be self-explanatory.

出版物向けのアイデアは制作の初期段階で生まれました。最初のアート・ディレクター、Mike Wellsはポップアートに良く似た、分かりやすく明瞭なものが必要だと考えていました。ポスターを含めた表現スタイルは、ビール自体の色である非常に深い金色を使った印象的なビジュアル、完全な黒を背景にしたクリーミーな「泡」などを用いました。文字広告の部分は、黄色の帯で商品と同様の文字とマークを入れています。初期のビジュアルは「クリーム」というテーマが打ち出されたもので、「アイスクリーム」コーン、ビール・グラスの一部を切り取った「クリームケーキ」などが含まれており、その後さらにシュールな「ハンドクリーム」になりました。広告の中にはタイトルは印刷しておらず、画像による語呂合わせだけで分かるようにしました。

Despite the simple-looking finished image much work was required for the complex models/sets. The model-maker worked with the photographer to achieve an aesthetic, be-lievable model. The photographer took several Polaroids and test shots to discuss with the BBH creatives before agreeing the final shot. The 'poster' effect is achieved by media space being booked on the back of reviews/week-end magazines. When the magazine is turned over it pro-vides effortless visibility and offers more exposure than a normal press execution would demand. The Boddingtons brand 'owns' the backs of magazines, and consumers ex-pect to see a Boddingtons advertisement there.

仕上がったビジュアルの見た目はシンプルですが、手の込んだ模型やセットのためにかなりの作業が必要でした。模型製作者はカメラマンと共同で作業を行い、美術的に優れた模型を作りました。カメラマンはポラロイド撮影やテスト撮影を何度か行い、BBHの製作者と話し合った後、最終的な写真について意見を統一しました。「レビュー／ウィークエンド・マガジン」の裏面に掲載されることで、「ポスター」の効果が生まれました。雑誌を裏返せばすぐ目に付くため、通常の雑誌広告よりも宣伝効果は高くなります。バディントンズは雑誌の裏面を確保しており、消費者はその場所にバディントンズの広告があることを知っています。

THE CREAM OF MANCHESTER.
Boddingtons Draught Bitter. Brewed at the Strangeways Brewery since 1778.

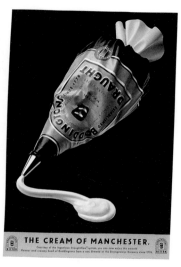

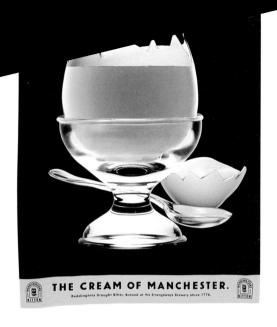

THE CREAM OF MANCHESTER.
Boddingtons Draught Bitter. Brewed at the Strangeways Brewery since 1778.

THE CREAM OF MANCHESTER.
Boddingtons Draught Bitter. Brewed at the Strangeways Brewery since 1778.

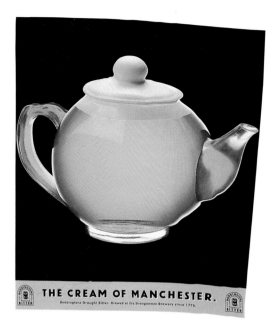

THE CREAM OF MANCHESTER.
Boddingtons Draught Bitter. Brewed at the Strangeways Brewery since 1778.

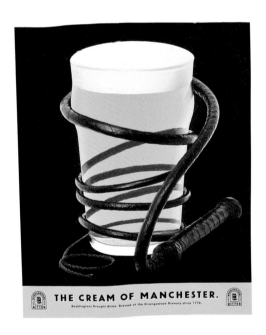

THE CREAM OF MANCHESTER.
Boddingtons Draught Bitter. Brewed at the Strangeways Brewery since 1778.

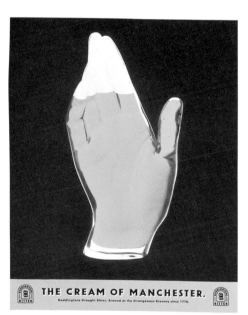

THE CREAM OF MANCHESTER.
Boddingtons Draught Bitter. Brewed at the Strangeways Brewery since 1778.

THE CREAM OF MANCHESTER.
Boddingtons Draught Bitter. Brewed at the Strangeways Brewery since 1778.

THE CREAM OF MANCHESTER.
Boddingtons Draught Bitter. Brewed at the Strangeways Brewery since 1778.

VANISHING CREAM.
Boddingtons. The Cream of Manchester. Brewed at the Strangeways Brewery since 1778.

THE CREAM OF MANCHESTER.
Boddingtons Draught Bitter. Brewed at the Strangeways Brewery since 1778.

THE CREAM OF MANCHESTER.
Boddingtons Draught Bitter. Brewed at the Strangeways Brewery since 1778.

■ DF: Bartle Bogle Hegarty UK (1996) ■ CD: John Hegarty ■ AD: Graham Watson ■ P: Tif Hunter ■ CW: Bruce Crouch

Recent studies have shown that communication intented to correct irresponsible behaviour of young drivers during the weekend has no effect when directed straight at them. They deny that they behave irresponsibly when drinking and driving and have the impression that they are fully in control at all times. So if you can't talk sense to the driver, talk sense to his friends. Make them realise that they're the only ones who can prevent someone drunk from driving and that a friend is

worth all the on...
やめさせようという呼びかけ...
飲酒や運転の際に無責任な行動はとって...
ると思っている。ドライバーに言ってもだめなら、...
酔っぱらった友人に運転を止めさせることのできる唯一の人で...
それだけの努力をする価値があるということを理解させるのだ。

ROUGH SKETCHES

FINAL PRESENTATION

After exploring several directions we arrived at the idea that you can't do enough to prevent a friend from driving when he's drunk. We imagined how far you could go in preventing him from driving. This is the way we prefer to present our work: a plain and simple line drawing presenting the idea as clearly as possible. Everything that might obstruct the idea is left out.

いくつかの方向から検討した結果、友人の飲酒運転を止めるためにいくら努力してもしすぎることはない、というコンセプトにたどり着いた。友人の飲酒運転を止める時、どの程度までできるものか我々は考えた。こうした方法で作品のプレゼンテーションを行うことは我々の望むところである。簡単明瞭なラインで、可能な限り明確にこのコンセプトを打ち出すのである。このコンセプトの邪魔になるものはすべて取り除いた。

After the first meeting the general approach was approved. Other themes were created while the remaining ideas were further developed. The projects still remained basic in appearance.

最初のミーティングで、コンセプト全体が承認された。その他のテーマの制作を行う一方で、残った構想を発展させた。プロジェクトは一見したところまだ基本的な段階に留まっている。

After the pictures were shot different lay-out approaches were tried. The design had to get rid of any possible patronizing tone and be in line with current youth culture. The challenge was to go graphically as far as possible without creating interfering noise, and at the same time remain relevant. After consideration of a more colourful approach, I decided to tone the design down and let the white border neutralise the busy surroundings of billboard sites. At the same time it gives the vivid colours in the pictures more power. The sentence was split in two to help improve legibility.

写真撮影の後、様々なレイアウトを試みた。偉そうな感じではなく、現代の若者文化に沿ったものでなければならない。干渉的に聞こえないよう、おしつけがましくなく、できるだけ写実的な路線で行くことにした。色とりどりのアプローチを考えたが、その後デザインのトーンを落とし、ビルボードのごてごてした周辺を白枠で抑えることにした。これにより、同時に、写真のビビッドなカラーがさらに際立つようになった。コピーは読みやすいように2つに分けた。

■ DF: n.v. Van Hees Vlessing Lagrillière/BBDO s.a. Belgium (1995)
■ CD: Willy Coppens ■ AD: Peter Aerts ■ P: Danny Willems ■ CW: Philip Maes

If you have a car of this calibre you know it has to dominate the poster. A quick scribble to represent this is sufficient. The car and a line should be able to communicate the idea in a snap. A simple line drawing was enough to represent the car. ▬▬　こんな車だったら、ポスター全体を占め

るのが当然だと思うだろう。車を表現する走り書きで十分である。車と1本の線で即座にそのコンセプトを伝えることができるに違いない。それには、シンプルなラインで描くだけで十分であった。

R O U G H   S K E T C H E S

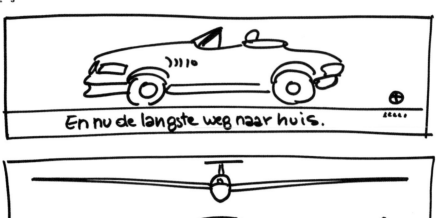

F I R S T   P R E S E N T A T I O N

In the conceptual phase we were looking for a way to show off the breathtaking beauty of the car. Everything that made immediate reference to the car seemed to make it less desirable. We always got confronted with the fact that words made the car less precious. At the same time we were working on a poster for the convertible and found that the headline for that one worked better with Z3. And the swap was proposed to the client.

コンセプトの段階で、この車の息をのむような美しさを引き立たせる方法を模索した。車を直接表現するものはすべて、魅力を半減させるように思われた。言葉にすると車の価値が減少するという事実を我々はいつも見てきた。同時進行で、コンバーティブルのポスターも手掛けており、コンバーティブルの見出しがBMW Z3の方にふさわしいことに気がついた。そこで、クライアントに変更を提案した。

After the photo was taken we made a straight comp with the notice neatly across the poster. And it worked. But you always wonder if the work can be improved. And it could. Finally it became a poster with only a picture of an incredible car, its name, the BMW tag line, and a notice screwed on asking people not to climb on the poster.

写真撮影の後、ポスターをあざやかに横切って注意書きをつけたストレートなカンプを制作した。これはうまくいった。しかし、他にいい案はないだろうか。まだある。最終的に、すばらしい車の写真と名前とBMWの文字、それにポスターに登らないでくださいという注意書きをねじで留めただけのポスターとなった。

■ DF: n.v. Van Hees Vlessing Lagrillière/BBDO s.a. Belgium (1996) ■ CD: Willy Coppens ■ AD: Peter Aerts ■ P: Christophe Gilbert ■ CW: Philip Maes

The premium image of the Carlsberg brand had its limitations in the Belgian lager market, where a lot of Belgian common lager brews rule. To enlarge its share we opted for a slight image change to position Carlsberg as the most attractive common lager and discontinue the absolute premium positioning. ■ 数多くの大衆的なベルギーラガーが優勢なラガー市場で、カールスバーグブランドの高級なイメージには限界があった。そこで我々はシェアの拡大のために、カールスバーグのイメージを若干変更し、最も魅力のある大衆ラガーとして位置づけ、最高級のポジショニングを廃止することにした。

FIRST PRESENTATION: IDEA 1

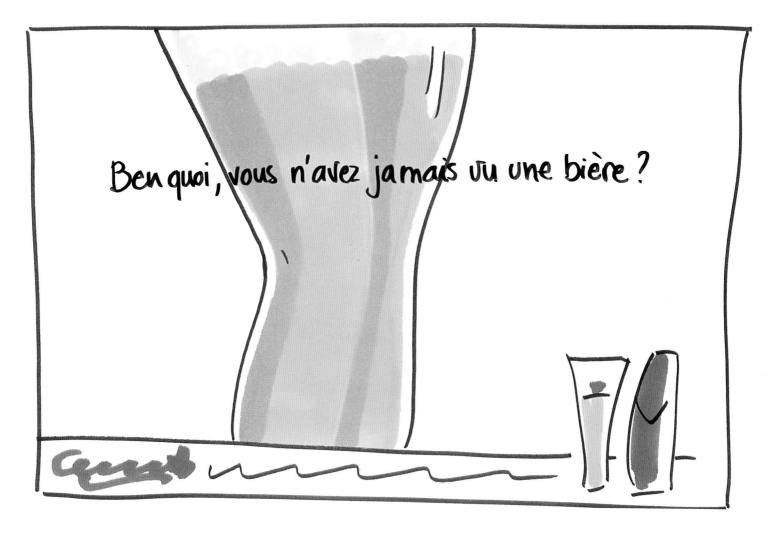

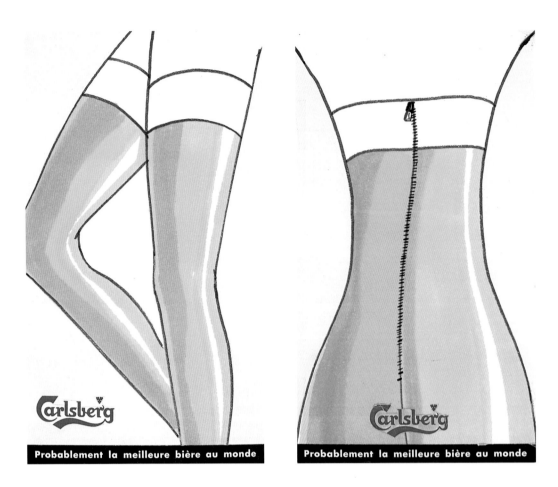

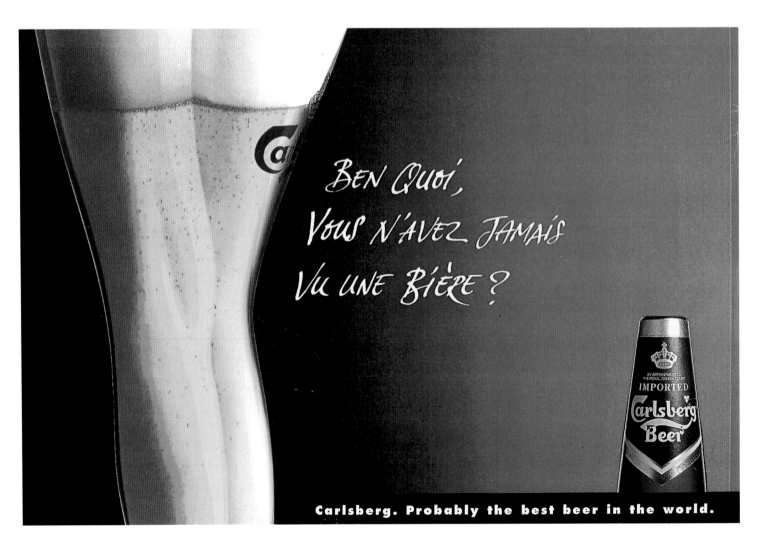

These were two of the angles taken on the project. In all cases the known tag line was kept as a reference point. The meaning of 'The best beer' had to be adjusted and translated in common lager terms. One way to do this was to use a more slapstick kind of humour that played on 'Probably the best beer in the world'. The incapability of tasting the best lager in the world was an interesting way to play down the premium image whilst creating a lot of sympathy. The other direction obtained the same goal by interpreting the premium lager as purely attractive. So an attractive female was created out of the beer. At this stage still without text.

以下は、プロジェクトに基づいて取り上げられた2つの観点である。様々な面から検討して、知名度の高いタグライン（標語）は、ブランドを示すものとして残した。「最高のビール」という考えを改め、大衆的なラガーという言葉に変更しなければならなかった。これを実現する一つの方法が、どたばた調のユーモアを使い、「たぶん世界最高かもしれないビール」と冗談の種にしたことである。世界最高のラガーを味わうことができないという設定は、高級イメージをトーンダウンする一方で共感を呼び起こす面白い方法であった。もう一つの方法は、高級ラガーを純粋に魅力的であると解釈して表現すること。そこで、魅力的な女性をビールから誕生させた。この段階ではまだコピーはつけていない。

Finally it was decided that we would go for the sexy approach if we could make it a bit more down to earth. The solution came in the form of quotes from a 'femme fatale'. This way we popularised the classy looking visuals. Since the campaign was considered a relaunch it was found essential to create a female silhouette resembling the elegant lines of the Carlsberg glass.

最終的に、もう少し現実的なものにできればという条件で、我々はセクシー路線で行くことに決定した。『ファム・ファタール（運命の女）』から引用することによって解決法が見つかった。こうして、見た目に高級なビジュアルを大衆化したのである。キャンペーンは再出発と考えられていた、女性のシルエットに似せた、カールスバーググラスのエレガントなラインを作る事を必要とされた。

Different approaches were tested, each trying to get the voice and tone of our female across. Set type seemed less appropriate because of its harshness. The simple handwriting gave it the personality we were looking for.

様々なタイプのアプローチが試みられた。それぞれに女性の声と調子を合わせようとした。活字は味気ないためにふさわしいとは思えなかった。我々の求めていたパーソナリティーを与えてくれたのは単純な手書き文字である。

■ DF: n.v. Van Hees Vlessing Lagrillière/BBDO s.a. Belgium (1996)
■ CD: Willy Coppens
■ AD: Peter Aerts / Dominique Vandoormael / Christina Gesulfo / Fred Van Have
■ P: Pascal Demeester / Jean Pierre Vanderelst ■ CW: Vincent Abrams / Willem de Geyndt

Pepsi / Pepsi Max Product Ad ■ ペプシ／ペプシ マックス　商品広告

Pepsi has a small share of the soft drink market in Belium. The introdution of Pepsi Max was an ideal opportunity to reinforce the brand's image with primarily teen soft-drinkers. Max is a sugarless soft drink but the no sugar route was avoided to widen the appeal among the youth target.　The brief boiled down to 'the soft drink for people *with guts'.*　■■■■■　ベルギーのソフトドリンク市場では、ペプシはシェアが小さい。ペプシマックスの紹介は、主にティーンエージャーのソフトドリンク愛好者にブランドイメージを浸透させる絶好の機会であった。ペプシマックスはシュガーレスのソフトドリンクだが、若者に広くアピールするためにシュガーレス路線は避けた。検討した結果「ガッツのある人のソフトドリンク」に落ちついた。

C O L O R   C O M P S

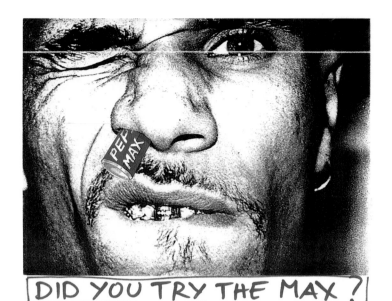

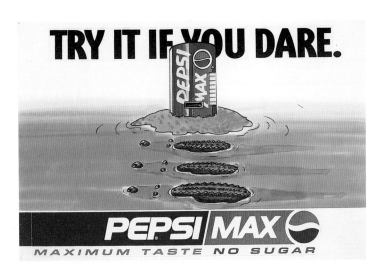

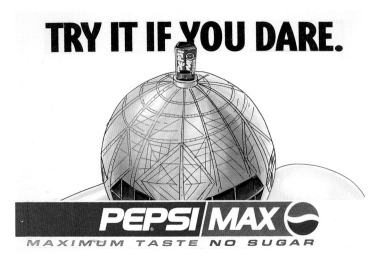

In the initial phase a lot of approaches were tried to convey the balsy character of the brand. One denied that Max was a 'soft-drink' and therefore for gutsy characters. And two concepts put the drink forward as a challenge, something you certainly must have tried. Rough photo comps and traditional marker lay outs were made for in-house evaluation.

最初の段階では、このブランドの威勢の良さを伝えるために様々なアプローチを試みた。その中の一つは、ペプシマックスが「ソフトなドリンク」であることを否定する、そして結果的に威勢の良さを売りものするというものである。そして、この２つのコンセプトによってこの飲み物を、チャレンジ、絶対試しておかねばならないものとして前面に押し出した。ラフ・写真・カンプと昔ながらのマーカーによるレイアウトを、社内で検討するために制作した。

It was decided that the physical challenge had the most scope. This axis was conceived as a 3-D poster concept actually challenging those who dare. In this instance we tried to convey as much as possible of the three-dimensional feeling.

最も有望なものとして、立体的な制作をしてみようということになった。この方針は３Ｄポスター構想として考え出されたものであるが、これは挑戦する者にとっては実に困難な仕事である。この場合は、できるだけ３次元の感じを伝えようと努力した。

Additional 3D executions were developed together with 2D variants. The final type was designed once the pictures were taken. We made sure that this approach also worked on the 3D posters. I finally designed the headline as a caption. In the end two 2D and two 3D posters with 1 - metre - high cans attached to them were created. And these proved to be a success. They all got stolen and on one poster someone wrote 'I did it'. Apparently the balsy youngsters got the message.

２Ｄ版と共に３Ｄ版をさらに発展させて制作が行われた。最終版は撮影終了後に立案されたものである。このアプローチもまた３Ｄポスターに合うように努力をした。最終的にヘッドラインをキャプションとしてデザインすることにした。最後に、２Ｄと３Ｄのポスターがそれぞれ２種づつ、高さ１ｍの缶をつけて制作された。そして後にこれは大成功であったことが判明した。それはポスターがすべて盗まれたからである。あるポスターには「おれがやった」と落書きがあった。威勢の良い若者からメッセージを受け取ったのは明らかである。

■ DF: n.v. Van Hees Vlessing Lagrillière/BBDO s.a. Belgium (1994)
■ CD: Willy Coppens ■ AD: Peter Aerts
■ P: Georges Charlier / J. F. De Witte ■ CW: Willem de Geyndt

Suntory Ltd. / Suntory C. C. Lemon Canned Drink Packaging ■ サントリー㈱／サントリーC.C.レモン パッケージ

Suntory C.C. Lemon is a new product directed at the high turnover carbonated drinks section of the soft drinks market. It was developed out of a study into the views and feelings of male and female junior and senior high school students, the mass target of soft drinks consumption. The market for carbonated drinks has previously been focused on strongly carbonated drinks, but it is now seeing a major reorientation towards more natural, health-promoting drinks. The concept developed for this market was a carbonated health drink with

a high level of vitamin C, and regarded as thirst-quenching, refreshing, fruity, and healthy. It was launched in March 1994. ■■■■ サントリーC.C.レモンは、飲料市場のボリュームゾーン、炭酸飲料市場に向けた新製品です。飲料消費のマスターゲットの中高生男子の感性と意見を取り入れ開発しました。強炭酸を中心とした従来の炭酸市場が、自然、健康志向にそって大きく変化し始めています。その市場に対して開発したコンセプトは、止渇感、清涼感、果実感、健康感をもち、ビタミンCたっぷりの、健康炭酸飲料としました。（1994年3月新発売）

COLOR COMPS

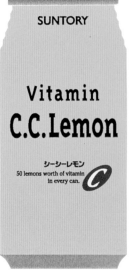

C.C. Lemon was chosen as the product name, with the C repeated to increase the sense of lots of vitamin C. Yellow was selected as the main design color because it most closely puts over the idea of vitamins.

ビタミンCのたっぷり入った飲料を表現するネーミングとして、C.C.と繰り返す表現をし、ビタミンを感じる色彩として黄色をメインカラーに感じるデザインを基本としました。

We decided to use a combination of green and red to set off the main yellow color. We brought in variation by re-arranging the layout, and emphasizing or de-emphasizing the logo, checking to ensure the end-result remained true to the product concept.

黄色を生かす色として、グリーン、赤をコンビネーションとすることにしました。またロゴの強弱、レイアウトの変化により、「商品コンセプトが表現できているか」を常に考え、バリエーションを広げました。

It was important that the product should be distinctive among other brands. We decided to keep the design far simpler than usual, and at the presentation we used simplicity as the key that would differentiate the product.

他社製品と差別化することがポイントです。その為に、今までにないシンプルなデザインを決定する事、シンプルこそが差別化になることを、プレゼンテーションしました。

■ DF: サントリー㈱ Suntory Ltd. Japan (1994)
■ CD: 大門敏彦 Toshihiko Daimon ■ CD, AD: 加藤芳夫 Yoshio Kato ■ D: 前田英樹 Tsuneki Maeda

Suntory Ltd. / Suntory Coffee Boss Packaging ■ サントリー㈱／サントリーコーヒーボス パッケージ

Canned coffee has a large share of the canned drinks market and consumption continues to grow steadily. The heavy drinkers of canned coffee represent only 17.9% of the total, but they account for 60% of the consumption. To promote a new brand of canned coffee with these heavy drinkers as the target audience, comprehensive market research was carried out to decide the taste, the product name and the design. The underlying product concept was 'aiming to be top brand' or becoming the 'boss' of canned coffees. It was launched in September 1992.

■■■ 飲料市場の中で、大きな割合を占め、着実な伸びを見せているのが、缶コーヒーです。この缶コーヒー市場に対し、新ブランドを開発することになりました。缶コーヒーユーザーの中のヘビーユーザーは、全体の17.9％に過ぎませんが、消費量は、全消費量の60％に達している市場であることが、確認されました。このヘビーユーザーをターゲットに、中味、ネーミング、デザインを徹底した市場調査により開発、決定しました。「ブレンドの頂点をめざす」「缶コーヒーのボスになる」を商品コンセプトとしました。（1992年9月新発売）

THUMBNAIL SKETCH

ビジュアルコンセプトスケッチ

FIRST PRESENTATION

キャラクタースケッチの一部

デザインスケッチ案の一部

カラー バリエーション案の一部

グラフィック アイデンティティーの展用

To convey the idea of the 'boss' of canned coffees, it was thought that a design centered around a face would catch the eye and be most effective.

缶コーヒーのボスを表現する為に、アイキャッチャーとして、キャラクター表現を中心にしたデザインが有効であると考えました。

We used very simple colors and logo in order to focus the design on a face that conveyed the idea 'boss', a man with discriminating taste. The underlying message was of setting a standard and being of high quality.

「"ボス"を感じる顔」「こだわりのある男」を表現したデザインをするために、単純化された色彩、ロゴを採用し、「スタンダードを感じ」「上質であること」を基本としました。

Distinguishing it from other companies' products was seen as the essence of success for this new product launch. The central point of the presentation was that the design would appeal to the heavy drinkers.

他社製品と差別化することが、新製品として成功するポイントであること。しかも、そのデザインがヘビーユーザーに受け入れられているということをプレゼンテーションの核としました。

■ DF: サントリー㈱ Suntory Ltd. Japan (1992)
■ CD, CW: 藤田芳康 Yoshiyasu Fujita ■ CD, AD: 加藤芳夫 Yoshio Kato ■ D, I: 石浦弘幸 Hiroyuki Ishiura

Toyo Suisan Kaisha, Ltd. / Hot Noodles Packaging ■ 東洋水産㈱／ホットヌードル パッケージ

The logo character Maru-chan had been introduced 4 years before. In spring 1996 a new communication strategy was wanted for the 'summer salty' and 'summer vegetable curry' flavors. We reached the conclusion that the character should not be changed (in fact minimal changes were made) and the whole visual appearance, including the packaging, should be freshened up with a TV commercial. For the packaging, we started with the first important element, the name, and decided to make the names the largest feature, and use the character as a small brand logo positioned at the top and less conspicuously.

The guiding principle was designing something that would sell.

東洋水産のマルちゃん「ホットヌードル」は'93年ロゴキャラクターを開発してから4年目を迎え、'96年春の「夏しお」「夏野菜カレー」から新しいコミュニケーション戦略で登場することになった。キャラクターは変えるべきではないという結論に達し、（実はほんのわずか変えてある）、全体の見え方をパッケージを含めTV-CFも新鮮なものにすることになった。パッケージにおいては、まず重要な要素であるネーミングの開発から入り、ネーミングを一番大きくし、キャラクターは小さくブランドロゴマークとして上部に小さめに扱うことになった。何しろまず「売れる」ことが第一なのである。

LOGO TREATMENT

MONOCHROME COMPS

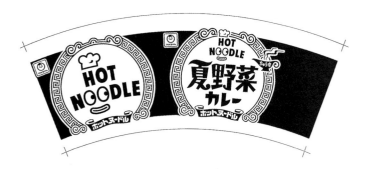

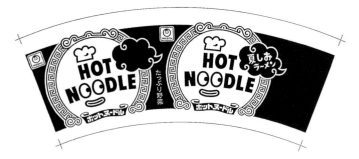

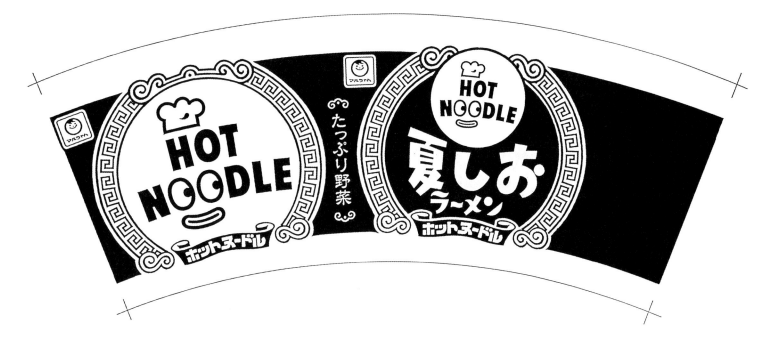

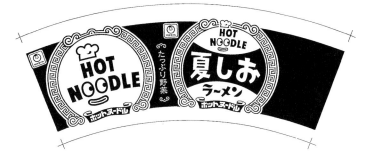

We studied the logo character and searched for a new design format. At this stage the names had not been finally decided. We were also debating how prominently to use the character. We tried out different ideas, adding further colors to color copies.

ロゴキャラクターの検討と共に、新しいデザインフォーマットを探る。この段階では、まだネーミングは決定していない。キャラクターを大きく扱うべきかどうかも検討中のもの。カラーコピーで色も仮に付けて検討してみる。

The new format was agreed in principle, the likely names were designed and we tried fitting them into the new format. Using a very large name logo gives a strong impact. When we're short of time we get an interim OK on the basis of black and white comps as here.

新しいフォーマットの方向性が決まり、決定しそうなネーミングをロゴ化し、フォーマットに入れ込んでみて検討。ネーミングロゴを大きく扱う方向が有力になる。時間が無い場合は、このようにモノクロで途中チェックを受ける。

We made 3D dummies from color copies. With the client we considered them from all possible angles, including coloring: whether they looked like what they were, whether they would stand out, whether they would appeal to shoppers from supermarket shelves, and whether they made the product look tasty. Then we decided on the final details.

カラーコピーレベルで立体ダミーを制作する。しおラーメンがしおラーメンらしいか、目立つか、手に取ってみたくなるか、おいしそうかなど、色も含めいろいろな角度からクライアントとスタッフで検討し最終方向を決定する。

■ DF：㈱佐藤 卓デザイン事務所 Taku Satoh Design Office Inc. Japan (1996)
■ AD, D：佐藤 卓 Taku Satoh ■ D：古賀 友規 Tomoki Koga
■ CW：山田紀子 Noriko Yamada ■ PL：西橋裕三 Yuzo Nishihashi

Nakayama Co.,Ltd. / Mónte Mezzo Label Promotion ■ ㈱中山／モンテメッツオ　ブランドプロモーション

These posters were produced for display within the shops, but were also used at the show launching the new Mónte Mezzo collection. The client, haute couture fashion manufacturer Nakayama, requested something that would look fresh to the eye and we decided on B-size (1030mm X 728mm) half-width posters. As they were to be image posters we had a free hand with the design and were able to produce what we wanted.　■　オートクチュールの服飾メーカーである㈱中山のブランド、"モンテメッツオ" のためのイメージポスターです。店頭用を目的に制作したのですが、実際には、店頭以外に、"モンテメッツオ" の新作発表会にも使用しました。目新しさが望まれていたので、B全1/2という変形のポスターの形態を選出しました。イメージポスターということで、表現等はこちらにまかせていただき、自由に制作させてもらいました。

THUMBNAIL SKETCHES

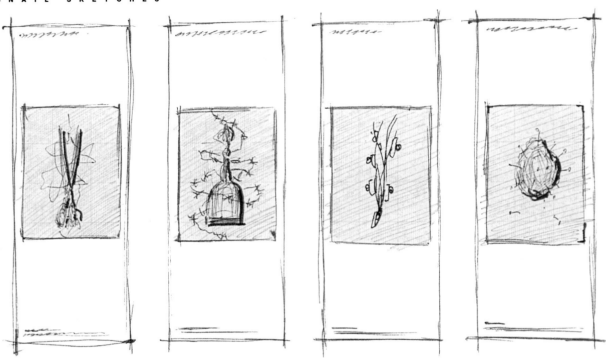

COLOR ROUGHS & TYPE TREATMENT

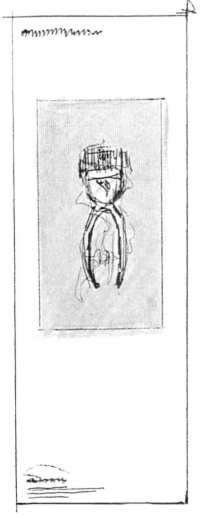
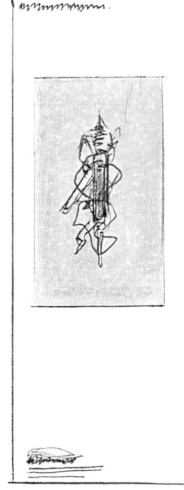
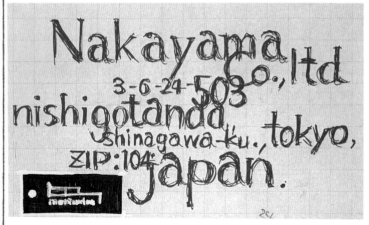

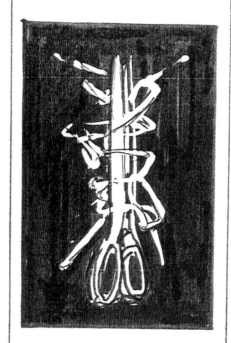

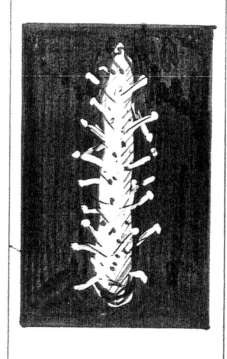

とりあえずだったら、欲しくない。

Nakayama co., ltd.
#503, 3-6-24,
nishigotanda,
shinagawa-ku, Tokyo,
ZIP:141 Japan.

動機は、不純な方がうまくいく。

The unusual tall shape had been decided at the outset, and next we looked for an effective way to put over the right image for Mónte Mezzo haute couture clothes.

あまりないＢ全1/2という変形はアイデアの段階から決めてあり、"モンテメッツオ"というオートクチュールの服のイメージをどの様に表現しようかと、映像を考えていきました。

We decided we would avoid the mix of models and clothes that other fashion labels go for, and at the same time thought the trend in fashion advertising to avoid copy would in this case hamper us from communicating the haute couture quality of this label, and so we planned to use both visuals and copy.

他のファッションブランドの様に"人と服"のからみだけはさけると同時に、ファッション広告にありがちな「コピーなし」では、このオートクチュール感を表現できないと考え、"コピー"と"ビジュアル"を考えてゆきました。

The client left the design entirely to us, so we didn't prepare any comps but did a presentation on the proofs. I felt that we produced fashion posters with a distinctively different feel about them.

表現にいたっては、クライアント側からすべてまかせていただいたので、カンプは作らず校正でお見せしました。ファッションブランドのポスターとしては、風変わりなものが出来たと思います。

■ DF: ㈱マグナ Magna, Inc. Advertising / ビームX10 Beam X10 Inc. Japan (1996)
■ CD, AD, D: 工藤規雄 Norio Kudo ■ P: 佐藤孝仁 Takahito Sato ■ CW: 田中裕子 Yuko Tanaka

Nakayama co., ltd.
#503, 3-6-24,
nishigotanda,
shinagawa-ku, Tokyo,
ZIP:141 Japan.

The client wants to remove the association in people's minds between agricultural studies and farming. The University PR staff and the agency, Recruit, all agreed that as before they wanted to place the emphasis on putting over the great potential of agricultural studies. This was not the first time for the research that students were undertaking to be publicized through the medium of advertising, but everyone involved agreed that this was the quickest way of putting over

the right message. ■ 農学＝農業というイメージをなくすために、クライアントである東京農業大学の広報の担当者や、代理店であるリクルートの人等、スタッフ全員が"農学のすばらしさ"を表現することに今回も力点をおいて制作しました。実際に農学を実戦している学生の研究を、広告という媒体を使って伝えてゆくという方法は、今回が初めてではないが、やはりその方法が伝え方として一番早いと、スタッフ全員の判断で決定しました。

THUMBNAIL SKETCHES

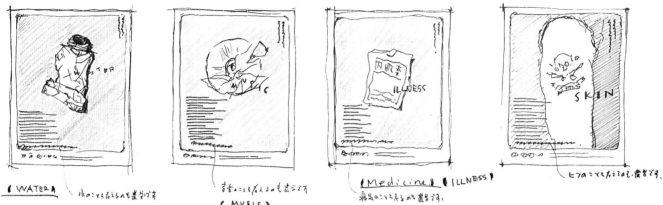

COLOR ROUGHS

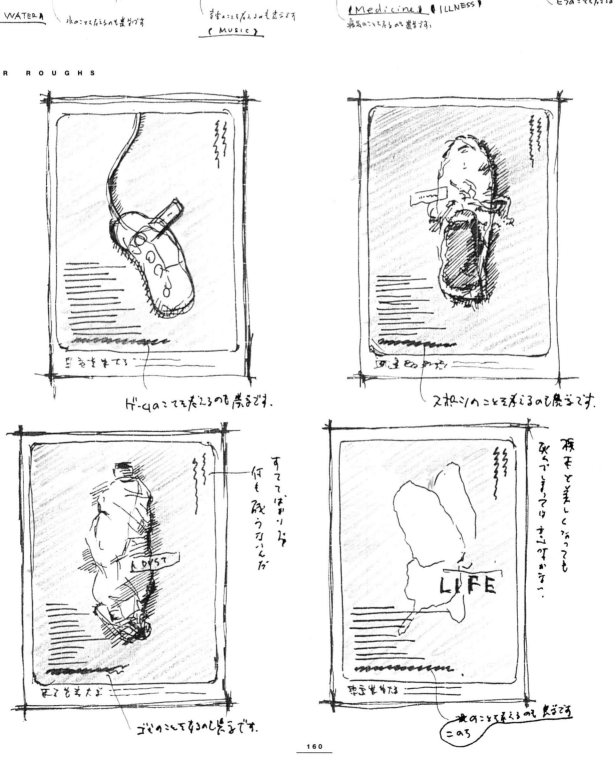

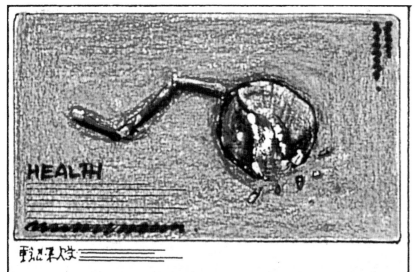

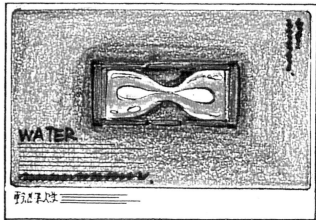

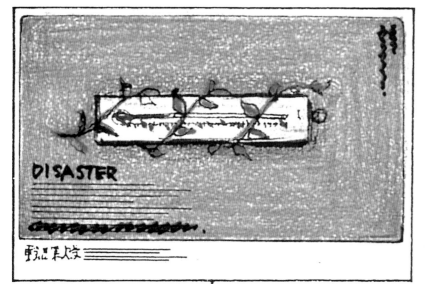

The issue was to design an ad around the message 'such-and-such research is also part of agricultural studies'. We tried out some idea sketches, talked to 20 or 30 students, and gradually worked up our ideas.

「農学はこんなこともやっているのです。」ということを、どの様に表現するかがポイントでした。アイデアスケッチを進行と同時に学生数十人の取材も同時に進行しアイデアをツメてゆきました。

The copy was decided quite early on, and after completing interviews with the students we had a far clearer idea of how to approach the design.

「○○○も、農学です。」というコピーをキーワードとして使うことは早い時点で決まり、学生への取材も終えると、伝えたい内容はよりしぼられてきました。

We agreed on the themes water, health, and natural disasters and used some aspect of the students' research in each field in the visuals. In this way we wanted to achieve something that was not merely visually arresting but would generate interest in the content, and we stressed this in the presentation.

「水」、「災害」、「健康」とテーマは決まり、その学生の研究の内容をビジュアルに融合させることで、単なるおどかしや、見た目だけではなく、内容に興味を持ってもらうことに重点をおいてプレゼンテーションしました。

■ DF: ㈱マグナ Magna, Inc. Advertising / ㈱サン・アド Sun - Ad Co., Ltd. Japan (1996)
■ CD, AD, D: 工藤規雄 Norio Kudo ■ CD, CW: 笠原千昌 Chiaki Kasahara
■ D: 日置好文 Yoshifumi Hioki ■ P: 泊 昭雄 Akio Tomari ■ Stylist: 岡村雅人 Masato Okamura

The biggest point here was how to use posters, a printed medium, to demonstrate a high level of printing technology. They were not to be posters for public display, but something the company could give as small gifts to their customers. So an important condition was that they should be decorative, so people would enjoy displaying them. ▬

印刷会社である、錦印刷㈱の技術をＰＲするために制作したポスターです。印刷の技術の高さを、ポスターという実際の印刷でどの様に表現するかが最大のポイントでした。駅に貼る等のポスターではなく、「おとくい様に渡せるポスターを。」という要望もあり、もらった人が壁などに貼った時のポスターとしての装飾性も重要な条件となりました。

THUMBNAIL SKETCHES

COLOR ROUGHS

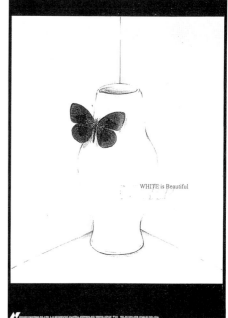

I first of all began to think up ideas that would stress beauty or decorativeness. The idea in my mind was to see the posters as having the role of something you would put on show in your home, like a painting or vase.

ポスターの美しさ（装飾性）をまず頭の中に入れて発想を初めました。絵画や花びんのように、部屋の中における役割に近いものをこのポスターに盛り込めたら…と発想をしました。

The biggest drawback of printing is the 4-color process. It often gives me headaches in the course of my work. Black doesn't turn out really black, or else the 4 colors of the process separate a fraction. I decided I would try to bring out both beauty and sophisticated printing technology in my designs.

印刷の最大の特徴であり、欠点であるのが4色分解です。私自身が通常の仕事で、悩みのタネである、「黒のシマリの悪さ」と「色ウキ」ということがよくあり、この辺を「印刷の技術」と「美しさ」で表現してみることに決めました。

Something that shows off black and white really beautifully will testify to high quality printing technology. I did a presentation on this, and got the OK to go ahead with 9-color printing for these posters.

本当に美しい"黒"と"白"が表現できれば、それは印刷の技術の高さを表していることになる…。とプレゼンテーションをし、そのための各ポスターの９色刷もＯＫをいただきました。

■ DF: ㈱マグナ Magna, Inc. Advertising Japan (1996)

■ CD, AD, D, CW: 工藤規雄 Norio Kudo ■ P: 泊 昭雄 Akio Tomari ■ Stylist: 岡村雅人 Masato Okamura

Murata MFG. Co., Ltd. / Corporate Promotion ■ ㈱村田製作所／企業広告

The theme of this year's advertising was to show where Murata electronic components go, introducing some major products and showing the benefit gained by using Murata components. A further aim was to project an international image. We started out with an idea for a TV ad. Various foreigners use broken Japanese to ask Japanese about the 'brand inside'. The Japanese get agitated. The words are unexpected. Famous brands don't appear on the 'outside' exclusively. Can't we see the inside? We decided the copy should be in katakana

script to exploit its 'foreign' feel. After some brisk discussion, the idea of seeing into the product came up. ■■■ 村田製作所の電子部品はどんな製品の中に入っているのか？それがこの年のテーマだった。（部品が使われている）代表的な製品を紹介すること。その性能に大きく貢献している ということ。加えて国際性というねらい。これらを軸にまずＴＶ案から考えた。いろんな外国人が日本人にカタコトの日本語で中のブランドを質問する。うろたえる日本人。唐突なコトバ。外だけがブランドじゃない。中ってどうして見えないの？じゃあコピーはカタカナか。的やりとりの末、透視するという考えが浮かんだ。

R O U G H   S K E T C H E S

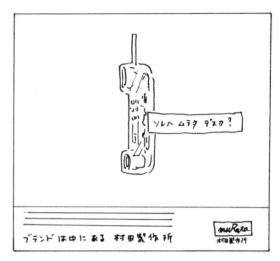

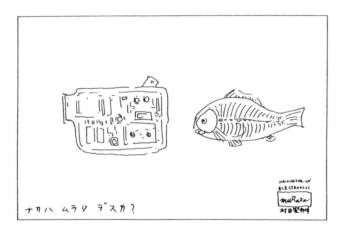

V I S U A L S

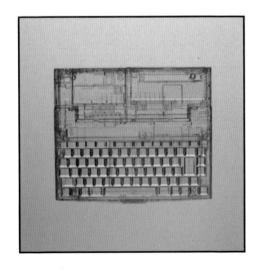

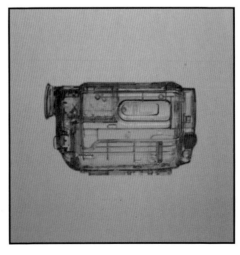

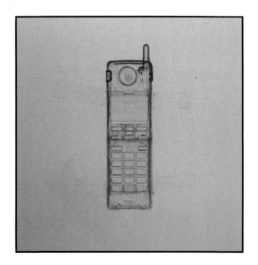

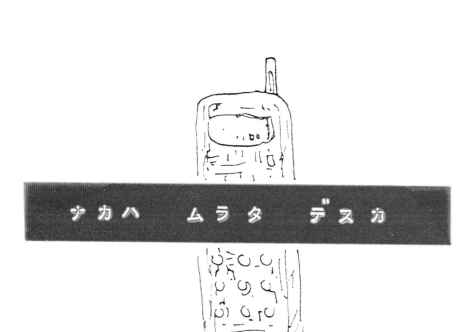

Put forward two proposals as ideas to stimulate interest in the 'inside': the X-ray idea and the skeleton-drawing idea. The X-ray idea compared the inside of a machine with the insides of plants and creatures. But it suffered the limitation of not allowing much photographic flexibility.

中に興味を持ってもらうアイデアとして、X線案とスケルトン案の2つを提案した。X線案は機械の中身と生物や植物の中を対比させるという考えがあった。しかし写真的なコントロールはあまりできないという制約もあった。

Recommended using photography of a transparent plastic model for a greater degree of freedom of expression. The dymo tape used for the copy was perfect because of the mechanical and stilted effect it gives. A concealed intention was bringing together the ideas of state-of-the-art precision equipment and an old-fashioned analog-based technique.

透明なプラスチックモデルを使って撮影すれば表現の自由度が増すだろうと考えて、これをおススメした。コピーに使ったダイモは、カタコト感と電気的イメージにぴったり。精密感とアナログ感の共存がかくれたねらいとしてあった。※ダイモ→ダイモテープ

Requested that the skeleton-drawing motif and the background should be the same tone. Photography using natural light passing through the transparent model gave better results than we expected.

モチーフのスケルトンとバックが統一のトーンになるようにお願いした。自然光を透過した撮影方法は、予想以上のクオリティだった。

■ DF: ㈱サン・アド Sun-Ad Co., Ltd. Japan (1994)
■ CD: 小森純夫 Sumio Komori
■ CD, CW: 安藤 隆 Takashi Ando
■ AD, D: 小塚重信 Shigenobu Kozuka
■ P: 藤井 保 Tamotsu Fujii
■ CW: 下堂貴政 Takamasa Shimodo

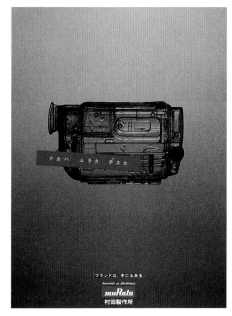

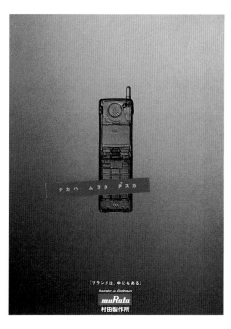

Using the theme of 'inside' for another year. So once again we're thinking about insides all the time. Working on the inside is pretty dull. What's going on inside these days? No-one's got a clue. It's all due to these components that telephones are smaller these days. It's amazing inside! An exhibition of inside parts? There's an inside and therefore there's an outside. It's the inside that counts. Everything's just a matter of what's in it. And so on. From these incoherent ramblings we drew some roughs. ■ 中をテーマにもう一年。ということで、また中のことばかり考えることになった。中の仕事って地味な商売だよね。最近中ってどうなってるの？誰も中のことなど知らんよ。この部品のおかげで電話は小さくなったらしいよ。中は不思議だ。部品の展覧会は？中があるから外がある。中が本質なんだ。やはり中身だよね、なにごとも。というとりとめのない中でラフを描きだした。

THUMBNAIL SKETCHES

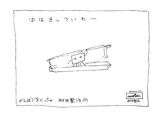

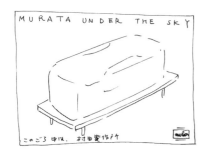

CFとは連動せず、新聞広告らしいシリーズとして、部品のスーパーリアリズムの絵で、ミクロの不思議感を伝えます。
「MURATA UNDER THE SKY」は、ついに白日のもとに堂々と自分をき張する村田の誇りを表現します。

「子供とフシギ」ということで、子供がフシギと出会う絵を、絵本風に展開します。続編としては、豆電球が、乾電池の⊕⊖で点灯したときのオドロキなど、素材で電気に関係するシーンをとりあげます。

PHS、カーナビ、パソコンなど、外のブランド名をモザイクで分らなくした（さらにモザイクアートにまで高めた）商品シリーズ。「そとはぴーつ　なかはむらた」と対のコピーにして、わかりやすくしました。

VISUAL CONCEPTS

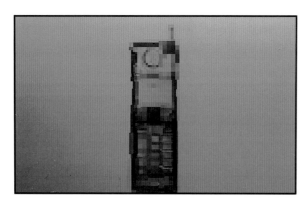

A

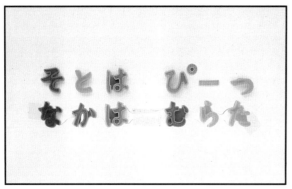

B

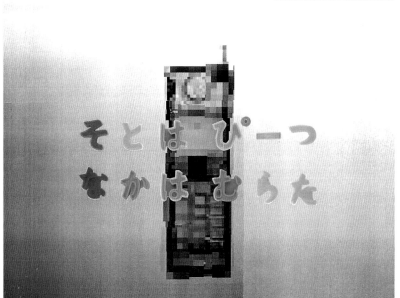

フシギは中にある

中をかんがえよう　村田製作所

Decided to go ahead with graphics on three ideas: the mosaic idea, the 'in-sides are amazing' idea, and the exhibition of inside parts idea. We pushed the mosaic idea. The 'It's tough inside!' idea was put forward at the first pre-sentation. Wanted to go with it.

モザイク案、中はフシギ案、部品の展覧会案、グラフィックはこの３案を出すことにした。おス
スメはモザイク案。「中はきっついわー」案は最初のプレゼンに出したもの。やりたかった。

Prepared the comps trying to bring out the importance of the different nuances in the designs. For the mosaic idea, we showed an example of a shot from last time that we had worked on. The toy letters used for the copy were to soften the seriousness of the wording.

それぞれ表現のニュアンスが大切だったこともあってカンプを作った。モザイクは例として前回の
写真に手を加えたものを見せた。コピーのおもちゃ文字はコトバのシリアスさをやわらげる為にも
必要な要素だった。※おもちゃ文字→文字を形どったおもちゃのブロック

Shot A was taken without the mosaic. Shot B was taken with a Polaroid with the wording put on top of the print. The cameraman could not have been keen on having the mosaic on the photo.

Aはモザイクをかける前のポジ。Bはプリントの上に文字をのせてポラで撮ったもの。カメラマン
としては、写真にモザイクがかけられるのは抵抗があったと思う。

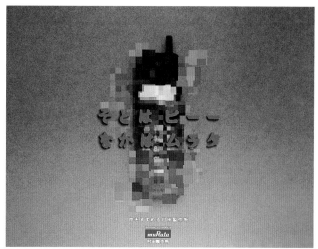

■ DF: ㈱サン・アド　Sun-Ad Co., Ltd. Japan (1995)
■ CD: 小森純夫　Sumio Komori　■ CD, CW: 安藤 隆　Takashi Ando
■ AD, D: 小塚重信　Shigenobu Kozuka　■ P: 藤井 保　Tamotsu Fujii

Suntory Ltd. / Whisky Promotion ■ サントリー㈱／シーズン プロモーション

One of several proposals put forward at a presentation we arranged to do for year-end gifts. Christmas and whisky. Night sky in winter. A castle made of bottles. Santa comes to call bringing whisky. Thought it was romantic. ■■■■■ 年末のギフトがらみの自主プレゼンテーションで、いくつか出した案の一つ。クリスマスとウイスキー。冬の夜空。ボトルのお城。サンタがウイスキーを持ってやってくる。ロマンチックだと思った。

ROUGH SKETCH

FIRST PRESENTATION

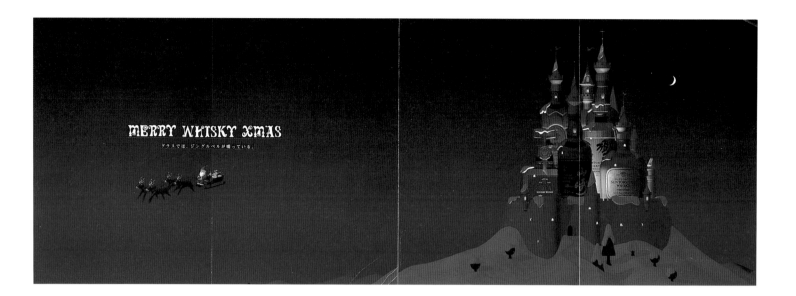

Did a presentation with these roughs. Thought at first we'd go for illustration, but when we couldn't find the right person we switched to photography. Then had the idea of trying computer graphics just before the presentation.

このラフでプレゼンテーション。当初イラストレーションにしようと作家を探していたが見つからず、ボツにしようと思っていた。ＣＧでやってみようと考えついたのはプレゼンテーションの直前だった。

Roughs for the computer assisted drawing. Had a vague idea how it would turn out, but I was still concerned: getting the right balance in using the product itself to create the castle, the Santa character, getting a sense of quality etc. Anyway, decided to see as things went along.

ポリゴンとの打ち合わせ用に描いたラフ。漠然としたイメージはあったが、どうなるか心配もあった。商品のデフォルメとお城の関係。サンタのキャラクター、質感の問題等。とにかく作りながら見ていくことにした。

Presentation for Suntory's confirmation. Thought we did well to get a representation of the product that needed virtually no changes. Color tones for the castle and the night sky remained an issue.

サントリーに確認の為プレゼンテーション。商品の印象をほとんど変えることなくできたのは、よかったと思う。お城と夜空の空間感、全体の色調が課題としてまだあった。

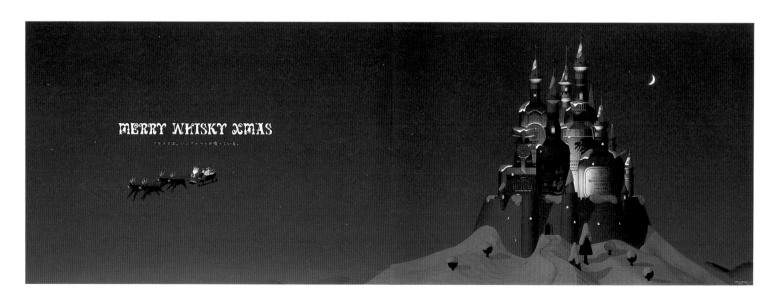

■ DF: ㈱サン・アド Sun-Ad Co., Ltd. Japan (1996) ■ CD, CW: 木村 昇 Noboru Kimura
■ AD, D: 小塚重信 Shigenobu Kozuka ■ CG: 今村卓也(ポリゴン・ピクチャーズ) Takuya Imamura (Polygon pictures) ■ PR: 小田桐 団 Dan Odagiri

Matsushita Seiko Co., Ltd. / Corporate Promotion　■　松下精工㈱／企業広告

The name Matsushita Seiko is not so well known, but it's the company that gave the extractor fan its Japanese name. Within the Matsushita group this company specializes in air- and water-related equipment, sort of 'environmental' issues. Our work started from collecting information, by checking on the company's wide-ranging products and technologies. To examine a tunnel air cleaning system, we were fully kitted out in protective clothing and went deep into one of Japan's longest tunnels. Using the knowledge gained through such experiences, we each tried out thumb nail sketches in our favorite medium and stuck them up on the board in the conference room.

■■■■　松下精工は、まだ広く知られていないが、初めて「換気扇」とネーミングした会社。松下グループの中では、空気と水を扱う、いわば環境問題の専門会社である。作業は、たいへん広い範囲にわたる製品や技術を調べ、取材するところから始まった。トンネルの空気浄化システムの時など、わが国有数の長さを誇る恵那山トンネルの奥深く、完全防護の服装で入っていった。このようにして体で得た知識をもとに、各自好みの筆記具でサムネイルをおこし、会議室のホワイトボードに貼っていく。

ROUGH SKETCHES

FIRST PRESENTATION

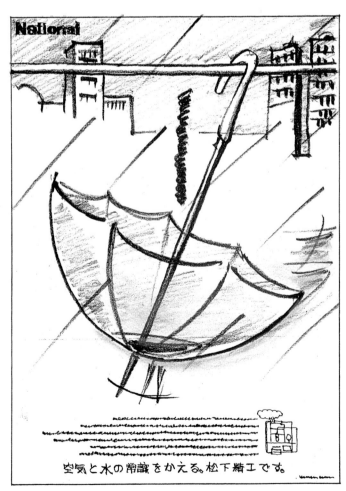

The rough sketches shown here represent only a small proportion of the total. Designers and copywriters got together and noisily worked them up. At this point, there were masses of ideas, including copy, stuck all over the board. The director and the client had to decide which way we should go.

ここに紹介したラフは、ごく一部である。デザイナー、コピーライターも一緒になって、侃々諤々やる。この時点では、コピー案も多数ボードに貼りだされている。ディレクターとクライアントが、方向づけを行なう。

This project was a full-page ad in the Nihon Keizai Shimbun (the leading business daily) in 2-color printing. The slogan was 'Matsushita Seiko: Changing our thinking on air and water'. We needed then just to work on individual points. Images of the musical 'Singin' in the Rain'.

この企画は日本経済新聞全15段、2色刷と決まった。スローガンは、「空気と水の常識を変える。松下精工」。あとは一点一点の精度を高めることが求められた。ミュージカル「雨に唄えば」のイメージもでてきた。

The suggestion was to make something direct that would elicit a response, using the umbrella idea that we'd had right from the start. We came up with the scene of a child playing with an umbrella. The word 'humanity' was a common theme running through the whole series.

当初からでていた傘を小道具として使いながら、素直で共感のあるものにできないかということで、子供が傘で遊んでいるシーンがでてきた。シリーズ全体を通じて「ヒューマン」が、合言葉のひとつとなった。

■ DF: ㈱中塚大輔広告事務所 Nakatsuka Daisuke Inc. / ㈱マック Maq Inc. / ㈱大広 Daiko Advertising Inc. Japan (1995)
■ CD: 中塚大輔 Daisuke Nakatsuka ■ AD: 東澤雅晴 Masaharu Higashizawa / 針谷辰志 Tatsushi Hariya
■ D: 本田邦人 Kunito Honda / 河方光治 Koji Kawakata
■ P: アリゾナ五郎 Goro Arizona ■ CW: 小川正廣 Masahiro Ogawa / 山阪佳彦 Yoshihiko Yamasaka

For this series of ads we started with an idea from Mr. Shu Uemura. He suggested a chart of the full line-up of 120 different lipstick colors arranged like a dart board. The chart was divided up into gloss, sheer and matt sections. To complement this we designed a kiss-mark poster. For the launch of a new range of foundations, we used the same idea with a chart showing the range of light tones. For the complementing poster we created a special image of a face.

一連の作品は、植村秀氏の発案によってスタートした。氏の発想は、120色に及ぶ口紅のラインアップをダーツのターゲットに見立て、チャート化しようというものであった。円は、グロス、シアー、マットなど質感によって分類されている。このポスターを補う形でキスマークのポスターが制作された。同様にファンデーションの新発売にあたって、明度の重要性に着目したチャートが制作された。対のポスターとして、私達が「顔拓」と名づけた顔型のポスターが制作された。

V I S U A L   I D E A S

F I N A L   P R E S E N T A T I O N

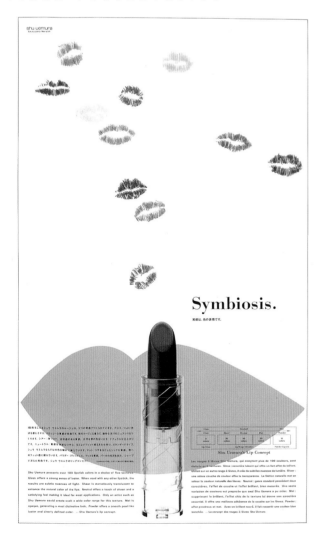

F I N A L   P R E S E N T A T I O N

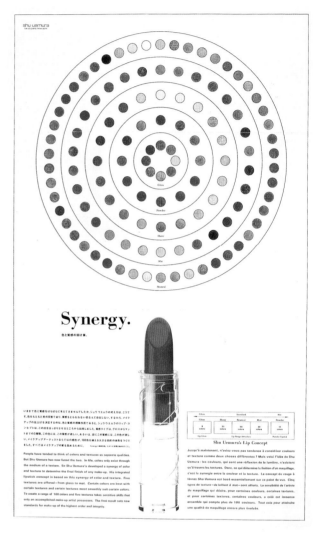

We don't always make pencil roughs. We make collages of the materials we have, and using Macs and copiers we work up the image we want.

ペンシルラフはつくらないこともある。既成の素材をコラージュしたり、MAC、コピー機などを使って、イメージを探りだしていく。

The poster combined the classic idea of the chart with the retro-feeling kiss-mark idea. We used chic color representative of Shu Uemura.

ターゲットという古典的なアイデアに合せて対になるポスターは、レトロ感覚をいかしたキスマーク案となった。シュウ ウエムラ的なシックな色使いとした。

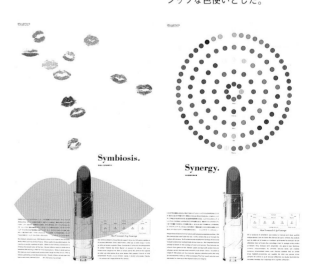

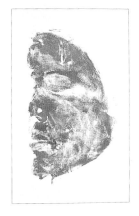

FINAL PRESENTATION

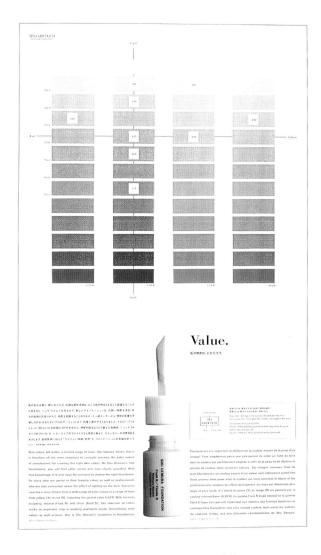

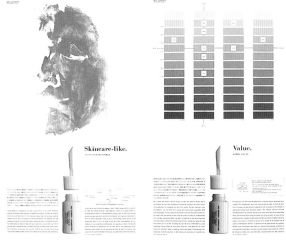

Even though we have to use equipment, we try as much as we can to use hands and bodies to produce ideas. For this, a face was covered thickly with foundation and then pressed on paper to get the facial mask image. The work took a number of days.

機械は使っても、なるべく手や体を使って発想するように心がけている。この作品では、顔にファンデーションを厚目に塗り、紙に転写した。この作業に日数をかけた。

This face was a big surprise for Mr. Uemura but it's certainly interesting and he thought it would work. Actually, this is the method used to make masks of characteristic Kabuki facial make-up.

「顔拓」の発見は、植村秀氏をおおいに驚かせたが、おもしろい。行こうではないかということになった。考えてみれば、この手法は、歌舞伎の隈取りの転写にもみられる。

■ DF: ㈱中塚大輔広告事務所 Nakatsuka Daisuke Inc. Japan (1996)
■ CD: 植村 秀 Shu Uemura ■ AD: 中塚大輔 Daisuke Nakatsuka
■ D: 沼尻かんな Kanna Numajiri ■ P: 中村彰三 Shozo Nakamura ■ CW: 中塚吐夢 Tom Nakatsuka

'I'd like to show plants': this task also started from something Mr. Uemura said. Not just simple plants shown in connection with natural cosmetics, but plants offering something artistic, in a design that evokes a feeling of harmony between nature and science. It was a big, heavy topic. What turned out to be the key to solving the difficulties was a virtually unprecedented printing method of multi-color printing on both sides of cardboard. The Osaka printer, Ueroku, renowned for cosmetics packaging, struggled intrepidly with a task that looked impossible, but after many attempts the dream was accomplished. ■ 　「植物をみせたい」。この仕事も、植村秀氏のひと言で始まった。植物といっても、自然化粧品のように素朴ではなく・アート的感性をそなえ、自然と科学の調和を暗示するデザイン。課題は、大きく重かった。難問を解く鍵となったのが、ダンボールの両面多色刷という、ほとんど前例のない印刷方式だった。化粧品のパッケージに実績をもつ大阪の上六印刷が、不可能に見えた仕事に果敢に取り組んだ。そして何度もトライを重ね、ついに夢が実現された。

P A T T E R N   C O M P S

The outside of the package was to portray a scientific, bio-tech image, while the inside was to portray nature and plants. It was Mr. Uemura's artistic vision that combined the two. This simple formula turned the task into something easy to understand. For the inside of the package we ordered a large quantity of palm leaves from Okinawa and photographed them in black and white. We roughened the grain using a photocopier and readied the photos for printing. To hide the joins we used the method used for textiles: dozens of photocopies had to be attached by hand. The logo mark was created with the letters SS, the initial letters of Shu Uemura Skincare. The logotype was original, based on Franklin Gothic. From start to finish this project took nearly six months.

パッケージの外側は、科学、ハイテクをイメージし、内側は、自然、植物をイメージする。パッケージの内外を結合するのがシュウ ウエムラのアート性である。この単純な図式が作業をわかりやすいものにした。パッケージの内側には、沖縄から大量の椰子の葉をとり寄せ、モノクロ撮影。コピー機を使って粒子をあらし、入稿原稿とした。版下は絵柄のつなぎ目をわからなくするため、テキスタイルの手法を採用。数十枚のコピーを手作業で貼りこんでいった。マークは、シュウ ウエムラ スキンケアの頭文字Ｓ・Ｓを組合せたもの。ロゴタイプは、フランクリン・ゴシックをベースにオリジナルに書きおこした。企画から完成まで約半年の仕事だった。

LOGO PRESENTATION

SHU UEMURA SKIN CARE

Cleansing Beauty Oil Fresher

Huile Démaquillante Fraîche

since 1960

SHU UEMURA SKIN CARE

Cleansing Beauty Oil Fresher

Huile Démaquillante Fraîche

since 1960

SHU UEMURA SKIN CARE

Cleansing Beauty Oil Balancer

Huile Démaquillante Equilibre

since 1960

■ DF: ㈱中塚大輔広告事務所 Nakatsuka Daisuke Inc. Japan (1996)
■ CD: 植村 秀 Shu Uemura ■ AD: 中塚大輔 Daisuke Nakatsuka ■ D: 沼尻かんな Kanna Numajiri
/ 桑田 修 Osamu Kuwata ■ P: 中塚吐夢 Tom Nakatsuka ■ Artist: 中塚純子 Junko Nakatsuka

Anchor Foods Ltd. / Butter Product Ad ■ アンカーフーズ／バター　商品広告

Anchor's spreadable butter, when it came onto the market in 1995, was unique in being the only pure butter that spreads straight from the fridge. A one-page colour press campaign was required to drive product awareness, establish the butter's credibility as truly spreadable—unlike any of the competition—and encourage consumers to try it via a coupon included in the ad. There were two target audiences: existing butter users who could now benefit from the convenience of spreadable butter, and users of butter-like spreads—generally younger than users of standard packet butter. The ad had to include a 20 pence-off coupon, and a brief explanation of the two varieties of Anchor Spreadable Butter. The desired brand image was 'newsy, modern, celebratory, natural and brand leader assumptive,' following the single-minded proposition that Only Anchor Make Pure

Butter That Spreads Straight From the Fridge. ▬▬▬ アンカーのスプレッダブル・バターは、市場に登場した1995年ごろは、冷蔵庫から出してすぐに塗れる唯一のピュア・バターでした。要望は出版物用の1ページ・カラー広告で、製品の認識度を深め、このバターの塗りやすさに関する信頼性 ―競合品との違い― を浸透させ、広告についているクーポン券を使って製品を試すよう消費者を促すものでした。ターゲットになる人たちには2種類あり、スプレッダブル・バターの便利さをすぐに活用できる既存のバター利用者よりも若い世代に多い人たちです。広告には20ペンス割引クーポン券と2つの姉妹品に関する簡単な説明を入れる必要がありました。望まれるブランドイメージは「話題になる、モダン、称賛に値する、ナチュラル、ブランドリーダーと考えられる」で、テーマを「冷蔵庫から出してすぐ塗れるピュア・バターをつくるのはアンカーだけ」という目的を絞ったものにしました。

CONCEPT IDEAS

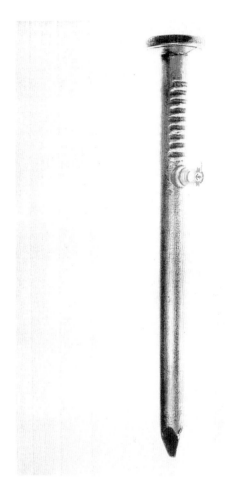

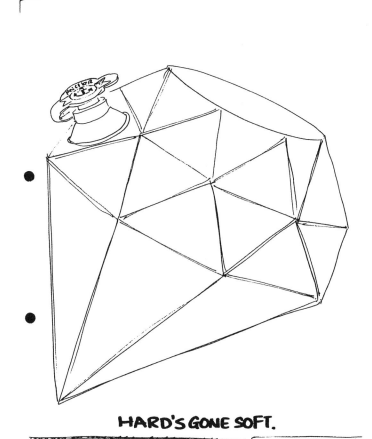

We wanted to do something that would be different from traditional food ads so that it would be highly visible. It had to be a simple expression of the recognisable truth that butter is hard straight from the fridge and Anchor had made it soft and spreadable.

従来の「食品」広告とは違うものにしたかったため、ビジュアル的にすぐれたものにする必要がありました。冷蔵庫から出したばかりのバターは固いけれど、アンカーならやわらかく塗りやすいという分かりやすい事実をシンプルに表現しなくてはなりませんでした。

Keep it clean. Keep it simple. Keep it understandable.

すっきりさせる。
シンプルにする。
分かりやすくする。

Great modelmaker for the diamond. Great photographer for the shot. Brave client for buying the idea. This ad was incredibly successful, doubling the expected number of responses to a coupon.

ダイヤモンドのモデルを作った優秀な模型製作者。撮影を行ったすばらしいカメラマン。アイデアを採用してくれた勇気あるクライアント。この広告は驚くほどの成功をおさめ、クーポン券の反響は予想した量の2倍に達しました。

■ DF: Saatchi + Saatchi Advertising UK (1995)
■ CD: Adam Kean / Alex Taylor ■ AD: John Messum ■ P: Mark Mattock
■ CW: Joe Tanner ■ Model maker: Nancy Fowler

Digitalogue Co., Ltd. / "Jungle Park" packaging ■ デジタローグ／ジャングルパーク　パッケージ

The package for this Jungle Park game, and the CD-ROM inside, have been produced by Saru Brunei, and it all arose out of a desire to make this sticker. A package for a CD-ROM usually involves the latest computer technology--a million polygons per second, 1.064 billion different colors, putting in 100 screen shots, and so on. What we came up with is what you see here, and we have had some very favourable reactions. One store asked 'Don't you want this to sell?', and a cute 12-year-old boy sent a postcard with the message 'You should at least have the front cover in color!' A senior citizen commented, 'You haven't taken the slightest trouble over the wrapping. It's a disgrace!'　　　　ジャングルパーク（CD-ROMで、中身もサルブルネイが作ってる）って、要はこのシールが作りたくて始めたようなモノ。通常この手のモノのパッケージって秒数100万ポリゴンとか、空気までレイトレーシングでレンダリングしてますだとか、10億6,400万色だとか、画面写真100枚入れなきゃいけないとかなんだけど、出来上がりはご覧のとおりで、ショップからは「売る気ないンすか？」とか、小学6年生のカワイイ男の子からはユーザーハガキに「表紙はせめてカラーじゃなきゃね。」とか、お年寄りの方からは「包装に全く気をつかっとらん。ひどすぎる。」等、好評をいただきました。

THUMBNAIL SKETCHES

COLOR STUDIES

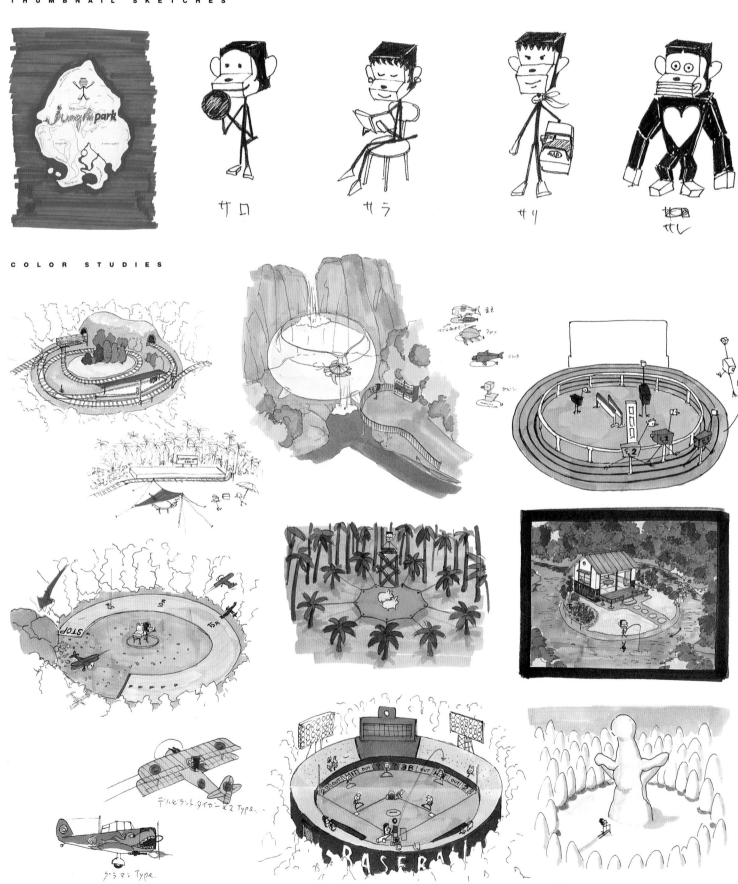

Sticker

Of course the concept for the packaging should come from what's inside, but it doesn't sound very appealing to say it's an 'interactive movie role-playing game with no treasure and no dragons', so we are just calling it an 'island'. I don't like the sorts of games you play once and forget about. I want this to go on selling for 100 years so I decided on a package that would last 100 years. I liked the idea that this 'welded' finish on the sticker will look black with age in 100 years' time. This is a technique that may have completely disappeared within ten years, so I thought it interesting to put it into a design likely to last much longer.

もちろん内容からのコンセプトが出ちゃうんだけど、『宝物とかドラゴンが出てこないインタラクティブムービー・ロールプレイングゲーム』とか言ってもアヤシイだけだから、『島を作った』って言ってるのね。1回クリアしたら終わりっていうのもイヤで、100年くらい売れ続けるつもりだから、100年もつパッケージにしようって思った。100年たったくすんだウェルダー加工シールとか、そーとーイイんじゃないかね。10年後に全くなくなっちゃいそうな技術って興味があって、そーゆーモノを長く持つデザインにオトシこみたいっていつも思ってる。

■ DF: ㈱サルブルネイ　Saru Brunei Co., Ltd.　Japan (1996)
■ AD, D: 松本弦人　Gento Matsumoto

The product being what it is, the fashion wear business is pretty tricky. There's no way I could be art director for DKNY! The way I see it, you can either just do the logo and finish, or else you get deeply involved and then you have to see it through. In that case you certainly have more problems, but you do get to go to unusual places, like an embroidery workshop way out in the suburbs, a factory famous for making the bags the Aum cult used for their sarin gas, or the Turbine

shop in the Odakyu department store in Shinjuku. ■ ファッションメーカーってケッコウビミョウでしょ。商品が商品なだけに。さすがにオイラDKNYのアートディレクター出来んよね。ロゴだけスパっとやって終わるか、深く関わるならとことんやっちゃわないとダメかなって思って。そーなるといろいろ大変なんだけど、桐生の刺繍工場とか、成田の袋工場（オウムサリンの袋つくったとこ）とか、新宿小田急百貨店タービン売場とか、ふだん行けないとことか行けてオモシロイけどね。

COLOR COMPS

Having various designers produce a series of T-shirts is not such an attractive proposition, even for the designers. An overall design strategy that will motivate everyone is crucial if you're going to get different people to work on the project.

I was first asked to design an art T-shirt series (!), a point-of-purchase display and a shopping bag, so I put them all together and this is what I got. Even though the individual budgets are small, when you combine them you arrive at a reasonable sum. It's fun to think up print designs for pants, it's the first time to print something on a combustible garbage bag, and I'm glad there are different shopping bags for each season.

Tシャツをいろいろなクリエーターにデザインしてもらったシリーズとか、メディアとしてそんなに魅力ないでしょ、作り手にとっても。「よし、いっちょきばるか!」って気にさせるフィールドデザインが、いろんな人に頼む場合の基本。最初アートTシャツシリーズ（笑）、店頭POP、ショッパーのデザインを頼まれてたんだけど、それを全部一緒にしたのがコレ。個々の予算が少なくてもグロスにすればまーまーのギャラ出せるし、パンツにプリントの柄考えるのも楽しいし、炭酸カルシウムのゴミ袋のインクのノリは初めてのカンジだし、季節ごとに変わるショッパーとかまーなんかウレシイじゃない。

■ DF: ㈱サルブルネイ　Saru Brunei Co., Ltd.　Japan (1994-1995)
■ AD, D: 松本弦人　Gento Matsumoto
■ P: 井上よういち　Yoichi Inoue

We have a mission at Recruit: to create a new set of values. All the magazines we publish--ABroad, Car Sensor, Recruit Book, Jutaku Joho, etc. seek to further this mission. What 'creating a new set of values' means within the context of society is that up till now just a handful of people have had control of important information and privileges. This is how Japanese society has been structured: only a special class of people get the opportunities and ordinary people rarely benefit. For a long time people didn't even notice. But now we want to put across the message that actually, anybody can take advantage of opportunities. This is our starting point. ■■■■

『新しい価値観の創造』というテーマが私たちリクルートにはあります。このテーマは、私たちの事業テーマといってもいいものです。皆さんが目にするエービーロード、カーセンサー、リクルートブック、住宅情報など、私たちが発行する全ての情報誌がこの使命をもっています。『新しい価値観の創造』というテーマを社会との関係の中でお話しすると、今までごく一握りの人々が、大切な情報や権利を抱え込んでいる。これが、いままでの日本社会の構造でした。高い壁の中にすんでいる人だけがチャンスを享受し、一般の人々にはなかなか恩恵がもたらされない。しかも、人々はそんな構造があることさえ、長い間気づかずにきました。でも本当はこんなことできるのだよ。それを静かに伝えていきたいという気持ちが出発点でした。

ROUGH SKETCHES

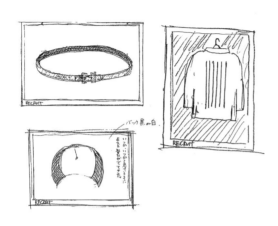
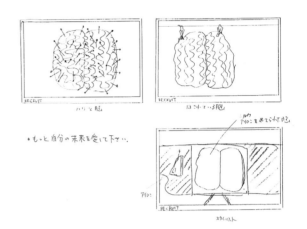

FINAL PRESENTATION

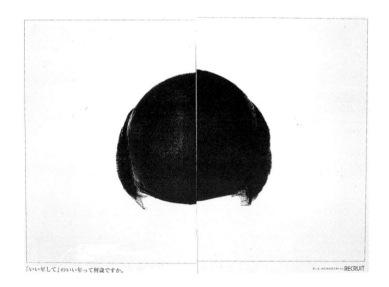
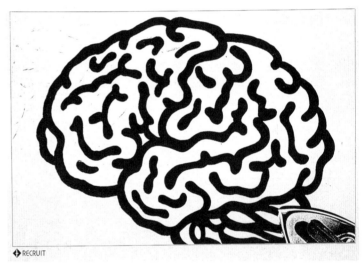

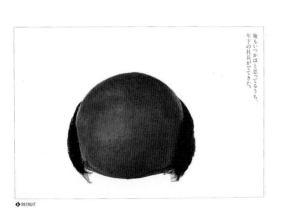
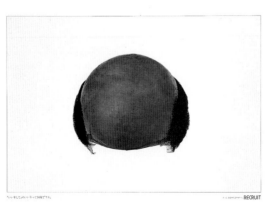

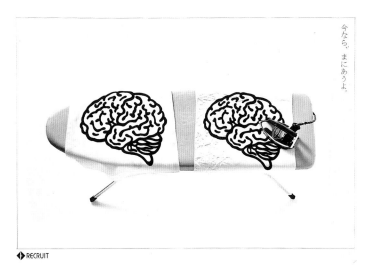

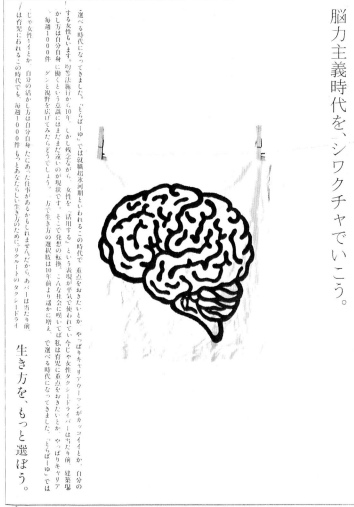

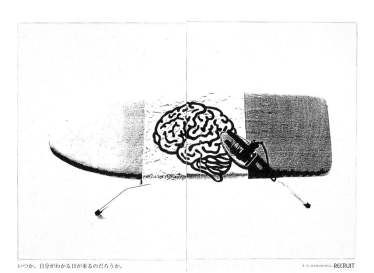

Job hunting, choosing a school or college, researching the latest in travel, cars or books... When this sort of information is passed through the Recruit filter, a new yardstick is apparent and a wealth of options become available. The people who have these lifestyle options are those who read the information magazines. Of course, we cannot directly change our readers' lifestyles. What we can do is help people to recognize for themselves how they want to lead their lives. We can encourage those pursuing their own individual ideals and changing to a new lifestyle. Through this sort of work, little by little we can make society a little freer. And this is the message that underlies our corporate advertising.

仕事探しも学校選びも、旅行や車や本の情報もリクルートの情報誌のフィルターを通してみると、新しい基準が見えてきます。そして豊富な選択肢が供給されるようになってくる。でも、その生き方の選択肢を選ぶのは、あくまで情報誌の利用者です。あたりまえですが、読者の生き方そのものを変えることは私たちにはできません。私たちがやれることは、どんな人生を描くのか、自分探しのお手伝いをすることです。自分らしい価値を求め、新しい生き方をしようとする人の背中をそっと押してあげること。そんな仕事をとおして少しでも自由な社会を実現していくことなのです。これがこの企業広告のテーマであり、表現なのです。

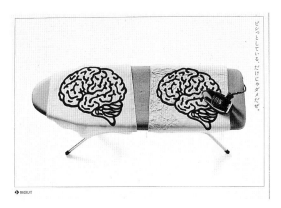

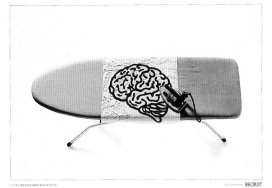

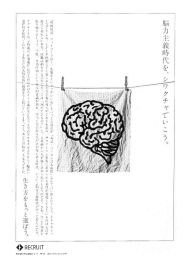

■ DF: ㈱リクルート Recruit Co., Ltd. Japan (1995)
■ CD: 渡邊嘉子 Yoshiko Watanabe (magazine)   ■ AD, D: 柏本郷司 Satoji Kashimoto (magazine / poster)   ■ P: 下梁健一 Kenichi Shimoyana (magazine / poster)
■ CW: 紫垣樹郎 Jurou Shigaki (magazine) / 下澤宏之 Hiroyuki Shimosawa (magazine) / 名雪祐平 Yuhei Nayuki (poster)

The Levi's 501 campaign was created for a very exclusive target: the opinion leaders, the trendsetter consumers who are extremely critical and hate to feel as if they are being manipulated by advertising. We had to present the well-known qualities of the product in a way that was entirely new.　■■■■　リーバイス501のキャンペーンは、限られたターゲット向けに行われました。オピニオンリーダーであり、トレンドの流れを決める消費者で、批判的で広告に操作されたと感じるのを嫌う人たちです。そのため、良く知られている製品の品質をまったく新しい方法で提示する必要がありました。

R O U G H S K E T C H E S

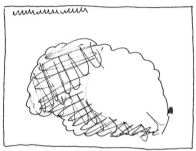

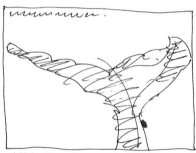

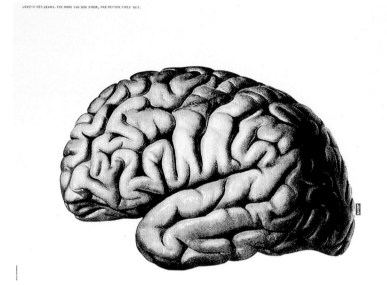

There is nothing new to tag lines such as *The More You Wash Them the Better They Look*. But what's new is the way we linked the qualities of the product (strength, etc.) without showing the product itself—just the Red Tab, and the 501s replaced by an object.

ブレーンストーミング、アイデアの仕上げ「洗うほどに味がでる」といったキャッチフレーズに新しさはまったくありません。新しさは、製品自体を見せずに赤いラベルだけを使って、（丈夫さなどの）製品の品質と代替物で表現した501を結びつけた方法にあるのです。

The campaign appeared as double-page spreads in Spanish magazines in September 1994. The punching ball photograph was done by Arará Pelegrin. The whale's tail is a stock colour photograph retouched on Photoshop. The brain is a hyper-re-alistic illustration.

このキャンペーンは1994年9月にスペインの雑誌の見開きページに登場しました。パンチング・ボールの写真はArará Pelegrinによって撮影されました。クジラの尾はストックフォトのカラー写真をフォトショップ上で修正したものです。脳はハイパーリアリズム風のイラストレーションです。

The campaign won numerous awards around the world, including the Grand Clio 95, the Bronze Lion at Cannes in 1995 and a Gold Medal at the Art Directors Club of New York.

このキャンペーンは95年グランドクリオ、95年カンヌの銅獅子賞、アートディレクターズ・クラブ・オブ・ニューヨークの金メダルなど世界中でたくさんの賞を獲得しました。

■ DF: Bassat, Ogilvy & Mather Spain (1994)
■ CD, CW: Gustavo Caldas ■ CD, AD: David Ruiz
■ P: Arará Pelegrin / Horrillo Riola / Carlos Suarez

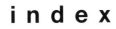

index of submittors

Art Director	Douglas Gordon
Designer	Douglas Gordon
Editor	Kaoru Yamashita　山下かおる
Photographer	Kuniharu Fujimoto　藤本邦治
English Translator	Sue Herbert
Typesetter	Yutaka Hasegawa　長谷川豊
Publisher	Shingo Miyoshi　三芳伸吾

1997年5月14日初版第一刷発行

発行所　ピエ・ブックス

〒170 東京都豊島区駒込4-14-6 ビラフェニックス301

編集　TEL:03-3949-5010　FAX:03-3949-5650

営業　TEL:03-3940-8302　FAX:03-3576-7361

©1997 P・I・E BOOKS

Printed in Hong Kong

本書の収録内容の無断転載、複写、引用等を禁じます。

落丁、乱丁はお取り替え致します。

ISBN4-89444-045-8 C3070

CORPORATE IMAGE DESIGN
世界の業種別CI・ロゴマーク
Pages: 336 (272 in Color)　￥16,000
An effective logo is the key to brand or company recognition. This sourcebook of total CI design introduces pieces created for a wide range of businesses - from boutiques to multinationals - and features hundreds of design concepts and applications.

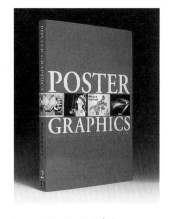

POSTER GRAPHICS Vol. 2
好評！業種別世界のポスター集成、第2弾
Pages: 256 (192 in Color)　￥17,000
700 posters from the top creators in Japan and abroad are showcased in this book - classified by business. This invaluable reference makes it easy to compare design trends among various industries and corporations.

BROCHURE & PAMPHLET COLLECTION Vol. 4
好評！業種別カタログ・コレクション、第4弾
Pages: 224 (Full Color)　￥16,000
The fourth volume in our popular "Brochure & Pamphlet" series. Twelve types of businesses are represented through artwork that really sells. This book conveys a sense of what's happening right now in the catalog design scene. A must for all creators.

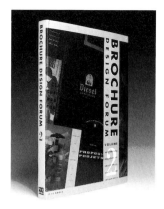

BROCHURE DESIGN FORUM Vol. 2
世界の最新カタログ・コレクション
Pages: 224 (176 in Color)　￥16,000
A special edition of our "Brochure & Pamphlet Collection" featuring 250 choice pieces that represent 70 types of businesses and are classified by business for handy reference. A compendium of the design scene at a glance.

A CATALOGUE AND PAMPHLET COLLECTION
業種別商品カタログ特集／ソフトカバー
Pages: 224 (Full Color)　￥3,800
A collection of the world's most outstanding brochures,catalogs and leaflets classified by industry such as fashion, restaurants, music, interiors and sports goods.Presenting each piece in detail from cover to inside. This title is an indispensable sourcebook for all graphic designers and CI professionals.

COMPANY BROCHURE COLLECTION
業種別（会社・学校・施設）案内グラフィックス
Pages: 224 (192 in Color)　￥16,000
A rare selection of brochures and catalogs ranging from admission manuals for colleges and universities, to amusement facility and hotel guidebooks, to corporate and organization profiles. The entries are classified by industry for easy reference.

COMPANY BROCHURE COLLECTION Vol. 2
業種別会社案内グラフィックス　第2弾！
Pages: 224 (Full Color)　￥16,000
Showing imaginative layouts that present information clearly in limited space,and design that effectively enhances corporate identity,this volume will prove to be an essential source book for graphic design work of the future.

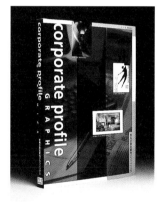

CORPORATE PROFILE GRAPHICS
世界の会社案内グラフィックス
Pages: 224 (Full Color)　￥16,000
A new version of our popular "Brochure and Pamphlet Collection" series featuring 200 carefully selected catalogs from around the world. A substantial variety of school brochures, company profiles and facility information is offered.

CREATIVE FLYER GRAPHICS Vol. 2
世界のフライヤーデザイン傑作選
Pages: 224 (Full Color)　￥16,000
A pack of some 600 flyers and leaflets incorporating information from a variety of events including exhibitions, movies, plays, concerts, live entertainment and club events, as well as foods, cosmetics, electrical merchandise and travel packages.

EVENT FLYER GRAPHICS
世界のイベントフライヤー・コレクション
Pages: 224 (Full Color)　￥16,000
Here's a special selection zooming in on flyers promoting events. This upbeat selection covers wide-ranging music events,as well as movies,exhibitions and the performing arts.

ADVERTISING FLYER GRAPHICS
衣・食・住・遊の商品チラシ特集
Pages: 224 (Full Color)　￥16,000
The eye-catching flyers selected for this new collection represent a broad spectrum of businesses,and are presented in a loose classification covering four essential areas of modern lifestyles: fashion,dining,home and leisure.

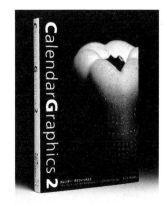

CALENDAR GRAPHICS Vol. 2
好評カレンダー・デザイン集の決定版、第2弾
Pages: 224 (192 in Color)　￥16,000
The second volume of our popular "Calendar Graphics" features designs from about 250 1994 and 1995 calendars from around the world. A rare collection including those on the market as well as exclusive corporate PR calendars.

DIAGRAM GRAPHICS Vol. 2
世界のダイアグラム・デザインの集大成
Pages: 224 (192 in Color)　￥16,000
The unsurpassed second volume in our "Diagram Graphics" series is now complete, thanks to cooperation from artists around the world. It features graphs, charts and maps created for various media.

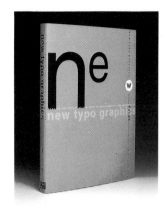

NEW TYPO GRAPHICS
世界の最新タイポグラフィ・コレクション
Pages: 224 (192 in Color)　￥16,000
Uncompromising in its approach to typographic design, this collection includes 350 samples of only the very finest works available. This special collection is a compendium of all that is exciting along the leading edge of typographic creativity today.

1, 2 & 3 COLOR GRAPHICS
1・2・3色グラフィックス
Pages: 208 (Full Color)　￥16,000
Featured here are outstanding graphics in limited colors. See about 300 samples of 1,2 & 3-color artwork that are so expressive they often surpass the impact of full four-color reproductions. This is a very important book that will expand the possibilities of your design work in the future.

1, 2 & 3 COLOR GRAPHICS Vol. 2
1・2・3色グラフィックス、第2弾
Pages: 224 (Full Color)　￥16,000
Even more ambitious in scale than the first volume, this second collection of graphics displays the unique talents of graphic designers who work with limited colors. An essential reference guide to effective, low-cost designing.

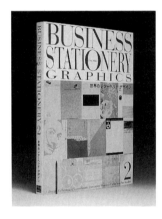

BUSINESS STATIONERY GRAPHICS Vol. 2
世界のレターヘッド・コレクション、第2弾
Pages: 224 (176 in Color)　￥16,000
The second volume in our popular "Business Stationery Graphics" series. This publication focuses on letterheads, envelopes and business cards, all classified by business. Our collection will serve artists and business people well.

BUSINESS CARD GRAPHICS Vol. 1 / Soft Jacket
世界の名刺コレクション／ソフトカバー
Pages: 224 (160 in Color)　￥3,800
First impressions of an individual or company are often shaped by their business cards. The 1,200 corporate and personal-use business cards shown here illustrate the design strategies of 500 top Japanese, American and European designers. PIE's most popular book.

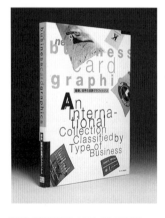

NEW BUSINESS CARD GRAPHICS
最新版！ビジネスカード グラフィックス
Pages: 224(Full Color)　￥16,000
A selection of 900 samples representing the works of top designers worldwide. Covering the broadest spectrum of business categories, this selection of the world's best business cards ranges from the trendiest to the most classy and includes highly original examples along the way.

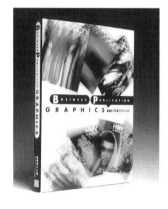

BUSINESS PUBLICATION GRAPHICS
業種別企業ＰＲ誌・フリーペーパーの集大成！
Pages: 224 (Full Color)　￥16,000
This comprehensive graphic book introduces business publications created for a variety of business needs, including promotions from boutiques and department stores, exclusive clubs, local communities and company newsletters.

POSTCARD GRAPHICS Vol. 4
世界の業種別ポストカード・コレクション
Pages: 224 (192 in Color)　￥16,000
Our popular "Postcard Graphics" series has been revamped for "Postcard Graphics Vol. 4." This first volume of the new version showcases approximately 1,000 pieces ranging from direct mailers to private greeting cards, selected from the best around the world.

POSTCARD COLLECTION Vol. 2
ポストカードコレクション／ソフトカバー
Pages: 230 (Full Color)　￥3,800
Welcome to the colorful world of postcards with 1200 postcards created by artists from all over the world classified according to the business of the client.

TRAVEL & LEISURE GRAPHICS
ホテル＆旅行 案内 グラフィックス
Pages: 224 (Full Color)　￥16,000
A giant collection of some 400 pamphlets, posters and direct mailings exclusively delivered for hotels, inns, resort tours and amusement facilities.

SPECIAL EVENT GRAPHICS
世界のイベント・グラフィックス
Pages: 224 (192 in Color)　￥16,000
A showcase for event graphics, introducing leaflets for exhibitions, fashion shows, all sorts of sales promotional campaigns, posters, premiums and actual installation scenes from events around the world. An invaluable and inspirational resource book, unique in the world of graphic publishing.

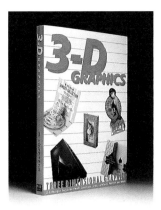

3-D GRAPHICS
3Dグラフィックスの大百科
Pages: 224 (192 in Color) ￥16,000
350 works that demonstrate some of the finest examples of 3-D graphic methods, including DMs, catalogs, posters, POPs and more. The volume is a virtual encyclopedia of 3-D graphics.

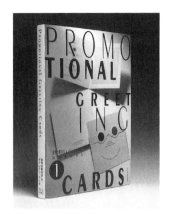

PROMOTIONAL GREETING CARDS
ADVERTISING GREETING CARDS Vol. 4
(English Title)
厳選された世界の案内状＆DM
Pages: 224 (Full Color) ￥16,000
A total of 500 examples of cards from designers around the world. A whole spectrum of stylish and inspirational cards, are classified by function for easy reference.

DIRECT MAIL GRAPHICS Vol. 1
衣・食・住のセールスDM特集
Pages: 224 (Full Color) ￥16,000
The long-awaited design collection featuring direct mailers with outstanding sales impact and quality design. 350 of the best pieces, classified into 100 business categories.
A veritable textbook of current direct-marketing design.

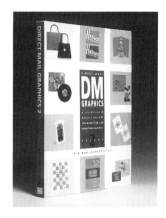

DIRECT MAIL GRAPHICS Vol. 2
好評！衣・食・住のセールスDM特集！第２弾
Pages: 224 (Full Color) ￥16,000
The second volume in our extremely popular "Direct Mail Graphics" series features a whole range of direct mailers for various purposes; from commercial announcements to seasonal greetings and are also classified by industry.

T-SHIRT GRAPHICS / Soft Jacket
世界のTシャツ・コレクション／ソフトカバー
Pages: 224 (192 in Color) ￥3,800
This stunning showcase publication features about 700 T-shirts collected from the major international design centers. Includes various promotional shirts and fabulous designs from the fashion world and sporting-goods manufacturers as well. This eagerly awaited publication has arrived at just the right time.

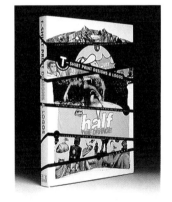

T-SHIRT PRINT DESIGNS & LOGOS
世界のTシャツ・プリント デザイン＆ロゴ
Pages: 224 (192 in Color) ￥16,000
Second volume of our popular "T-shirt Graphics" series. In this publication, 800 designs for T-shirt graphics, including many trademarks and logotypes are showcased. The world's top designers in the field are featured.

The Paris Collections / INVITATION CARDS
パリ・コレクションの招待状グラフィックス
Pages: 176 (Full Color) ￥13,800
This book features 400 announcements for and invitations to the Paris Collections, produced by the world's top names in fashion over the past 10 years. A treasure trove of ideas and pure fun to browse through.

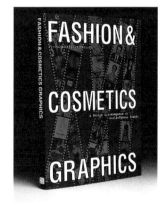

FASHION & COSMETICS GRAPHICS
ファッション＆コスメティック・グラフィックス
Pages: 208 (Full Color) ￥16,000
A collection of promotional graphics from around the world produced for apparel, accessory and cosmetic brands at the avant-garde of the fashion industry. 40 brands featured in this book point the way toward future trends in advertising.

SPORTS GRAPHICS / Soft Jacket
世界のスポーツグッズ・コレクション／ソフトカバー
Pages: 224 (192 in Color) ￥3,800
A collection of 1,000 bold sporting-goods graphic works from all over the world. A wide variety of goods are shown, including uniforms, bags, shoes and other gear. Covers all sorts of sports: basketball, skiing, surfing and many, many more.

LABELS AND TAGS COLLECTION Vol. 1 / Soft Jacket
ラベル＆タグ・コレクション／ソフトカバー
Pages: 224 (192 in Color) ￥3,800
Nowhere is brand recognition more important than in Japan. Here is a collection of 1,600 labels and tags from Japan's 450 top fashion names with page after page of women's and men's clothing and sportswear designs.

INSIGNIA COLLECTION
ワッペン＆エンブレム・コレクション／ソフトカバー
Pages: 224 (Full Color) ￥3,800
Over 3000 designs were scrutinized for this collection of 1000 outstanding emblems and embroidered motifs that are visually exciting, make innovative use of materials and compliment the fashions with which they are worn.

CD JACKET COLLECTION
世界のCDジャケット・コレクション／ソフトカバー
Pages: 224 (192 in Color) ￥3,800
Featuring 700 of the world's most imaginative CD and LP covers from all musical genres, this is a must-have book for all design and music professionals.

THE P·I·E COLLECTION

TYPO-DIRECTION IN JAPAN Vol. 6
年鑑 日本のタイポディレクション '94-'95
Pages: 250 (Full Color) ¥ 17,000
This book features the finest work from the international competition of graphic design in Japan. The sixth volume of our popular yearbook series is edited by the TOKYO TYPE DIRECTORS CLUB with the participation of master designers worldwide.

THE TOKYO TYPEDIRECTORS CLUB ANNUAL 1995-96
TDC 年鑑95-96
Pages: 250 (Full Color) ¥ 17,000
A follow-up publication to Japan's only international graphic design competition. Featuring 650 typographic artworks selected by THE TOKYO TYPEDIRECTORS CLUB, this book provides a window on the latest typographic design concepts worldwide.

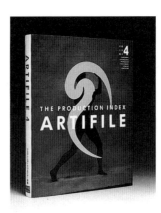

The Production Index ARTIFILE Vol. 4
活躍中！広告プロダクション年鑑、第4弾
Pages: 224 (Full Color) ¥ 12,500
The fourth volume in our "Production Index Artifile" series features vigorously selected yearly artworks from 107 outstanding production companies and artists in Japan. An invaluable source book of the current design forefronts portraying their policies and backgrounds.

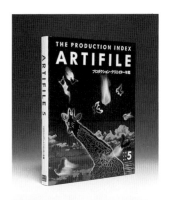

The Production Index ARTIFILE Vol.5
最新版プロダクション・クリエーター年鑑
Pages: 224(Full Color) ¥ 12,500
ARTIFILE 5 features artwork from a total of 100 top Japanese production companies and designers, along with company data and messages from the creators. An invaluable information source for anyone who needs to keep up with the latest developments in the graphic scene.

SEASONAL CAMPAIGN GRAPHICS
デパート・ショップのキャンペーン広告特集
Pages: 224 (Full Color) ¥ 16,000
A spirited collection of quality graphics for sales campaigns planned around the four seasons and Christmas, St. Valentines Day and the Japanese gift-giving seasons, as well as for store openings, anniversaries, and similar events.

SHOPPING BAG GRAPHICS
世界の最新ショッピング・バッグデザイン集
Pages: 224 (Full Color) ¥ 16,000
Over 500 samples of the latest and best of the world's shopping bag design from a wide selection of retail businesses! This volume features a selection of shopping bags originating in Tokyo, NY, LA, London, Paris, Milan and other major cities worldwide, and presented here in a useful business classification.

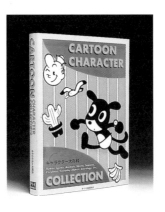

CARTOON CHARACTER COLLECTION
5500種のキャラクターデザイン大百科
Pages: 480 (B&W) ¥ 9,800
A total of 5,500 cartoons and illustrations from some of the most successful illustrations in the industry have been carefully selected for this giant, new collection. The illustrations included are classified by animals, figures, vehicles, etc, for easy reference.

カタログ・新刊のご案内について

総合カタログ、新刊案内をご希望の方は、はさみ込みのアンケートはがきを
ご返送いただくか、90円切手同封の上、ピエ・ブックス宛お申し込み下さい。

CATALOGUEŞ ET INFORMATIONS SUR LES NOUVELLES PUBLICATIONS

Si vous désirez recevoir un exemplaire gratuit de notre catalogue général ou des détails sur nos nouvelles publications, veuillez compléter la carte réponse incluse et nous la retourner par courrierou par fax.

CATALOGS and INFORMATION ON NEW PUBLICATIONS

If you would like to receive a free copy of our general catalog or details of our new publications, please fill out the enclosed postcard and return it to us by mail or fax.

CATALOGE und INFORMATIONEN ÜBER NEUE TITLE

Wenn Sie unseren Gesamtkatalog oder Detailinformationen über unsere neuen Titel wünschen, fullen Sie bitte die beigefügte Postkarte aus und schicken Sie sie uns per Post oder Fax.

ピエ・ブックス

〒170 東京都豊島区駒込 4-14-6-301
TEL: 03-3940-8302 FAX: 03-3576-7361

P·I·E BOOKS

#301, 4-14-6, Komagome, Toshima-ku, Tokyo 170 JAPAN
TEL: 813-3940-8302 FAX: 813-3576-7361